PENGUIN CLASSICS

THE OBEDIENCE OF A CHRISTIAN MAN

WILLIAM TYNDALE was born in Gloucestershire in 1494. He spent over ten years at Magdalen Hall, Oxford, and may then have gone on to Cambridge. By the early 1520s Tyndale was back in Gloucestershire serving as tutor to the children of Sir John and Lady Walsh, for whom he translated Erasmus's *Enchiridion*. He was ordained priest. Using Erasmus's newly-printed Greek text, Tyndale began to translate the New Testament into English, at that time a forbidden, heretical undertaking. Having failed in an attempt to gain the support of the Bishop of London for his endeavours to print an English New Testament for the first time, he left England for Germany in about 1524. In Cologne in 1525 his printing was stopped by the authorities. In 1526, Tyndale, now living in Worms, printed his English translation of the New Testament, which was smuggled into England in bales of cloth. It was swiftly denounced in Britain as heretical and many copies were burned. In Antwerp in 1530, having by then learnt Hebrew (impossible in England), he produced his Pentateuch (the first five books of the Old Testament), which, like his other works, was then smuggled into Britain. His knowledge of Hebrew also lay behind his revised edition of the New Testament in 1534, this time including prologues and notes. In May 1535, having completed his translation of the remainder of the Old Testament historical books, Tyndale was tricked into arrest and imprisoned in Vilvoorde Castle near Brussels. He was interrogated by Catholic heresy-hunters for sixteen months. Denounced as a heretic, he was passed to the secular authorities, and, on 6 October 1536, having been stripped of his priesthood, he was publicly strangled and burned.

His treatise *The Obedience of a Christian Man* was first printed in Antwerp in October 1528. In it he set down the religious principles that made it one of the most important books of the first phase of the English Reformation. His *Parable of the Wicked Mammon*, published earlier that same year, and other books, strongly influenced English religious life. Seventy-five years after his death, his translation of the New Testament was taken almost unchanged, and what he had translated of the Old Testament only slightly altered, into the King James Version (the 'Authorized Version').

DAVID DANIELL is Emeritus Professor in the University of London, and Honorary Fellow of Hertford College Oxford. He read English, and then Theology, at Oxford. His Ph.D., in Shakespeare, is from London. He has published extensively on Shakespeare (including the Arden edition of *Julius Caesar*), on John Buchan and on the English Bible. His editions of Tyndale's New and Old Testaments and his biography of Tyndale were published by Yale University Press. He is Chairman of the Tyndale Society, which has members worldwide.

WILLIAM TYNDALE

The Obedience of a Christian Man

Edited and with an Introduction and Notes by
DAVID DANIELL

PENGUIN BOOKS

In memory of my father,
Eric Daniell, 1892–1960

PENGUIN BOOKS

Published by the Penguin Group
Penguin Books Ltd, 80 Strand, London WC2R 0RL, England
Penguin Putnam Inc., 375 Hudson Street, New York, New York 10014, USA
Penguin Books Australia Ltd, 250 Camberwell Road, Camberwell, Victoria 3124, Australia
Penguin Books Canada Ltd, 10 Alcorn Avenue, Toronto, Ontario, Canada M4V 3B2
Penguin Books India (P) Ltd, 11 Community Centre, Panchsheel Park, New Delhi – 110 017, India
Penguin Books (NZ) Ltd, Cnr Rosedale and Airborne Roads, Albany, Auckland, New Zealand
Penguin Books (South Africa) (Pty) Ltd, 24 Sturdee Avenue, Rosebank 2196, South Africa

Penguin Books Ltd, Registered Offices: 80 Strand, London WC2R 0RL, England

www.penguin.com

First published in Antwerp, 1528
Published in Penguin Books 2000

025

Introduction and editorial matter copyright © David Daniell, 2000
All rights reserved

The moral right of the editor has been asserted

Set in 10/12.5 pt PostScript Monotype Garamond
Typeset by Rowland Phototypesetting Ltd, Bury St Edmunds, Suffolk
Printed and bound in Great Britain by Clays Ltd, Elcograf S.p.A.

ISBN 978-0-14-043477-4

www.greenpenguin.co.uk

MIX
Paper from
responsible sources
FSC   FSC® C018179
www.fsc.org

Penguin Books is committed to a sustainable
future for our business, our readers and our planet.
This book is made from Forest Stewardship
Council™ certified paper.

CONTENTS

ACKNOWLEDGEMENTS

I am glad to acknowledge here the help that I have received. Sir Christopher Zeeman, former Principal of Hertford College, Oxford (which owns a rare copy), has been continually encouraging. The computer skills of Dr Deborah Pollard of Queen Mary and Westfield Colleges, London, have been invaluable. Robert Ireland of the Department of Greek and Latin at University College London told me about Aristotle. My son Christopher answered historical questions immediately. Lucy Davies helped with the iconography of the title page.

To four people I am especially indebted. The Rt Rev. Dr Rowan Williams, Bishop of Monmouth, in his Fifth Annual Lambeth Tyndale Lecture, 'Tyndale and the Christian Society', alerted me to one of the significances of the *Obedience* which I was in danger of bypassing. Ellen Herron, Managing Director of the Van Kampen Foundation at the Scriptorium: Center for Christian Antiquities, Grand Haven, Michigan, keyed in a basic modern-spelling version from a facsimile of the original in all its problematic peculiarities of type, spellings, and abbreviations, and sent it to me on disk. Daniel Bryant made me a present of his own facsimile copy of the *Obedience*. My greatest debt, as always, is to my wife, Dorothy, without whose support over some years this edition would never have happened.

ABBREVIATIONS

A&M *The Acts and Monuments of John Foxe*, edited by George Townshend, 8 vols. (1843–9); revised and corrected by J. Pratt, with an introduction by J. Stoughton (1887)

Answer *An Answer to Sir Thomas More's Dialogue* ... by William Tyndale, edited for the Parker Society by Henry Walter (Cambridge University Press, 1850)

Duffy Eamon Duffy, *The Stripping of the Altars: Traditional Religion in England 1400–1580* (Yale University Press, 1992)

Mammon *The Parable of the Wicked Mammon* by William Tyndale, edited for the Parker Society by Henry Walter (Cambridge University Press, 1848)

OED *Oxford English Dictionary*

PS *Doctrinal Treatises*, etc., by William Tyndale, edited for the Parker Society by Henry Walter (Cambridge University Press, 1848–50). This volume includes the *Obedience*

Practice *The Practice of Prelates* by William Tyndale, edited for the Parker Society by Henry Walter (Cambridge University Press, 1849)

TNT *Tyndale's New Testament: a modern-spelling edition* (Yale University Press, 1989)

TOT *Tyndale's Old Testament: a modern-spelling edition* (Yale University Press, 1992)

WTB David Daniell, *William Tyndale: a Biography* (1994)

INTRODUCTION

It is commonly said that William Tyndale's *The Obedience of a Christian Man*, published in 1528, was the first, and the most important, book in the earliest phase of the English Reformation.

That is true – except that it does not take into account what had happened shortly before. In 1525, Tyndale's English translation of the New Testament, the first from the original Greek rather than from the church's Latin version, and the first to be printed, was on Peter Quentell's presses in Cologne. The work was stopped as heretical by the city authorities. The materials were confiscated. Some sheets of the Prologue and the translation as far as Matthew 22 reached England, and became the first printed Lutheran tracts in circulation in London.[1] A year later, in 1526 and in Worms, Tyndale successfully saw through the press of Peter Schoeffer his complete New Testament, this time without Prologue or notes. Several thousand of these small books were smuggled into England in bales of cloth. This English New Testament, in its accuracy, simplicity and grace, has been the foundation of most English versions that followed. It gave English readers and hearers at every social level full access to the whole of New Testament theology, without restriction or intermediary. That access, building on the Lollard movement which had been continuously active during the hundred and fifty years before Tyndale, was the first significant popular 'Protestant' development in the British Isles.[2]

It is in the light of the sudden availability of the New Testament in English that Tyndale's books must be seen. Tyndale's *Obedience* was first printed in Antwerp on 2 October 1528, but it was not his first large essay. Five months before, on 8 May 1528, the same Antwerp press had produced Tyndale's *The Parable of the Wicked Mammon*. (The parable referred to is known to us as 'The Unjust Steward', Luke 16.) It is

Tyndale's declaration of the New Testament teaching – as the first line of the first leaf has it (there is no title page): 'That faith the mother of all good works justifieth us, before we can bring forth any good work'. Although this is what the New Testament teaches, in 1528 it was startling, strange – and heretical, as thought to be developed from Luther. But Tyndale's pages are rich with New Testament quotations in English, effectively making scripture speak for itself. Good works are necessary, but follow faith as the fruit comes from the tree. Mammon (riches) is wicked 'principally because it is not bestowed unto our neighbour's need'. Tyndale's new vision of the oldest roots of Christian life is central also to the *Obedience*, which runs alongside and overlaps *Mammon*, as will be seen. *Mammon* is a thoughtful working-out of the teaching of Christ, and to a lesser extent Paul, about such deeds as should follow faith. It is a systematic analysis of what ordinary Christian living should be, entirely according to what the New Testament (and not the church) says – and says in English. Tyndale writes for inquiring believers on, for example, fasting, watching, prayer, almsgiving (not just how much to donate; Christ teaches that 'everyman is other's debtor since love maketh all things common' – Christian society is still trying to catch up with that). A low-key book in appearance, it was revolutionary. Circulating secretly in England, it was soon officially banned. It continued to be widely read in spite of severe interrogations and punishments.

The Obedience of a Christian Man is on a larger scale than *Mammon*. As the title declares, Tyndale looks, again systematically, at English social and political life through New Testament doctrine. Martin Luther had written sixteen pages *On the Liberty of a Christian Man*, in November 1520. The third, and shortest, of his three treatises in that year – the other two were the better-known *Address to the Christian Nobility of the German Nation* and *The Babylonian Captivity of the Church* – it was dedicated to Pope Leo. The first sentence, 'A Christian man is a free lord over everything and subject to no one', became a rallying-call to his supporters. The second sentence, however, is 'A Christian man is an obedient servant in everything and subject to everyone.'

There is, says Tyndale in his own book of *Obedience*, one social structure, created by God, to which everyone has to be obedient simply by being God's creature – you cannot exist on earth without having a father and mother: he begins his treatise, movingly, with the moment of the reader's conception. The God-given structure is a simple one of 'degrees' (that is, steps or ranks). From children obedient to parents, through the obedience of wives to husbands and servants to masters, to subjects obedient to 'Kings, Princes and Rulers' – already we see that what he writes will be strange to readers in the twenty-first century. Tyndale pauses at this point to explain the New Testament doctrine of social responsibility: what do you do if the King, Prince or Ruler is evil? He answers by out-Luthering Luther: you must disobey, but not resist, even tyrannical rulers, lest God in his wrath make it worse. Into the discussion of this New Testament question there cuts a long jagged point which has nothing to do with the New Testament at all: what do you do with 'the Pope's false power'?

Seeing obediences from below, however, from children and subjects, is only a way in. The book then turns round, going from 'them that are under power and rule' to 'how the rulers ought to rule' (p. 59). Discussion of the offices of fathers, husbands and masters leads briefly to the duty of landlords, and then, at length, the duty of 'kings, and of the judges and officers'. These, in all the diversity of callings, are personally responsible to God. At this point the jagged problem again intrudes. Those whose place is to be pastors and teachers have left those vocations and become rulers. 'To preach God's word is too much for half a man. And to minister a temporal kingdom is too much for half a man also. Either other requireth an whole man. One therefore cannot well do both' (p. 68). There has been laid across English society an alien structure, in no way authorized by the New Testament. This has had two effects: it has meant that the God-given rulers are interfered with at every moment, unable to be as God made them – good or bad – because they are controlled by the Pope and his prelates. And it has meant that there are two nations, not one. The split between church and state has given the former the authority both to intervene at every level and to be exempt from all challenge. Worse, the bishops themselves claim that the Pope is authorized by the New Testament, even created by Christ himself – a dogma challenged by Martin Luther. So Tyndale in a long digression attacks the Bishop of Rochester for a sermon, delivered at a burning of Luther's books, stating just that.

At root is the clash over works, on which 'the Pope's false power' depends. As Tyndale had explained in his 'book of the justifying of faith', which is *Mammon*, the New Testament teaches as its strong main current that it is faith alone that justifies – this is what is unique about the New Testament. Good works should follow personal faith, but a Christian is not saved by performing ceremonies, paying money or listening to Latin. He is saved by the work of Christ in his undeserving heart, which favour then leads to his understanding and growth as he searches and knows God's word.

Tyndale explains in *Obedience* that two things should happen. First, the unity of God's kingdom should be declared. 'The most despised person in his realm is the king's brother and fellow member with him and equal with him in the kingdom of God and of Christ' (p. 63). As always, Tyndale makes his own, and extends, the thinking of Luther. There should not be two kingdoms, one secular and one run by the Pope and the prelates. 'The powers that be are ordained by God.' Secondly, England should wake up to the extent of the evil intrusion of pope and prelates into daily life, national and ordinary, and to the thoroughness with which the gospel has been distorted. Powerfully, Tyndale's *Obedience* does both these things. Explaining that the Pope does the work of an 'Antichrist', Tyndale analyses at length the falsehoods that control the church's teaching on the sacraments and other practices, and ends with a long attack on the source of all the distortions: the authorized, and by then traditional, misreading and misinterpreting of scripture by seeing everything as an allegory, making it mean whatever you want.

While scripture was entirely in Latin, few could object. Now, however, the Bible was arriving printed in English, and eagerly, indeed desperately, being read and heard. That changed everything. Tyndale did not write from himself. His *Obedience* is made of scripture. The Bible is everywhere, in the words and the phrases, in the stories quoted and the references made. Sometimes, as in the first paragraphs of the book, and elsewhere, they are very thick on the page, but they are never far away. Scripture, in English, abundantly known and quoted, is the authority by which Tyndale refutes error, whether the widespread corruptions of popes, bishops or clergy, or that sermon by the Bishop of Rochester. (To Fisher's apparent error of Latin grammar, reversing the New Testament doctrine of faith, Tyndale responds with two pages of solid Pauline and Johannine theology in quotation: pp. 79–81.) Tyndale understood his authority: he was an outstanding scholar of the original, Greek, New Testament, and by 1528 it seems he was already reading the Hebrew scriptures in the original, almost the only Englishman to do so at the time.

As Tyndale writes, 'the scripture giveth record to himself, and ever expoundeth itself by another open text' (p. 172). For that to happen, of course, the whole of scripture has to be freely available. It is striking that while usually expositing and spelling out scripture passages, Tyndale also expects his readers to know the Bible well. How they did that when the Constitutions of Oxford of 1408, forbidding access to any Bible in English, were still so powerfully in force is a question even now awaiting adequate answer. By the last years of our twentieth century, the Bible printed in English has been for so long automatically available, and to many so familiar, that it needs saying strongly that in 1528 to know a Bible in English was both arrestingly new, and dangerous.

For Tyndale and all the Reformers, the Bible – the whole Bible – was the first and only authority for belief and practice. This needs to be re-emphasized here for two reasons. First, Tyndale is packing his text with the Bible not for affectation or ornament, as someone might use quotations from Virgil or Ovid, or (later) Shakespeare. Tyndale's Bible is the living Word. To make whole paragraphs out of Bible sentences is for Tyndale to declare that what he writes is God's truth – and God's truth as it is now accessible to every reader and hearer of English. Secondly, the Catholic church for centuries had claimed another authority altogether. Since Tyndale in the *Obedience* spends many pages attacking what he finds as the false doctrine of the Bishop of Rochester in his sermon against Luther, we might conveniently quote that sermon to set out the standard Catholic doctrine:

After this the second person the son of God our saviour Christ Jesu was sent by his father into this world to instruct man, both by himself and by his apostles, the which were conversant with him (as the gospel here sayeth) from the beginning. Those blessed apostles left unto us also many things by mouth, which is not written in the bible . . .

St Paul in 2 Thessalonians *sive per sermonem sive per epistolam nostram*, that is to say, be ye constant and keep those instructions and eruditions that ye have learned of us, either by mouth, or else by writing . . .

. . . Here ye may see by express scripture of St Paul that we be bound to believe many more things than be written and put in the bible . . .

A marginal note refers to the 'Unwritten traditions left to the church by Christ and the apostles'. Another, beside a reference to the third-century theologian Origen on observances, has 'kneeling towards the east, words, gestures, questions, answers in the sacrament'.[3]

The Reformers were absolutely against this. For them, the only authority was what was in the Bible – and the whole Bible, not selected texts. The whole Bible, they believed with passion, could interpret itself, particularly through the guidance of the Holy Spirit working to edify local congregations in the working-out of faith. So every man, woman and child should have access to the whole Bible in their own tongue, to read it or hear it read, for their own salvation. All the Reformers scorned the claim by the great hierarchical structure that was the church that it had an alternative, superior and secret authority stemming from what another marginal note in Fisher's sermon calls 'the traditions of the great Bishop Christ' – especially as those traditions were a mesh of practices, observances, gestures, or whatever, which the Reformers saw had nothing to do with the New Testament and its central doctrine of justification by faith alone.

The second thing to recognize is that Tyndale was an outstanding writer of English prose: that is, prose in English, not, as characteristic of the early 1500s, in the vocabulary and heavily subordinated syntax dependent on Latin, on top of an uncertain form that was half Saxon and half Norman French. His Bible translations, of which his Gospel narratives, and especially the parables, are models, can be shown to have affected the general development of an English Plain Style in the decades that followed. In his *Obedience*, as everywhere in his writings, he used the tropes and figures of classical rhetoric. When Tyndale was young, this craft was freshly taught to English boys by Erasmus in his schoolbook *De Copia*. That book and that craft were in Latin. Tyndale made a prose in English. Remarkable enough in 1528, it still feels both effective and modern, crying out to be spoken aloud. See for example the paragraph beginning 'To preach God's word . . .', p. 68; and the passages on extortion of money from the poor (pp. 91–4).

Tyndale had something clear to say, of course, which always helps. Part of the power of his prose comes from his wide landscape, dense with thought and life, rich with existential experience. In these pages is high theology and pastoral wisdom, from Paul and the Gospels. Here is much of the New Testament, and also the Old. Here are the Fathers, from Origen to Aquinas; the late medieval schoolmen, and the squabbling metaphysicians. Literature in England, and English history, are part of his picture. Above all, here in a broad unrolling tapestry is the contemporary church in so many of its practices, from pope to deacon, through bishop, priest, monk and friar, limiter and pardoner, and not all of them condemned. The national structure of civil law, too, from judges to 'sheriffs, baily-errants and constables' is set in the domestic structure of husbands and wives, fathers and mothers, sons and daughters, and servants. This daily life of England in detail is often a list of gross abuses of the common people by the church. This is the now neglected side of English life at the time. A powerful modern view has given us a picture of bewildered people in mourning for the loss of their beloved religious practices at the hands of a few noisy politicians who made the English Reformation.[4] Tyndale, throughout his writings, is ruthless and thorough in his attack on the church of which he was a priest. Spiritual leaders did not trust in God, or preach his gospel. They had been seduced at every level by worldly power. Internationally, popes and prelates successfully schemed to their own advantage, accumulating vast wealth at a huge cost in lives and livelihoods. Large numbers of 'the spirituality' were pursuing only their own comfort and power. In every town and village, a root of hypocrisy could be the clergy's official celibacy – and the scriptures, it was being discovered, said that priests should be married (for instance 1 Timothy 3:2). At every level, abuses of power were a scandal. Powerfully expressed anticlericalism had a history in England from at least the time of Chaucer and Langland in the 1380s. It reached print in England with Tyndale's *Obedience*. His strong and extensive New Testament theology gives him a cogency in attacking the corruptions in the church of his day that puts him well above other printed works that followed: for example *The Supplication of Beggars* (1529), attributed to Simon Fish, and even Robert Barnes in his short *What the church is* and *Men's constitution*, both also of 1529. Tyndale is in a different league from the doggerel *Rede me and be not wroth* (1527), probably by Jerome Barlow and William Roye – the latter a former helper of Tyndale's whom he was glad to lose.

Because almost all the English nation, including the priesthood, was ignorant of almost all the Bible, and nobody taught it, traditional religion had often become superstition. In a passionate early passage in *Answer*, Tyndale wrote:

Judge whether it be possible that any good should come out of their dumb ceremonies and sacraments into thy soul. Judge their penance, pilgrimages, pardons, purgatory, praying to posts, dumb blessings, dumb absolutions, their dumb pattering, and howling, their dumb strange holy gestures, with all their dumb disguisings, their satisfactions and justifyings. And because thou findest them false in so many things, trust them in nothing; but judge them in all things.[5]

In saying all this: giving laymen the Bible in English, pointing out that the church could err, Tyndale's *Obedience*, like his *Mammon*, was forbidden, and read dangerously in secret.

Stylistically, his immersion in scripture means that it is easy to see that the writer of the *Obedience* has translated the New Testament. When he is not directly quoting he is often, or even usually, echoing biblical words and phrases. This is a very different thing from the 'biblical rhythms' sometimes noted in modern writers, where 'the + noun + of + the + noun' forms ('the fish of the sea', 'the fowls of the air'), which are English shapes made from Hebrew, are used for sentimental effect. Tyndale's 'biblical rhythms' are not surface imitation so much as the result of Bible forms having seeped far down into his mind. Moreover, Tyndale's 'biblical' sentences are made of hard theological truths. Consider the following, from Tyndale's section 'Of anoiling':

The promise of God is the anchor that saveth us in all temptations. If all the world be against us, God's word is stronger than the world. If the world kill us, that shall make us alive again. If it be possible for the world to cast us into hell from thence yet shall God's word bring us again. Hereby seest thou that it is not the work but the promise that justifieth us through faith. Now where no promise is there can no faith be and therefore no justifying, though there be never so glorious works (p. 131).

The words 'God', 'promise' and 'anchor' echo Hebrews 6:17–19; 'saveth' and 'in all temptations' pick up statements in Hebrews before (3:8, 5:7), and after (7:25). 'If all the world be against us' echoes Romans 8:31. The 'word/world' opposition is from John 1 and elsewhere. And so on – the same tracing of the origins of the vocabulary can be done throughout the passage, as throughout many paragraphs of the book. But look also at the forms of the sentences. They are founded on New Testament Greek syntax. In Greek the verb is paramount: 'If the world kill us' (unlike Latin, where the noun dominates, producing as it might be 'cause our deaths'). New Testament Greek syntax, like English, is a basic subject–verb–object sequence, 'The promise of God is the anchor', without elaborate subordination which Latin prefers. The three sentences beginning with 'If' imitate many sentences by Paul – see 1 Corinthians 15:12–19, to look no further. 'Hereby seest thou . . .' reflects forms in 1 John 3 and 4 (for example, 1 John 4:13, 'Hereby know we, that we dwell in him . . .'). More than this: the pattern of logical argument, saying 'this, therefore that' or 'not this, that', or 'this, then not that', ringingly echoes Paul, as that same passage from 1 Corinthians 15 shows.

Though in the notes that follow the text in this edition many of his phrases are given their scripture origin, it would have become tedious to try to locate in the *Obedience* – as in any book by Tyndale – every single New Testament word or phrase which is echoed. Occasional small discrepancies between his quotations and what appears in his own translations suggest that he is quoting from memory, which is not unlikely.[6] And of course there are in his book long stretches of attack on corrupt dealings or superstitions or peasant suffering where scripture is irrelevant to his subject – significantly so, indeed.

Life

To understand his work better, and in particular this book of *Obedience*, we should know something of Tyndale's life. He was born in Gloucestershire in 1494. He spent more than ten years at Magdalen Hall, Oxford (which later became Hertford College), where in the course of his BA and MA he learned the new, good, humanist Latin, and Greek, then newly being taught in Oxford. He may have gone on to Cambridge, where Greek had been taught by Erasmus. Though it seems unlikely that they met, that great scholar permanently influenced Tyndale in several important ways. It is probable that Tyndale is the author of the English translation of the *Enchiridion militis Christiani* ('A Handbook for a Christian soldier') in the course of which Erasmus argues that the scriptures in the vernacular should be available to everyone. Erasmus in 1516 had published in Basel his *Novum instrumentum*, a 'new instrument' in the work of reforming the church from within. This was his own translation of the New Testament into Latin, a challenge to the church's 'common version', the Latin Vulgate, which had been the only Bible the church had known, or permitted, since the fourth century. Erasmus's translation was influential: but far more powerful in its effect on Europe was his printing of the original Greek alongside the Latin. This Greek 'Textus Receptus', as it became, is in some details flawed: but that the movers of reform throughout Europe could use an easily available Greek New Testament for translation into national vernaculars was effective in ways that remain incalculable. Luther led the way in 1522 with his German 'September Testament': by 1526 Tyndale had followed.

In the early 1520s Tyndale, back in Gloucestershire from Oxford and possibly Cambridge, and ordained priest, had served as tutor to the children of Sir John and Lady Walsh. His duties were light. His work with the Greek New Testament text sealed his vocation to bring that book to the English. To one learned clergyman at the Walshes' table who remarked that 'we were better without God's law than the Pope's', Tyndale famously retorted, 'I defy the Pope and all his laws. If God spare my life ere many years, I will cause a boy that driveth the plough shall know more of the scripture than thou dost.' Reading any part of the Bible in English (that is, in the manuscript 'Lollard' versions from the Latin made in the 1380s, popularly ascribed to John Wyclif and still circulating), never mind freshly translating, were activities, uniquely in Britain, punishable by the severest penalties, including being burned alive. Needing a bishop's permission, Tyndale left Gloucestershire to carry out his intentions. He took with him his translation (since lost) of the difficult Greek of an oration by Isocrates as a demonstration of his skill, and hoped to approach the Bishop of London, Cuthbert Tunstall (who had, incidentally, helped to find Greek manuscripts of the New Testament for Erasmus). Tunstall would not see him. Tyndale recognized that, as he wrote, 'there was no place in all England' for such work, and he left for Germany in about 1524. In 1525 he was in Cologne, and in 1526 in Worms, as we saw. In Britain, possession of a copy of his 1526 New Testament meant punishment. The Bishop of London collected all he could, and in a ceremony at St Paul's Cathedral, burned them.[7] Tunstall himself preached a sermon denouncing Tyndale's New Testaments as heretical. From these events we can date Tyndale's more aggressive anticlericalism.

Probably in Germany, Tyndale learned Hebrew. In Antwerp in 1530 he produced his Pentateuch, again smuggled into Britain. These small volumes had prologues, woodcuts and some explanatory marginal notes, a few of them (no more) anti-papal. His Hebrew understanding meant that as he revised his New Testament, Tyndale became aware of the Hebrew affecting the Greek, a new insight at the time. This 1534 revision of his New Testament, also from Antwerp, now had prologues and marginal notes: the often-reported offensiveness of those notes is largely a modern invention, handed on by those who cannot have studied a copy. A greater number of these New Testaments survived, including one owned and inscribed by Queen Anne Boleyn.

Tyndale had printed his translation of Jonah, and already in manuscript was his translation of the Old Testament historical books, Joshua to 2 Chronicles, when in May 1535 he was tricked into arrest and incarcerated in Vilvoorde Castle, outside Brussels. Attempts from the English court to get him released were blocked locally. Leading heresy-hunters, principally from the Catholic University of Leuven, interrogated him over sixteen months: they confirmed him a heretic, and handed him over to the secular arm. On the morning of 6 October 1536, having been degraded from the priesthood, he was led out before a grand assembly, strangled and burned.

On Tyndale's death, John Rogers, Chaplain to the English House at Antwerp (and seventeen years later to become himself the first martyr under Queen Mary), gathered up all Tyndale's translations, that is, his revised New Testament and half the Old Testament. Adding the rest of the Old Testament from the work of Miles Coverdale, Rogers had the whole Bible printed in 1537 to carry forward Tyndale's versions, even obtaining a licence from King Henry VIII. Tyndale the heretic could not be mentioned, so Rogers used the names of two disciples, Thomas and Matthew, to make 'Thomas Matthew's Bible'. The story of the succession of Tyndale's Bible translations after this volume, through sixteenth-century versions, and even until today, does not belong here. It has to be understood, however, that Tyndale's texts went forward, often little changed, as the foundation of all succeeding English Bibles, including the celebrated 1611 Authorized Version, or King James Version, of which the New Testament is 83 per cent Tyndale.[8] Thus the wide dissemination across the globe for nearly four hundred years of that version has assured the transmission of Tyndale's original translations, frequently taken over by King James's scholars word for word. Tyndale has reached more people than Shakespeare.

Other works

Tyndale wrote a number of other books, all attacked in England and denounced as heretical. From Worms in 1526 came a development of his prologue to the abandoned 1525 Cologne translation, *A compendious introduction, prologue or preface unto the epistle of Paul to the Romans*. This small, slim book, of which one copy exists,[9] is based fairly freely on the prologue to Romans which appeared in all editions of Luther's German New Testament. Tyndale expanded it into the prologue to Romans in his own 1534 New Testament. The popular Reformation in Europe can be summarized as 'people studied Paul', whose Epistle to the Romans was the most important document for all reformers. That epistle dominates

Tyndale's further extension of the 1525 prologue into *A Pathway to Holy Scripture* of 1531. Tyndale published in Antwerp two other biblical commentaries, *The Exposition of the First Epistle of John* in 1531, and *An Exposition upon the V, VI, VII Chapters of Matthew* (that is, the Sermon on the Mount), in 1533.

Four more books came from Tyndale in Antwerp. The first, *The Parable of the Wicked Mammon*, also partly dependent on Luther, we have considered above. Two years after *Mammon* and *Obedience*, in 1530, Tyndale's short book, *The Practice of Prelates*, ostensibly argued that Henry VIII could not divorce Catherine of Aragon. It is an attack on a historic European Catholic conspiracy, as he sees it, to manipulate princes and rulers everywhere to the prelates' own advantage. A recurrent image is the pope's ivy strangling a nation's living tree. 'Practice' carries, as well as its meaning as the exercise of a profession, the Shakespearean meaning of scheming through trickery. In 1528, the London lawyer Thomas More, who had been knighted in 1521 and was already a seasoned opponent of Luther in Latin, received permission by Cuthbert Tunstall to read heretical books in English. More found it in his heart to crush heretics, 'if need be to burn heresy out of England with fire'.[10] The first result was his *Dialogue Concerning Heresies* of 1529, in which some of the third book, with heavy hitting elsewhere, is More's wholesale attack on Tyndale's 1526 New Testament as a Lutheran book. To this Tyndale replied two years later, in 1531, with *An Answer to Sir Thomas More's Dialogue*, in which, after an introductory essay, Tyndale replied point by point. More, who within weeks of the publication of the *Dialogue* had been made Chancellor, replied to Tyndale's *Answer* the following year, 1532, with his endless *Confutation of Tyndale's Answer* totalling (even unfinished) half a million words. More's *Apology* and his *Debellation of Salem and Bizance*, both of 1533, still attacked Tyndale. Tyndale had made no further reply after his 80,000-word *Answer*. All More's writings against Tyndale, almost three-quarters of a million words – frequently intemperate, as even his supporters, early and late, acknowledge[11] – can be boiled down to his objection to Tyndale's translation of six words. In place of the standard 'priest', 'church', 'charity', 'grace', 'confess' and 'do penance' from the fourth-century Latin, deeply built in to the church's practice for centuries, Tyndale from the original New Testament Greek gave 'senior' (later 'elder'), 'congregation', 'love', 'favour', 'knowledge' and 'repent'.[12] The difference between Tyndale and More was absolute and irreconcilable. More insisted that the church could not err in one jot or one tittle, and scripture had to be interpreted by the infallible church. Tyndale declared, from scripture itself, that scripture belongs to the whole body of Christian people, guided by the Holy Spirit in their congregations, and the activities of the church have to be based on, and judged by, scripture. Moreover, for Tyndale scripture can be, indeed has to be, reinterpreted in every generation. He speaks for all believers together in an open, expanding, Christian society.[13] This is why he is still important. He was releasing theology, looking forward. As will be seen, his understanding of the scriptural view of the common life of Christians is still, at the end of the twentieth century, a challenge – and has been almost totally ignored.

Thus three strands should run through discussion of *The Obedience of a Christian Man*: that the book is rooted in scripture; that the book contains English prose remarkable for 1528; and that the book was part of Tyndale's larger enterprise, breaking new ground in expounding the biblical Christian commonwealth, necessarily challenging the established order of the Catholic church.

The book

Like all Tyndale's books, his *Obedience* is a small volume. It is octavo, measuring about five and a half inches by four, the size of smaller prayerbooks found in Anglican church pews. It was made to be held in the hand. It has just over three hundred cleanly printed black-letter pages with wide margins which are often empty: sometimes they have one or two (occasionally more) marginal notes. The restraint in Tyndale's margins is important. After further editions following his death in 1536, some printed in London, the prolific London Protestant printer John Day issued in 1572 a new edition as part of his *The Whole Works of W. Tyndall, John Frith, and Doct. Barnes, three worthy Martyrs . . .* in double-column folio, with introductory matter from Foxe's *Acts and Monuments* (which Day also printed). It had some tiny variants in the text, and some new marginal notes obviously not by Tyndale. This version was the basis for the most used edition to date, that made by Henry Walter for the Parker Society in 1848.[14] Walter not only added unauthorized notes (even some of those he marks 'W.T.' are misplaced), and coyly omitted a mild scurrility (see below, p. 138). Worse, he promoted single subheadings in the text to running heads over many pages, altering the emphasis: for example, his eleven pages headed 'Against the pope's false power' would be better headed 'Christian responsibility'. Worse, he silently emended, changing 'to' to 'unto' for example, 'exempt' to 'except', 'stole' to 'stool', 'antetheme' to 'antitheme', 'chopological' to (once) 'tropological' (thus killing Tyndale's joke there), 'mighty' to 'naughty', 'bells tink' to 'bellies think', and so on. Worse still, he put into the margins Tyndale's internal biblical references, giving the impression they were somehow secondary. Worst of all, he interfered with every phrase and sentence by introducing heavy Victorian punctuation. This rash of commas on every page, with many semicolons (not invented in Tyndale's day) and the frequent lowering of full stops to colons (thus recasting sentences entirely), destroys the possibility of response to Tyndale's phrasing and rhythms. The original Antwerp printer's punctuation is erratic, but spare – not an impression a reader receives from Walter's pages. Nevertheless we must be grateful to him, for without the three Parker Society volumes of all Tyndale's works (and two that we now know were not by Tyndale) outside the Bible translations, any version of the *Obedience* and the rest would have been difficult for the general public to find. (A facsimile of the first 1528 edition has been available, without modern introduction or notes and in the original black letter, since 1977.)[15]

At the end of Tyndale's own 1528 edition, after fourteen pages of index and half a page of errata, the colophon reads, 'At Marlborow in the land of Hesse The second day of October . Anno. M. CCCCC.xxviij by me Hans Luft'. There was a Hans Luft of Wittenberg, of course, who was Luther's assiduous and wealthy printer: but 'Hans Luft of Marlborow' is an invention. Such a fiction was a frequent device of the printers of 'Protestant' books – another example is 'Adam Anonymous, Basel'. The invisible printer 'Hans Luft of Marlborow' (his name means 'John Air') was until recently thought to have been Johannes Hoochstraten of Antwerp. He is now more plausibly understood to have been Martin de

Keyser ('Martin L'Empereur'), one of the main Antwerp printers of 'Lutheran' books, and the printer of Tyndale's *Mammon, Practice, Answer* – and, as we now know, of his 1530 Pentateuch, as well as his 1534 New Testament.

The original 1528 title page of the *Obedience* calls, rather loudly, for comment. The central title block is reasonably straightforward. Where the author's name might have been, the space is blank, not uncommon in books of the time. The woodcut panels bordering it, however, show little else but thirteen naked ladies. The bottom block has, scratched on, the Greek word χαριτες (*charites*), that is, the three Graces: not that that helps much, and a fourth is bathing in a fountain. The top block possibly shows them dancing before Apollo, the movement continued in the side blocks. Martin de Keyser, for his own reasons, used crudely locked blocks which had already, as frequently happened, passed from printer to printer. These rather shop-worn nymphs had already appeared round the titles of books in Germany as well as Antwerp, Catholic and Protestant, and would go on to decorate the titles of others – seven in all. There seems to have been no greater significance in their use beyond the supposed attraction of faintly fetching decoration.

On publication, the *Obedience* was strongly received in Britain. (About ten copies of the original 1528 edition have survived, out of a print-run of unknown size.) It appeared regularly, with all Tyndale's other works, on official lists of banned books.[16] John Foxe, in his *Acts and Monuments*, tells, for example, the story of James Bainham, a virtuous London lawyer, who was arrested, kept imprisoned at Sir Thomas More's house at Chelsea, and tortured. The nine articles of his interrogation by John Stokesley, Bishop of London, printed by Foxe, conclude with his confession that he had 'the New Testament translated by William Tyndale'. He also 'had in his keeping . . . the Wicked Mammon, the Obedience of a Christian Man, the Practice of Prelates, the Answer of Tyndale to Thomas More's Dialogue' and books by John Frith and George Joye. 'Neither did he ever know (said he) that Tyndale was a naughty fellow.' After months in prison, and under great pressure (his wife had been imprisoned elsewhere, and their goods confiscated) he abjured and did public penance, and was allowed home. His conscience, however, would not let him rest: within a month he had recanted his abjuration, and the next Sunday after, he came to St Austin's, with the New Testament in his hand in English, and the Obedience of a Christian Man in his bosom, and stood up there before the people in his pew, there declaring openly, with weeping tears, that he had denied God.[17]

He wrote a letter to the Bishop, was again arrested and, according to Foxe, interrogated further and 'very cruelly handled'. On 1 May 1532 he was burned at the stake.

Foxe also possessed a manuscript, first printed by Strype in his *Ecclesiastical Memorials* in 1821, which told the romantic story connecting Tyndale's *Obedience*, Anne Boleyn, and her husband-to-be, Henry VIII. It is corroborated by a history of Anne Boleyn published in the 1590s. Briefly, it tells how Anne loaned her personal copy of the *Obedience* to a young lady in her service, whose suitor took the book and was found reading it. Cardinal Wolsey confiscated it. Anne went to the king, who had the book restored to her. She then 'besought his grace most tenderly to read it. The king did so, and delighted in the book. For, saith he, this is a book for me and all kings to read.'[18]

Structure

The *Obedience* has two preliminary sections (like later divisions, each begins with an illuminated capital letter). First is a preface entitled 'William Tyndale other wise called William Hychins unto the Reader', thirty-six pages long in the original, about a tenth of the whole volume. The tenor of this preface (pp. 3–25) is the double point that reading the scriptures (which everyone should be able to do) reveals the amazing power of God, and that the expositions of biblical faith on these pages are a personal address to each reader from 'William Tyndale other wise called William Hychins' – the author, who uses both his names, is not hiding. It is important not to disregard the bravery of Tyndale, and of other 'Lutherans' of the time like John Frith, in putting a name to work which attracted inevitable, and fearful, punishment.[19]

This is followed by 'The prologue unto the book', eight pages long in the original (pp. 26–30). This locates disobedience not in the teaching of God's word, as the church then had it, but in 'the bloody doctrine of the Pope which causeth disobedience, rebellion and insurrection'.

The book proper, also starting with an illuminated letter, has the heading, 'The obedience of all degrees proved by God's word and first of children unto their elders'. In working with the doctrine of degree, Tyndale was of his time. Sir Thomas Elyot, for example, in his famous *The book named the governour* (1531), essentially a plan for bringing up gentlemen's sons, elaborated how 'God . . . had set degrees and estates in all his glorious works'.[20] Luther had written that the secular authorities must be obeyed.[21] Tyndale characteristically makes an abstract remark startlingly concrete. His book starts with God, like the Epistle to the Hebrews, but far less grandly: it also starts from living human beings. New in this book is Tyndale's intermeshing of God's amazing presence, expressed in scripture, and lived experience.

The book has three large sections. The first (pp. 31–59) explains God's law of obedience, from which no one is exempt. The second (pp. 59–108) sets out how to rule as father, husband, master, landlord, king or judge. The third (pp. 108–191) discusses signs: true like those sacraments that are scriptural, or false like the worship of saints; true like the literal sense of scripture, or false like the allegorizing of it. The whole treatise is then summarized in the last twenty pages, and the fourteen pages of 'The table of the book' make an index.

The immediacy of the tone of Tyndale's voice can conceal the careful scheme. It is easy to demonstrate in a diagram the systematic headings, subheadings and further subdivisions, often balancing in pairs. Tyndale was a clever Oxford man of the time, trained in both late-medieval schemes of expression and the new humanist ways of logic and rhetoric. It would be unusual if he were not writing to a firm and detailed pattern of argument.[22]

The *Obedience* and political thought

Tyndale's book came at the time when what we understand as modern political thought was first becoming visible. It is a central document in that process. Crucially, we can watch in that period, throughout northern Europe, and here at the heart of the *Obedience*, the emergence of the modern concept of the state. Tyndale does not see a fractured nation, ruled by a monarchy that is itself fighting for independence from a church. He is not even what would later be called Erastian, arguing for the subordination of the jurisdiction of the church to the state. Yes, he wants England free of the pope, and he is withering about the papacy and all its manifestations in corrupt prelates, priests and monks. But that power of the pope is a late accretion on, and an irrelevance in, the congregation of believing Christians as seen in the New Testament: the rock and the keys of the kingdom in Matthew 16:18 are Peter's faith, not his person. The whole Christian community, Tyndale argues from the New Testament, is one. There is no parallel, holy, body with quite separate authority and powers. True, some have a special calling in Christ: but that is to preach the gospel, to educate their little flocks in the doctrines of Paul, flat contrary to what the prelates and priests were doing. Everyone, from the prince to the poorest infant, is part of the same commonwealth of Christians, as the gospels make so clear.

The word 'obedience' might suggest that Tyndale canvassed a blind patriarchy. Certainly there is one such elementary sense in the title of his book, to counter the accusations, coming from 'our holy prelates and our ghostly religious' as Tyndale puts it at the start of his prologue, that all the reformers were preaching sedition: that God's word itself, the bishops and 'religious' were saying,

causeth insurrection and teacheth the people to disobey their heads and governors, and moveth them to rise against their princes and to make all common and to make havoc of other men's goods (p. 26).

Thomas More stated the common Catholic view that the Peasants' Uprising of 1525 (in which between 70,000 and 100,000 peasants died) was caused by Luther.[23] It was important to Tyndale to be heard explaining that that was untrue. He begins his prologue to *Obedience* by stating that prelates, monks and friars are teaching that 'God's word ... causeth insurrection ... Therefore have I made this little treatise ... containing all obedience that is of God. In which (whosoever readeth it) shall easily perceive ... that they lie' (p. 26). Thomas More went on to attribute the sack of Rome and its exceptional cruelties to Luther, which Tyndale refuted, citing the responsibility of the pope.[24] As he explained later, 'God is not the author of dissension and strife, but of unity and peace and of good order' (p. 136). 'Give therefore to Caesar', Tyndale had translated Matthew 22:21 (and Mark 12:17, and Luke 20:25) 'that which is Caesar's.' Tyndale gave us the English of the verse from Romans 13, 'Let every soul submit himself unto the authority of the higher powers. For there is no power but of God. The powers that be, are ordained of God.' In that sense his political meaning might be seen as patriarchal. But he finds in the social and political structures adumbrated in the New Testament a hierarchical form different from patriarchy, something that has not even yet been taken seriously, as we shall see in a moment.

Tyndale's book went on to be popularly imitated: in, for example, the anonymous *The institution of a christian man* (1537). In John Bale's play *King John* (*c.* 1540), Tyndale's *Obedience* is quoted on stage. Shakespeare's pragmatist Ulysses in *Troilus and Cressida* (1601) expounds what would happen if degree were broken: 'Take but degree away, untune that string,/And hark what discord follows' (I.iii.109–10: see 83–137). A good argument can be made for Tyndale's book affecting seventeenth-century thinkers: Hobbes's horror of civil war 'seems . . . to have an emotional affinity with Tyndale's "It is better to have somewhat than to be clean stripped out of all together"'.[25]

Unlike the many complications of the church's pattern in the fabric of English life, the Christian commonwealth, holds Tyndale, is simple. Throughout the book he states again and again the central message of the Christian gospel – as, for example, on page 124: 'if any man have sinned, yet if he repent and believe the promise, we are sure by God's word, that he is loosed and forgiven in Christ'. That echoes 1 John 1:9, as all his statements of faith echo or quote scripture. Tyndale always cuts back to 'God's word', which he, like all reformers, understood was the true source. There he finds what he frequently expounds in all his books, a 'feeling faith' (as opposed to what Melanchthon first called a 'historical faith'), that is, God operative, through his word, and joyfully responded to, in the living moment (as opposed to faith in a 'story'). It is notable how often Tyndale in all his writing stresses the response to God in feelings, to 'feel the goodness of God and his help and the working of his spirit', as he puts it early on (p. 10). Many of his illustrations are bodily, of God as physician or surgeon treating illness, or the joy of recovery of health. A frequent Bible phrase is 'written in the heart', ultimately from Hebrews 8:10.

The signs of feeling faith in action are good deeds performed, not for personal gain, but for a neighbour. This is a central theme of *Mammon*. Riches are wicked if they are not given to fill a neighbour's need. Tyndale is everywhere savage about how this has been reversed by the prelates of Antichrist. In *Obedience* he writes:

. . . let any man eat flesh but on a Saturday or break any other tradition of theirs, and he shall be bound and not loosed, till he have paid the uttermost farthing, other with shame most vile or death most cruel, but hate thy neighbour as much as thou wilt and thou shalt have no rebuke of them, yea rob him, murder him, and then come to them and welcome (p. 99).

As modern readers we are aware of a passage like that set in its historical context. We should, as well, be formidably challenged. Tyndale's gender-politics may today be seen as derisory, but his point is the responsibilities that go with power. The Christian commonwealth that Tyndale expounds is not so visible in Christian countries where the rich get richer and the poor poorer; where such countries can use Third World debt as a tool of oppression; where, to come closer to home, ostentatious personal wealth can be declared a sign of Christ's personal approval.

The deepest core of this book, deeper even than the heart of *Mammon*, is the challenge of living as Christ. This is where 'the spirituality' have failed.

He that avengeth himself on every trifle is not meet to preach the patience of Christ, how that a man ought to forgive and to suffer all things. He that is overwhelmed with all manner riches and doth but seek more daily, is not meet to preach poverty (p. 68).

Tyndale wrote that of the prelates. Inside those words, as inside everything Tyndale wrote, including all the quoting from Paul, Peter and John in this book, is what is so lightly pictured there, the living Christ of the Gospels. And further inside still is the undeserved and unearned gift of God's love towards us.

Though Henry Walter's 1848 version for the Parker Society has been studied, and sometimes reprinted, William Tyndale's *The Obedience of a Christian Man* is given here, in the first months of a new millennium, as something new. It has a historical significance still not properly understood. For the first time it stated the two great principles of the English Reformation: the supreme authority of scripture in the church, and the supreme authority of the king in the state. More importantly, it challenges our twenty-first-century Christian commonwealth in its proper, biblical, source. Tyndale asks in this book what Christendom would look like if the base were the fullest Christian faith.

NOTES

1. Bound into a volume in Victorian times, they can be seen in the British Library in London.

2. 'Lollard' was initially the popular, and intentionally rude, name for the heretical followers of Wyclif, and then for members of the widespread underground movement that developed. They were believers in personal faith and the free availability of the Bible, and thus necessarily critical of church practices. Severely persecuted, they were nevertheless a foundation for the reception of Lutheran ideas. The word 'Protestant', in the sense wider than simply German opposition to the church, is not recorded by *OED* as being in use until 1553.

3. *The English Works of John Fisher . . .*, ed. John E. B. Mayor, Part 1 (EETS, Oxford University Press, 1876/1935), 322.

4. Eamon Duffy's remarkable study, *The Stripping of the Altars: Traditional Religion in England 1400–1580* (Yale University Press, 1992), in 650 pages mentions the Bible hardly at all, and gives no sense of the English Bible's widespread reception. In his index, there are only six entries under 'Bible-reading': they are 'unpopularity'; 'forbidden during services'; 'disparaged'; 'proclamation about, May 1541'; 'forbidden to women and lower orders'; 'discouraged in Kent'. Dense and valuable though Duffy's book is, this is a partisan view of Reformation England. Even assuming a lower figure (3,000 rather than Cochlaeus's 6,000) for the print-run of Tyndale's first (1526) New Testament from Worms, and then adding the print-runs of the piracies of it that came from Antwerp in the next few years, we easily reach a figure of at least 20,000 English New Testaments printed and

smuggled into England and Scotland in the early 1530s. Later in the century, over half a million English Bibles were bought. This represents an English experience of the Bible at the time that is worth more than six derogatory entries. Duffy, moreover, is said (see for example Clifford Longley, the *Tablet*, 14 August 1999, p. 1094) to have put paid to that 400-year-old version of English history which maintained that English religion prior to the Reformation was decadent and corrupt, and overripe for protest at the peddling of superstitious nonsense. Large sections of Tyndale's *Obedience*, written in 1528 at the height of the pre-Reformation Church's influence, will be seen to reveal just that decadence, corruption and superstition.

5. *Answer*, 9. It was on this passage that Thomas More commented: 'Judge, good Christian reader, whether it be possible that he [Tyndale] be any better than a beast, out of whose brutish beastly mouth cometh such a filthy foam of blasphemies . . .', in Louis A. Schuster, Richard C. Marius, James P. Lusardi and Richard J. Schoeck (eds.), *The Complete Works of St Thomas More*, vol. 8, Part 1 (Yale University Press, 1973), 135.

6. For detail about such biblical texture, see *WTB*, 122–8.

7. The one textually complete surviving copy was bought in 1994 by the British Library for over a million pounds (the greatest sum paid by the BL for a single volume) in order to preserve and display it. A second copy was found in 1996 in the Landesbibliotek in Stuttgart. This copy has a title page which reads: 'The new Testament as it was written and caused to be written by them which heard it. To whom our saviour Christ Jesus commanded that they should preach it unto all creatures.' See Eberhard Zwink, 'Confusion about Tyndale: The Stuttgart Copy of the 1526 New Testament in English', *Reformation* 3, 1998, 28–48.

8. See John Nielson and Royal Skousen, 'How much of the King James Bible is William Tyndale's?', *Reformation* 3, 1998, 49–74.

9. In the Bodleian Library, Oxford.

10. Richard Marius, *Thomas More* (1984), 338.

11. Nicholas Harpsfield (More's first biographer, who wrote some twenty-five years after More's death), *The Life and Death of Sir Thomas More*, ed. E. V. Hitchcock (1932), 117–18; L. A. Schuster, R. C. Marius, J. P. Lusardi and R. J. Schoeck (eds.), *The Complete Works of St Thomas More*, vol. 8, Part 3 (Yale University Press, 1973), 1260. For a discussion of More in relation to Tyndale, see *WTB*, 250–80.

12. Tyndale in several places elaborated and defended his translations: see the early pages of the essay that opens *Answer*, 11–24.

13. His enemy Thomas More's 'ideal', the 'No Place' which is Utopia, is an enclosed island, just as More's church is tightly enclosed, incapable of error.

14. *Doctrinal Treatises and Introductions to Different Portions of the Holy Scriptures by*

William Tyndale, Martyr, 1536, edited for the Parker Society by the Rev. Henry Walter (Cambridge University Press, 1848).

15. William Tyndale, *The Obedience of a Christian Man (Antwerp) 1528*, Theatrum Orbis Terrarum, Keizersgracht 526, Amsterdam, Holland; and Walter J. Johnson, 355 Chestnut Street, Norwood, New Jersey 07648, USA. ISBN 90 221 0897 x, LCCCN 77–007436 (both 1977).

16. As, for example, given by Foxe: G. Townshend (ed.), *The Acts and Monuments of John Foxe* (1846), V, 566.

17. ibid., IV, 697–702.

18. A slightly fuller account is in *WTB*, 244–7.

19. In his less attractive moments, Thomas More's sneers at the English reformers extended to accusing them of cowardice: see, for example, *A Dialogue Concerning Heresies*, in Thomas M. C. Lawler, Germain Marc'hadour and Richard C. Marius (eds.), *The Complete Works of St Thomas More*, vol. 6, Part 1 (Yale University Press, 1981), 201; answered by Tyndale in his *The Practice of Prelates*, 340, and in an assertive but dignified paragraph in his *Answer*, 113.

20. Sig. A2–A2v.

21. J. W. Allen, *Political Thought in the Sixteenth Century* (1928), 16.

22. For a demonstration of logical structure in *Obedience*, see *WTB*, 387–90.

23. More, *Dialogue*, op. cit., Part 1, 369. Tyndale, *Answer*, 188; figures from Steven Ozment, *The Age of Reform, 1250–1550* (1980), 284.

24. More, *Dialogue*, op. cit., 370–72, and Appendix C, 773–7. Tyndale, *Answer*, 188.

25. Anthea Hume, 'A Study of the Writings of the English Protestant Exiles, 1525–35', unpublished Ph.D. thesis, University of London, 1961, 170–71. See also Quentin Skinner, *The Foundations of Modern Political Thought*, vol. 11, *The Age of Reformation* (1978), 73–4 and *passim*.

FURTHER READING

On the English Reformation and its history, theology, politics and literature, A. G. Dickens, *The English Reformation* (2nd edn., 1989) remains the standard work. An excellent account of recent studies, including those by revisionists, is given by Nicholas Tyacke (ed.) in his introduction to *England's Long Reformation, 1500–1800* (1998). *The Age of Reformation*, volume 2 of Quentin Skinner's *The Foundations of Modern Political Thought* (1978), sets the political scene for Tyndale's *Obedience*. Tyndale's Pauline theology in this book is admirably discussed by David Knox in his *The Doctrine of Faith in the Reign of Henry VIII* (1961). The classic study of the output of printed reformed literature in England, effectively begun by Tyndale, is John N. King's *English Reformation Literature: The Tudor Origins of the Protestant Tradition* (Princeton, NJ, 1982).

On the life and work of Tyndale, see J. F. Mozley, *William Tyndale* (1937); and David Daniell, *William Tyndale: a Biography* (1994). Students of Tyndale should also look at *Tyndale's New Testament: a modern-spelling edition* (Yale University Press, 1989) and *Tyndale's Old Testament: a modern-spelling edition* (Yale University Press, 1992). For the other non-biblical works by Tyndale we still depend on the three volumes edited by Henry Walter for the Parker Society and Cambridge University Press: *Doctrinal Treatises* (1848), *Expositions of Scripture* and *The Practice of Prelates* (1849), and *An Answer to Sir Thomas More's Dialogue*, etc. (1850). Essays in *Word, Church, and State: Tyndale Quincentenary Essays*, ed. John T. Day, Eric Lund and Anne M. O'Donnell (Washington, DC, 1998), will be found useful.

Tyndale's major part in the history of the English Bible is still not widely known. On the Bible in English, B. F. Westcott's *A General View of the History of the English Bible* (3rd edn., revised W. A. Wright, 1905) remains invaluable. Gerald Hammond's *The Making of the English Bible* (1982), and the first hundred pages of the first volume of David Norton's *A History of the Bible as Literature* (1993), cast much light.

A NOTE ON THE TEXT

The text printed here is that of the first, 1528, edition, printed by Martin de Keyser in Antwerp, pseudonymously as 'Hans Luft of Marlborow'. Since Tyndale was then living in Antwerp, we can assume that he oversaw the printing, which was finished, as the colophon states, on 2 October 1528. Indeed, we may consider that the brief list of twelve errata, 'The faults of printing', are of Tyndale's detection (they are incorporated here). Tyndale's probable presence is important. The marginal notes added later by John Day in 1572 were further enlarged by Henry Walter in the Parker Society edition of 1848, and were not original. (The changes made by Walter are discussed above, p. xxii.)

The text printed here is without alteration except for light modernizing of spelling, in the hope of making something that keeps the original tone but can be followed easily. Martin de Keyser's punctuation was lighter than we are used to, and sometimes erratic: again it has been lightly regularized and modernized – only lightly, because it seemed important to preserve the rhythms of Tyndale's English. Occasional asterisks in the text indicating where marginal notes (here footnotes) apply have been replaced with alphabetical indicators. It should be noted that Tyndale's marginal notes are more in the nature of subheadings than explanatory glosses. Paragraph marks have been omitted. Some sections open with an illuminated capital – it seems, arbitrarily. These have not been indicated. The hand symbol is quite commonly found in the margins of books of the period. It points to matters felt to be important.

Opposite: title page of the first edition 1528, actual size

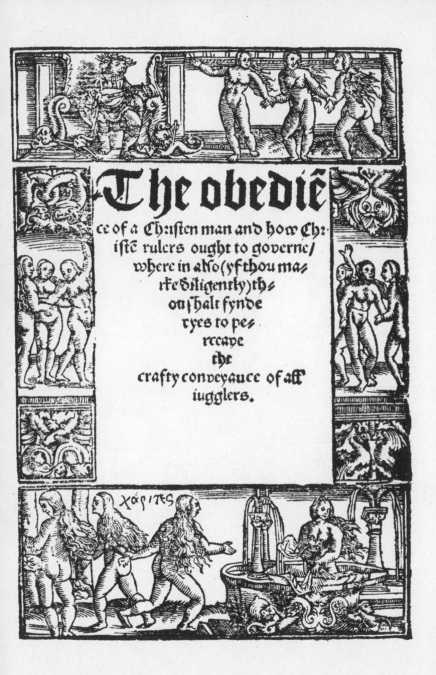

The obediē

ce of a Christen man and how Chr
istē rulers ought to governe/
where in also (yf thou ma
rke diligently) th
ou shalt fynde
eyes to pe
rceave
the
crafty conveyāuce of all
iugglers.

ΧΆΡΙΤΕΣ

The obedience[1] of a Christian man and how Christian rulers ought to govern, wherein also (if thou mark diligently) thou shalt find eyes to perceive the crafty conveyance of all jugglers.[2]

William Tyndale otherwise called William Hychins[3] unto the reader.

Grace, peace[4] and increase of knowledge in our Lord Jesus Christ[5] be with the reader and with all that call on the name of the Lord[6] unfeignedly and with a pure conscience,[7] Amen.

Let it not make thee despair neither yet discourage thee O reader, that it is forbidden thee[8] in pain of life and goods or that it is made breaking of the King's peace or treason unto His Highness to read the word of thy soul's health. But much rather be bold in the Lord[9] and comfort thy soul.[10] [a]Forasmuch[11] as thou art pure and hast an evident token[12] through such persecution[13] that it is the true word of God.[14] Which word is ever hated of the world,[15] neither was ever without persecution (as thou seest in all the stories of the Bible[16] both of the New Testament and also of the Old) neither can be, no more than the sun can be without his light. [b]And forasmuch as contrarywise thou art sure that the Pope's doctrine is not of God which (as thou seest) is so agreeable unto the world, and is so received of the world or which rather so receiveth the world and the pleasures of the world, and seeketh nothing but the possessions of the world, and authority[17] in the world, and to bear a rule in the world, and persecuteth the word of God, and with all wiliness[18] driveth the people from it, and with false and sophistical reasons maketh them afeared of it: yea curseth them and excommunicateth them, and bringeth them in belief that they be damned, if they look on it, and that it is but doctrine to deceive men, and moveth the blind powers of the world to slay with fire, water, and sword all that cleave unto it. For the world loveth that which is his, and hateth that which is chosen out of the world to serve God in the spirit. As Christ

a. The nature of God's word is to be persecuted.
b. The Pope is received and receiveth and persecuteth.

3

saith to his disciples (John 15)[19] if ye were of the world, the world would love his own. But I have chosen you out of the world and therefore the world hateth you.

[a]Another comfort[20] hast thou, that as the weak powers of the world defend the doctrine of the world so the mighty power[21] of God defendeth the doctrine of God.[22] Which thing thou shalt evidently perceive, if thou call to mind the wonderful deeds[23] which God hath ever wrought[24] for his word in extreme necessity[25] since the world began[26] beyond all man's reason. Which are written as saith Paul (Romans 15) for our learning[27] (and not for our deceiving) that we through patience, and comfort of the scripture might have hope. [b]The nature of God's word is to fight against hypocrites.[28] It began at Abel[29] and hath ever since continued and shall, I doubt not, until the last day.[30] And the hypocrites have always the world on their sides, as thou seest in time of Christ. They had the elders,[31] [c]that is to wit the rulers of the Jews, on their side. They had Pilate and the emperor's power[32] on their side. They had Herod[33] also on their side. Moreover they brought all their worldly wisdom[34] to pass and all that they could think or imagine to serve for their purpose. First to fear[35] the people withal, [d]they excommunicated[36] all that believed in him, and put them out of the temple,[37] as thou seest (John 9). Secondly they found the means to have him condemned by the emperor's power and made it treason to Caesar[38] to believe in him. Thirdly they obtained to have him hanged as a thief[39] or a murderer,[40] which after their belly wisdom[41] was a cause above all causes, that no man should believe in him. For the Jews take it for a sure token of everlasting damnation if a man be hanged. For it is written in their law (Deuteronomy 21) cursed is whosoever hangeth on a tree. Moses also in the same place commandeth, if any man be hanged, to take him down the same day and bury him, for fear of polluting or defiling the country, that is, lest they should bring the wrath and curse of God upon them. And therefore the wicked Jews themselves, which with so venomous hate persecuted the doctrine of Christ[42] and did all the shame that they could do unto him (though

a. God defendeth his doctrine himself.
b. God's word fighteth against hypocrites.
c. How our master Christ was entreated.
d. The craft of the hypocrites.

4

they would fain have had Christ to hang stiff on the cross and there to rot, as he should have done by the emperor's law), yet for fear of defiling their Sabbath and of bringing the wrath and curse of God upon them begged of Pilate to take him down (John 19), which was against themselves. Finally when they had done all they could and that they thought sufficient, and when Christ was in the heart of the earth and so many bills and poleaxes[43] about him, to keep him down, and when it was past man's help: then holp[44] God. When man could not bring him again, [a] God's truth fetched him again. The oath that God had sworn to Abraham,[45] to David and to other holy fathers and prophets raised him up again, to bless and to save all that believe in him. Thus became the wisdom of the hypocrites foolishness. Lo this was written for thy learning[46] and comfort.

[b]How wonderfully were the children of Israel locked in Egypt?[47] In what tribulation, cumbrance and adversity were they in? The land also that was promised them, was far off and full of great cities walled with high walls up to the sky and inhabited with great giants.[48] Yet God's truth brought them out of Egypt and planted them in the land of the giants. This was also written for our learning, for there is no power against God's[49] neither any wisdom against God's wisdom, he is stronger and wiser than all his enemies. What holp it Pharaoh to drown the men children?[50] So little, I fear not, shall it at the last help the Pope and his bishops to burn our [c]men children[51] which manfully confess that Jesus is the Lord and that there is no other name given unto men to be saved by, as Peter testifieth (Acts in the fourth chapter). Who dried up the Red Sea?[52] Who slew Goliath?[53] Who did all those wonderful deeds which thou readest in the Bible? Who delivered the Israelites evermore from thraldom and bondage, as soon as they repented and turned to God? Faith verily[54] and God's truth and the trust in the promises which he had made. Read the eleventh chapter to the Hebrews for thy consolation.

[d]When the children of Israel were ready to despair for the greatness

> a. God's truth worketh wonders and maketh the
> wisdom of the hypocrites foolishness.
> b. The captivity of the Israelites under Pharaoh.
> c. Pharaoh slayeth the men children.
> d. How Moses comforteth the Israelites.

and the multitude of the giants, Moses comforted them ever saying, Remember what your Lord God hath done for you in Egypt, his wonderful plagues, his miracles, his wonders, his mighty hand, his stretched out arm, and what he hath done for you hitherto. He shall destroy them, he shall take their hearts from them and make them fear and flee before you. He shall storm them and stir up a tempest among them and scatter them and bring them to nought.[55] He hath sworn, he is true, he will fulfil the promises that he hath made unto Abraham, Isaac and Jacob.[56] [a]This is written for our learning. For verily he is a true God, and is our God as well as theirs, and his promises[57] are with us as well as with them, and he is present with us as well as he was with them. If we ask we shall obtain, if we knock he will open, if we seek we shall find,[58] if we thirst, his truth shall fulfil our lust.[59] Christ is with us until the world's end, Matthew the last.[60] Let little flock[61] be bold therefore. For if God be on our side: what matter maketh it who be against us,[62] be they bishops, cardinals, popes or whatsoever names they will.

[b]Mark this also, if God send thee to the sea and promise to go with thee and to bring thee safe to land, he will raise up a tempest against thee, to prove whether thou wilt abide by his word, and that thou mayest feel thy faith and perceive his goodness, for if it were always fair weather and thou never brought into such jeopardy whence his mercy only delivered thee, thy faith should be but a presumption and thou shouldest be ever unthankful to God and merciless unto thy neighbour.[63]

[c]If God promise riches, the way thereto is poverty. Whom he loveth him he chasteneth,[64] whom he exalteth, he casteth down, whom he saveth he damneth first. He bringeth no man to heaven except he send him to hell first. If he promise life he slayeth first, when he buildeth, he casteth all down first. He is no patcher, he cannot build on another man's foundation. He will not work until all be past remedy and brought unto such a case, that men may see how that his hand, his power, his mercy, his goodness and truth[65] hath wrought all together. He will let

a. God's truth fighteth for us.
b. God trieth the faith of his children.
c. God worketh backward.

no man be partaker with him of his praise and glory. His works are wonderful and contrary unto man's works. Whoever save he delivered his own Son, his only Son,[66] his dear Son unto the death and that for his enemy's sake, to win his enemy, to overcome him with love, that he might see love and love again and of love to do likewise to other men, and to overcome them with well doing.

[a]Joseph saw the sun and the moon and eleven stars worshipping him.[67] Nevertheless ere that came to pass, God laid him where he could neither see sun nor moon neither any star of the sky, and that many years and also undeserved, to nurture him, to humble, to meek and to teach him God's ways, and to make him apt and meet for the room and honour against he came to it that he might perceive and feel that it came of God, and that he might be strong in the spirit to minister it godly.

[b]He promised the children of Israel a land with rivers of milk and honey.[68] But brought them for the space of forty years into a land where not only rivers of milk and honey were not, but where so much as a drop of water was not, to nurture them and to teach them as a father doth his son, and to do them good at the latter end,[69] and that they might be strong in their spirit and souls to use his gifts and benefits godly and after his will.

[c]He promised David a kingdom and immediately stirred up King Saul against him,[70] to persecute him, to hunt him as men do hares with greyhounds and to ferret him out of every hole and that for the space of many years to tame him, to meek him, to kill his lusts to make him feel other men's diseases, to make him merciful, to make him understand that he was made king to minister and to serve his brethren and that he should not think that his subjects were made to minister unto his lusts, and that it were lawful for him to take away from them life and goods at his pleasure.

[d]O that our kings were so nurtured nowadays, which our holy bishops teach of a far other manner saying, your grace shall take his pleasure: ye take what pleasure ye lust, spare nothing. We shall dispense with you:

a. Joseph.
b. Israelites.
c. David.
d. How bishops instruct kings.

7

we have power, we are God's vicars. And let us alone with the realm. We shall take pain for you and see that nothing be well. Your grace shall but defend the faith only.

[a]Let us therefore look diligently whereunto we are called,[71] that we deceive not ourselves.[72] We are called, not to dispute as the Pope's disciples do, but to die with Christ that we may live with him, and to suffer with him that we may reign with him.[b][73] We be called unto a kingdom that must be won with suffering only, as a sick man winneth health. God is he that doeth all things for us and fighteth for us[74] and we do but suffer only. Christ saith (John 20), As my father sent me, so send I you. And (John 15), If they persecute me then shall they persecute you. And (Matthew 10), saith Christ, I send you forth as sheep among wolves. The sheep fight not: but the shepherd fighteth for them[75] and careth for them. Be harmless as doves[76] therefore, saith Christ, and wise as serpents. The doves imagine no defence nor seek to avenge themselves. [c]The serpent's wisdom is to keep his head and those parts wherein his life resteth. Christ is our head and God's word is that where our life resteth. So cleave therefore fast unto Christ and unto those promises which God hath made us for his sake is our wisdom. Beware of men (saith he) for they shall deliver you up unto their councils and shall scourge you. And ye shall be brought before rulers and kings for my sake. The brother shall betray or deliver the brother to death and the father the son. And the children shall rise against father and mother, and put them to death. Hear what Christ saith more: The disciple is not greater than his master neither the servant greater or better than his lord. If they have called the goodman of the house Beelzebub, how much rather shall they call his household servants so? And (Luke 14), saith Christ, which of you disposed to build a tower, sitteth not down first and counteth the cost whether he have sufficient to perform it? Lest when he hath laid the foundation and then not able to perform it, [d]all that behold begin to mock him saying, this man began to build and was not able to make an end. So likewise none of you that forsaketh not all

a. Whereunto a Christian is called.
b. Our fighting is to suffer while God fighteth for us.
c. The wisdom of the serpent.
d. He maketh a mock of himself that casteth not the end ere he begin.

that he hath[77] can be my disciple. Whosoever therefore casteth not this aforehand, I must jeopard life, goods, honour, worship and all that there is for Christ's sake, deceiveth himself and maketh a mock of himself unto the godless hypocrites and infidels. No man can serve two masters God and Mammon, that is to say, wicked riches. Also (Matthew 6), Thou must love Christ above all things. [a]But that doest thou not if thou be not ready to forsake all for his sake, if thou have forsaken all for his sake, then art thou sure that thou lovest him. Tribulation[78] is our right baptism and is signified by plunging into the water: [b]we that are baptized in the name of Christ (saith Paul Romans 6) are baptized to die with him.

The spirit through tribulation purgeth us and killeth our fleshly wit,[79] our worldly understanding and belly wisdom, and filleth us full of the wisdom of God. Tribulation is a blessing that cometh of God, as witnesseth Christ (Matthew 5). [c]Blessed are they that suffer persecution for righteousness' sake, for theirs is the kingdom of heaven.[80] Is this not a comfortable[81] word? Who ought not rather to choose and desire to be blessed with Christ in a little tribulation, than to be cursed perpetually with the world for a little pleasure?

[d]Prosperity is a right curse and a thing that God giveth unto his enemies. Woe be to you rich saith Christ (Luke 6). Lo ye have your consolation, woe be to you that are full, for ye shall hunger, woe be to you that laugh, for ye shall weep, woe be to you when men praise you. For so did their fathers unto the false prophets: yea and so have our fathers done unto the false hypocrites. The hypocrites with worldly preaching have not gotten the praise only, but even the possessions also and the dominion and rule[82] of the whole world.

[e]Tribulation for righteousness is not a blessing only. But also a gift that God giveth unto none save his special friends. The apostles (Acts 5) rejoiced that they were counted worthy to suffer rebuke for Christ's sake. And Paul in the second epistle and third chapter to Timothy saith,

a. How is the Pope sure which taketh all for
Christ's sake but forsaketh nought?
b. Tribulation is our baptism.
c. Tribulation is a blessing.
d. Prosperity is a curse.
e. Tribulation is the gift of God.

All that will live godly in Christ Jesus must suffer persecution. And in the first chapter of his epistle to the Philippians he saith, Unto you it is given not only to believe in Christ, but also to suffer for his sake. Here seest thou that it is God's gift to suffer for Christ's sake. And Peter in the fourth chapter of his first epistle saith, Happy are ye, if ye suffer for the name of Christ, for the glorious spirit of God resteth in you. Is it not an happy thing to be sure that thou art sealed with God's spirit unto everlasting life? And verily thou art sure thereof, if thou suffer patiently for his sake. ªBy suffering art thou sure. But by persecuting canst thou never be sure.

For Paul in the fifth chapter to the Romans saith, Tribulation maketh feeling, that is, it maketh us feel the goodness of God and his help and the working of his spirit. And in the twelfth chapter of the second epistle to the Corinthians the Lord said to Paul, my grace is sufficient for thee. For my strength is made perfect through weakness. Lo Christ is never strong in us, till we be weak. As our strength abateth, so groweth the strength of Christ in us, when we are clean emptied of our own strength, then are we full of Christ's strength. And look how much of our own strength remaineth in us, so much lacketh there of the strength of Christ. Therefore saith Paul in the said place of his second epistle to the Corinthians, Very gladly will I rejoice in my weakness, that the strength of Christ may dwell in me. Therefore have I delectation saith Paul in infirmities, in rebukes, in need, in persecutions and in anguish for Christ's sake. For when I am weak, then am I strong, meaning that the weakness of the flesh is the strength of the spirit. ᵇAnd by flesh understand wit, wisdom and all that is in a man before the spirit of God come, and whatsoever springeth not of the Spirit of God and of God's word. And of like testimonies is all the scripture full.

Behold God setteth before us a blessing and also a curse.[83] A blessing verily and that a glorious and an everlasting, if we will suffer tribulation and adversity with our Lord and Saviour Christ. And an everlasting curse, if for a little pleasure's sake we withdraw ourselves from the chastening and nurture of God, wherewith he teacheth all his sons and

a. Whereby then are the Pope and bishops sure?
b. Flesh.

fashioneth them after his godly will and maketh them perfect[84] (as he did Christ) and maketh them apt and meet[85] vessels to receive his grace and his spirit, that they might perceive and feel the exceeding mercy which we have in Christ and the innumerable blessings, and the unspeakable inheritance[86] whereunto we are called and chosen and sealed[87] in our saviour Jesus Christ, unto whom be praise forever Amen.

Finally whom God chooseth to reign everlastingly with Christ him sealeth he with his mighty spirit and poureth strength into his heart to suffer afflictions also with Christ for bearing witness unto the truth.[88] [a]And this is the difference between the children of God and of salvation and between the children of the devil and of damnation, that the children of God have power in their hearts to suffer for God's word which is their life and salvation, their hope and trust and whereby they live in the soul and spirit before God. And the children of the devil in time of adversity flee from Christ whom they followed feignedly, their hearts not sealed with his holy and mighty spirit, and get them to the standard of their right father the devil, and take [b]his wages, the pleasures of this world. Which are the earnest[89] of everlasting damnation. Which conclusion the twelfth chapter to the Hebrews well confirmeth saying, My son despise not the chastising of the Lord, neither faint when thou art rebuked of him. For whom the Lord loveth him he chasteneth: yea and he scourgeth [c]every son whom he receiveth. Lo persecution and adversity for the truth's sake is God's scourge and God's rod and pertaineth unto all his children indifferently. For when he saith, he scourgeth every son, he maketh none exception. Moreover saith the text, if ye shall endure chastening, God offereth himself unto you, as unto sons.[90] What son is it that the father chastiseth not? If ye be not under correction (whereof all are partakers) then are ye bastards and not sons.

Forasmuch then as we must needs be baptized in tribulations and through the Red Sea and a great and a fearful wilderness and a land of cruel giants into our natural country: yea and inasmuch as it is a plain

a. The difference between the children of God and of the devil.
b. The devil's wages.
c. All God's children are under chastising.

earnest, that there is no other way into the kingdom of life, than through persecution and suffering of pain and of very death, after the example of Christ. ªTherefore let us arm our souls with the comfort of the scriptures. How that God is ever ready at hand in time of need to help us. And how that such tyrants and persecutors are but God's scourge and his rod to chastise us. And as the father hath always in time of correction the rod fast in his hand, so that the rod doth nothing but as the father moveth it: even so hath God all ᵇtyrants in his hand and letteth them not do whatsoever they would, but as much only as he appointeth them to do and as farforth it is necessary for us. And as when the child submitteth himself unto his father's correction and nurture and humbleth himself altogether unto the will of his father, then the rod is taken away: even so when we are come unto the knowledge of the right way and have forsaken our own will and offer ourselves clean unto the will of God, to walk which way soever he will have us: then turneth he the tyrants. Or else if they enforce to persecute us any further, he putteth them out of the way according unto the comfortable examples of the scripture.

Moreover let us arm our souls with the promises both of help and assistance and also of the glorious reward that followeth. ᶜGreat is your reward in heaven saith Christ (Matthew 5). And he that knowledgeth me before men him will I knowledge before my Father that is in heaven (Matthew 10). And call on me in time of tribulation and I will deliver thee (Psalm 65).⁹¹ And behold the eyes of the Lord are over them that fear him and over them that trust in his mercy. To deliver their souls from death and to feed them in time of hunger (Psalm 46). And in the forty-seventh Psalm saith David: the Lord is nigh them that are troubled in their hearts, and the meek in spirit will he save. The tribulations of the righteous are many, and out of them all will the Lord deliver them. The Lord keepeth all the bones of them, so that not one of them shall be bruised. The Lord shall redeem the souls of his servants. And of such like consolation are all the Psalms full: would to God when ye read them ye understand them. And (Matthew 10), When they deliver you take no

a. Which way go the bishops to heaven then?
b. The tyrants have not power to do what they would.
c. The promises of God are comfortable yea they are all comfort.

thought what ye shall say. It shall be given you the same hour what ye shall say. For it is not ye that speak: but the spirit of your Father which speaketh in you. The very hairs of your heads are numbered saith Christ also Matthew in the tenth. If God care for our hairs, he much more careth for our souls which he hath sealed with his holy spirit. Therefore saith Peter (1 Peter 4), Cast all your care upon him: for he careth for you. And Paul (1 Corinthians 10) saith: God is true he will not suffer you to be tempted above your might. And (Psalm 71), Cast thy care upon the Lord.

^aLet thy care be to prepare thyself with all thy strength for to walk which way he will have thee and to believe that he will go with thee and assist thee and strength thee against all tyrants and deliver thee out of all tribulation. But what way or by what means he will do it, that commit unto him and to his godly pleasure and wisdom and cast that care upon him.[92] And though it seem never so unlikely or never so impossible unto natural reason, yet believe steadfastly that he will do it. And then shall he according unto his old use change the course of the world, even in the twinkling of an eye,[93] and come suddenly upon our giants as a thief in the night,[94] and compass[95] them in their wiles and worldly wisdom: when they cry peace and all is safe, then shall their sorrows begin, as the pangs of a woman that travaileth with child.[96] And then shall he destroy them, and deliver thee, unto the glorious praise of his mercy and truth. Amen.

^bAnd as pertaining unto them that despise God's word, counting it as a fantasy or a dream, and to them also that for fear of a little persecution fall from it, set this before thine eyes. How God since the beginning of the world, before a general plague, ever sent his true prophets and preachers of his word, to warn the people, and gave them space to repent. But they for the greatest part of them hardened their hearts[97] and persecuted the word that was sent to save them. And then God destroyed them utterly and took them clean from the earth. As thou seest what followed the preaching of ^cNoah[98] in the old world, what

a. A Christian man's care.
b. The despisers persecutors and they that
fall from the word are threatened.
c. Noah.

followed the preaching of [a]Lot among the Sodomites and the preaching of Moses and [b]Aaron among the Egyptians, and that suddenly against all possibility of man's wit. Moreover as often as the children of Israel fell from God to worshipping of images, he sent his [c]prophets unto them. And they persecuted and waxed hard hearted. And then he sent them into all places of the world captive. [d]Last of all he sent his own Son out to them. And they waxed more hard hearted than ever before. And see what a fearful example of his wrath and cruel vengeance he hath made of them unto all the world now almost fifteen hundred years.

Unto the old Britons, also which dwelled where our nation now doth, preached [e]Gildas[99] and rebuked them of their wickedness and prophesied both unto the [f]spiritual (as they will be called) and unto the lay men also, what vengeance would follow except they repented. But they waxed hard hearted. And God sent his plagues and pestilences among them, and sent their enemies in upon them on every side and destroyed them utterly.

Mark also how Christ threateneth them that forsake him for whatsoever cause it be: Whether for fear, either for shame, either for loss of honour, friends, life or goods. He that denieth me before men, him will I deny before my father that is in heaven. He that loveth father or mother more than me, is not worthy of me. All this saith he (Matthew the tenth). And in the eighth of Mark he saith, Whosoever is ashamed of me or my words among this advoutrous[100] and sinful generation: of him shall the son of man be ashamed, when he cometh in the glory of his father with his holy angels. And (Luke 9) also: None that layeth his hand to the plough and looketh back, is meet for the kingdom of heaven.

[g]Nevertheless yet if any man have resisted ignorantly, as Paul did, let him look on the truth which Paul wrote[101] after he came to knowledge. Also if any man clean against his heart, but overcome with the weakness

a. Lot.
b. Moses and Aaron.
c. The prophets.
d. Christ.
e. Gildas.
f. They be spiritual: that is devilish: for the devil is a spirit.
g. God receiveth them that come again.

of the flesh for fear of persecution, have denied, as Peter did,[102] or have delivered his book or put it away secretly,[103] let him (if he repent) come again and take better hold and not despair or take it for a sign that God hath forsaken him. [a]For God ofttimes taketh his strength even from his very elect, when they either trust in their own strength or are negligent to call to him for strength. And that doeth he to teach them and to make them feel that in the fire of tribulation for his word's sake nothing can endure and abide, save his word and that strength only which he hath promised. For which strength he will have us to pray unto him night and day with all instance.

[b]That thou mayest perceive how that the scripture ought to be in the mother tongue and that the reasons which our spirits[104] make for the contrary are but sophistry and false wiles to fear thee from the light, that thou mightest follow them blindfold and be their captive, to honour their ceremonies and to offer to their belly.

First God gave the children of Israel a law by the hand of Moses[105] in their mother tongue. And all the prophets wrote in their mother tongue. And all the Psalms were in the mother tongue. And there was Christ but figured[106] and described in ceremonies, in riddles, in parables and in dark prophecies. What is the cause that we may not have the Old Testament with the New also, which is the light of the Old, and wherein is openly declared before the eyes that there was darkly prophesied? I can imagine no cause verily except it be that we should not see the work of Antichrist[107] and juggling of hypocrites. What should be the cause that we which walk in the broad day, should not see as well as they that walked in the night,[108] or that we should not see as well at noon, as they did in the twilight? Came Christ to make the world more blind? By this means Christ is the darkness of the world and not the light, as he saith himself (John 8).

Moreover Moses saith (Deuteronomy 6), Hear Israel let these words which I command thee this day stick fast in thine heart, and whet[109] them on thy children and talk of them as thou sittest in thine house, and as thou walkest by the way, and when thou liest down, and when

a. Why God letteth his elect fall.
b. That the scripture ought to be in the English tongue.

thou risest up, and bind them for a token to thine hand, and let them be a remembrance between thine eyes, and write them on the posts and gates of thine house. This was commanded generally unto all men. How cometh it that God's word pertaineth less unto us than unto them? Yea how cometh it that our Moseses forbid us and command us the contrary, and threat us if we do, and will not that we once speak of God's word? How can we whet God's word (that is put it in practice, use and exercise) upon our children and household, when we are violently kept from it and know it not? How can we (as Peter commandeth) give a reason of our hope[110] when we wot[111] not what it is that God hath promised or what to hope? Moses also commandeth in the said chapter: if the son ask what the testimonies, laws and observations of the Lord mean, that the father teach him. If our children ask what our ceremonies (which are more than the Jews' were) mean [a]no father can tell his son. And in the eleventh chapter he repeateth all again for fear of forgetting.

They will say haply,[112] the scripture requireth a pure mind and a quiet mind. And therefore the lay man because he is altogether cumbered with worldly business, cannot understand them. If that be the cause, then it is a plain case, that our prelates understand not the scriptures themselves. For no lay man is so tangled with worldly business as they are. The great things of the world are ministered by them. Neither do the lay people any great thing, but at their assignment.

If the scripture were in the mother tongue they will say, then would the lay people understand it every man after his own ways. Wherefore serveth the curate, but to teach them the right way? Wherefore were the [b]holy days made, but that the people should come and learn? Are ye not abominable [c]schoolmasters, in that ye take so great wages, if ye will not teach? If ye would teach how could ye do it so well and with so great profit, as when the lay people have the scripture before them in their mother tongue? For then should they see by the order of the text, whether thou jugglest or not. And then would they believe it, because it is the scripture of God, though thy living be never so

a. No nor Sir John his ghostly children.
b. Holy days.
c. Our schoolmasters take great wages but teach not.

abominable. ^aWhere now because your living and your preaching are so contrary, and because they grope out in every sermon your open and manifest lies, and smell your insatiable covetousness they believe you not, when you preach truth. But alas, ^bthe curates themselves (for the most part) wot no more what the New or Old Testament meaneth, than do the Turks. Neither know they of any more than that they read at mass, matins and evensong which they understand not. Neither care they but even to mumble up so much every day (as the pie and popinjay[113] speak they wot not what) to fill their bellies withal. If they will not let the lay man have the word of God in his mother tongue, yet let the priests have it, ^cwhich for a great part of them do understand no Latin at all:[114] but sing and say and patter all day, with the lips only, that which the heart understandeth not.

^dChrist commandeth to search the scriptures (John 5). Though that miracles bear record unto his doctrine, yet desired he no faith to be given either unto his doctrine or unto his miracles, without record of the scripture.[115] When Paul preached (Acts 17), the other searched the scriptures daily, whether they were as he alleged them. Why shall not I likewise, whether it be the scripture that thou allegest? Yea why shall I not see the scripture and the circumstances and what goeth before and after, that I may know whether thine interpretation be the right sense, or whether thou jugglest and drawest the scripture violently unto thy carnal and fleshly purpose? Or whether thou be about to teach me or to deceive me?

Christ saith that there shall come false prophets[116] in his name and say that they themselves are Christ, that is, they shall so preach Christ that men must believe in them, in their holiness and things of their imagination without God's word: yea and that against-Christ or Antichrist that shall come[117] is nothing but such false prophets that shall juggle with the scripture and beguile the people with false interpretations as all the false prophets, scribes and Pharisees did in the Old Testament. How shall I know whether ye are that against Christ or false prophets or no,

a. Why the preachers are not believed when they say truth.
b. The curates wot not what a Bible meaneth.
c. The priests understand no Latin.
d. Search the scriptures.

seeing ye will not let me see how ye allege the scriptures? Christ saith: [a]By their deeds ye shall know them.[118] Now when we look on your deeds, we see that ye are all sworn together and have separated yourselves from the lay people, [b]and have a several[119] kingdom among yourselves and [c]several laws of your own making, [d]wherewith ye violently bind the lay people that never consented unto the making of them. A thousand things forbid ye which Christ made free, and dispense with them again for money. Neither is there any exception at all, but lack of money. [e]Ye have a secret counsel by yourselves. All other men's counsels and secrets know ye and no man yours. Ye seek but honour, riches, promotion, authority and to reign over all, and will obey no man. If the father give you ought of courtesy, ye will compel the son to give it violently whether he will or not by craft of your own laws. These deeds are against Christ.

When an whole parish of us hire a schoolmaster to teach our children, what reason is it that we should be compelled to pay this schoolmaster his wages, and he should have licence to go where he will and to dwell in another country and to leave our children untaught? Doth not the Pope so? Have we not given up our tithes[120] of courtesy unto one for to teach us God's word? And cometh not the Pope and compelleth us to pay it violently to them that never teach? Maketh he not one [f]parson which cometh never at us? Yea one shall have four or six or as many as he can get and wotteth oftentimes where never one of them standeth. Another is made [g]vicar, to whom he giveth a dispensation to go where he will and to set in a [h]parish priest which can but minister a sort[121] of dumb ceremonies. And he because he hath most labour and least profit polleth[122] on his part and fetcheth here a mass penny[123] there a trental,[124] yonder dirige money[125] and for his bead roll[126] with a confession penny and such like. And thus are we never taught and are yet nevertheless

a. Against-Christ is known by his deeds.
b. A several kingdom.
c. Several laws.
d. What Christ looseth freely the Pope bindeth to loose it again for money.
e. A secret counsel.
f. Parson.
g. Vicar.
h. Parish priest.

compelled: yea compelled to hire many costly schoolmasters. These deeds are verily against Christ. Shall we therefore judge you by your deeds, as Christ commandeth? So are ye false prophets and the disciples of Antichrist or of against-Christ.

The sermons[127] which thou readest in the Acts of the Apostles and all that the apostles preached were no doubt preached in the mother tongue. Why then might they not be written in the mother tongue? As if one of us preach a good sermon why may it not be written? Saint Jerome[128] also translated the Bible into his mother tongue. Why may not we also? They will say it cannot be translated into our tongue it is so rude.[129] It is not so rude as they are false liars. For the Greek tongue agreeth more with the English[130] than with the Latin. And the [a]properties of the Hebrew tongue agreeth a thousand times more with the English[131] than with the Latin. The manner of speaking is both one, so that in a thousand places thou needest not but to translate it into the English word for word when thou must seek a compass[132] in the Latin, and yet shalt have much work to translate it well favouredly, so that it have the same grace and sweetness, sense and pure understanding with it in the Latin, as it hath in the Hebrew. A thousand parts better may it be translated into the English than into the Latin. Yea and except my memory fail me and that I have forgotten what I read when I was a child thou shalt find in the English chronicle how the king [b]Athelstan[133] caused the Holy Scripture to be translated into the tongue that then was in England and how the prelates exhorted him thereunto.

[c]Moreover seeing that one of you ever preacheth contrary to another. And when two of you meet, the one disputeth and brawleth with the other, as it were two scolds. And forasmuch as one holdeth this doctor and another that. [d]One followeth Duns,[134] another Saint Thomas,[135] another Bonaventure,[136] Alexander de Hales,[137] Raymond,[138] Lyre,[139] Brygot,[140] Dorbell,[141] Holcott,[142] Gorram,[143] Trumbett,[144] Hugo de Sancto Victore,[145] De Monte Regio,[146] De Nova Villa,[147] De Media Villa[148] and such like out of number. So that if thou hadst but of every

a. The properties of the Hebrew tongue agree with the English.
b. King Athelstan.
c. Contrary preaching.
d. Contrary doctors.

author one book thou couldest not pile them up in any warehouse in London, and every author is one contrary unto another. In so great diversity of spirits[149] how shall I know who lieth and who saith truth? Whereby shall I try them and judge them? Verily by God's word which only is true. But how shall I that do when thou wilt not let me see the scripture?

Nay say they, the scripture is so hard that thou couldest never understand it but by the doctors. That is I must measure the meteyard[150] by the cloth. Here be twenty cloths of diverse lengths and diverse breadths. How shall I be sure of the length of the meteyard by them? I suppose rather I must be first sure of the length of the meteyard, and thereby measure and judge the cloths. If I must first believe the doctor, then is the doctor first true and the truth of the scripture dependeth of his truth and so the truth of God springeth of the truth of man. ᵃThus Antichrist turneth the roots of the trees upward. What is the cause that we damn some of Origen's works[151] and allow some? How know we that some is heresy and some not? By the scripture I trow. How know we that Saint Augustine (which is the best or one of the best that ever wrote upon the scripture) wrote many things amiss at the beginning, as many other doctors do? Verily by the ᵇscriptures, as he himself well perceived afterward when he looked more diligently upon them, and revoked many things again. He wrote of many things which he understood not when he was newly converted, ere he had thoroughly seen the scriptures, and followed the opinions of Plato and the common persuasions of man's wisdom that were then famous.

ᶜThey will say yet more shamefully, that no man can understand the scriptures without *philautia*,[152] that is to say philosophy. A man must first be well seen in Aristotle ere he can understand the scripture say they. ᵈAristotle's doctrine is, that the world was without beginning and shall be without end,[153] and that the first man never was and the last shall never be.[154] And that God doth all of necessity, neither careth what we do neither will ask any accompts[155] of that we do. Without this

a. Antichrist turneth the roots of the tree upward.
b. The scripture is the trial of all doctrine and the right touchstone.
c. Philosophy.
d. Aristotle.

doctrine how could we understand the [a]scripture that saith, God created the world of nought,[156] and God worketh all thing of his free will and for a secret purpose,[157] and that we shall all rise again,[158] and that God will have accompts of all that we have done in this life.[159] [b]Aristotle saith, give a man a law and he hath power of himself to do or fulfil the law and becometh righteous with working righteously.[160] [c]But Paul and all the scripture saith, that the law doeth but utter sin and helpeth not.[161] Neither hath any man power to do the law, till the Spirit of God be given him through faith in Christ. Is it not a madness then to say that we could not understand the scripture without Aristotle? Aristotle's righteousness and all his virtues spring of a man's free will.[162] And a Turk and every infidel and idolater may be righteous and virtuous with that righteousness and those virtues. Moreover [d]Aristotle's felicity and blessedness[163] standeth in avoiding of all tribulations, in riches, health, honour, worship, friends and authority, which felicity pleaseth our spirituality well. Now without these and a thousand such like points, couldest thou not understand [e]scripture which saith that righteousness cometh by Christ and not of man's will[164] and how that virtues are the fruits and the gift of God's Spirit[165] and that Christ blesseth us in tribulations,[166] persecution and adversity? How, I say, couldest thou understand the scripture without [f]philosophy, inasmuch as [g]Paul, in the second to the Colossians warned them to beware lest any man should spoil them (that is to say, rob them of their faith in Christ) through philosophy and deceitful vanities, and through the traditions of men and ordinances after the world and not after Christ.

By this means then, thou wilt that no man teach another, but that every man take the scripture and learn by himself. Nay verily, so say I not. [h]Nevertheless, seeing that ye will not teach, if any man thirst for

a. Scripture.
b. Aristotle.
c. Paul.
d. Aristotle.
e. Scripture.
f. Philosophy.
g. Paul.
h. When no man will teach.
If we desire God will teach.

the truth,[167] and read the scripture by himself desiring God to open the door of knowledge unto him,[168] God for his truth's sake will and must teach him. Howbeit my meaning is that as a master teacheth his prentice to know all the points of the meteyard, first how many inches, how many feet and the half yard, the quarter and the nail, and then teacheth him to mete other things thereby: [a]even so will I that ye teach the people God's law, and what obedience God requireth of us unto father and mother, master, lord, king and all superiors, and with what friendly love he commandeth one to love another. And teach them to know that natural venom and birth poison[169] which moveth the very hearts of us to rebel against the ordinances and will of God, and prove that no man is righteous in the sight of God, but that we are all damned by the law. And then (when thou hast meeked them and feared them with the law) teach them the testament and promises which God hath made unto us in Christ, and how merciful and kind he is, and how much he loveth us in Christ. And teach them the principles and the ground of the faith and what the sacraments signify and then shall the Spirit work with thy preaching and make them feel.[170] So would it come to pass, that as we know by natural wit what followeth of a true principle of natural reason: even so by the principles of the faith and by the plain scriptures and by the circumstances of the text should we judge all men's exposition and all men's doctrine, and should receive the best and refuse the worst. I would have you to teach them also the properties and manner of speakings of the scripture, and how to expound proverbs and similitudes.[171] And then if they go abroad and walk by the fields and meadows of all manner doctors and philosophers they could catch no harm. They should discern the poison from the honey and bring home nothing but that which is wholesome.

[b]But now do ye clean contrary. Ye drive them from God's word and will let no man come thereto, until he have been two years master of art. First they nosel[172] them in sophistry and in *benefundatum*.[173] [c]And there corrupt they their judgments with apparent arguments and with alleging unto them texts of logic, of natural *philautia*, of metaphysic[174]

---

a. The order of teaching.
b. The disorder or overthwart [perverse] order of our schoolmen.
c. The school doctrine as they call it corrupteth the judgments of youth.

and moral philosophy and of all manner books of Aristotle and of all manner doctors which they yet never saw. Moreover one holdeth this another that. One is a Real, another a Nominal.[175] What wonderful [a]dreams have they of their predicaments,[176] universals,[177] second intentions,[178] quiddities, haecceities[179] and relatives.[180] And whether *species fundata in chimera* be *vera species*.[181] And whether this proposition be true *non ens est aliquid.* Whether *ens* be *equivocum* or *univocum. Ens* is a voice only say some. *Ens in univocum* saith another and descendeth into *ens creatum* and into *ens increatum per modos intrinsecos.* When they have this wise brawled eight, ten or twelve or more years and after that their judgments are utterly corrupt: then they beginneth their Divinity. [b]Not at the scriptures, but every man taketh a sundry doctor, which doctors are as sundry and as diverse, [c]the one contrary unto the other, as there are diversifications and monstrous shapes, none like another, among our sects of religion. Every religion, every university and almost every man hath a sundry divinity. Now whatsoever opinions every man findeth with his doctor, that is his gospel and that only is true with him and that holdeth he all his life long, and every man to maintain his doctor withal, corrupteth the scripture and fashioneth it after his own imagination as a [d]potter doth his clay. Of what text thou provest hell, will another prove purgatory, another *limbo patrum*[182] and another shall prove of the same text that an ape hath a tail. And of what text the greyfriar proveth that Our Lady was without original sin, of the same shall the blackfriar[183] prove that she was conceived with original sin. And all of this do they with apparent reasons with [e]false similitudes and likenesses, and with arguments and persuasions of man's wisdom. Now there is no other division or heresy in the world save man's wisdom and when man's foolish wisdom interpreteth the scripture. [f]Man's wisdom scattereth,

a. Dreams.

b. School divinity.

c. Yet in this they all agree: that no man is saved by Christ but by holy works. And that Christ hath given up his Godhead to the Pope and all his power and that the Pope may save Christ's merits to whom he will and take them from whom he will.

d. Potters: yea mockers or rather jugglers.

e. False similitudes.

f. Man's wisdom heresy.

divideth and maketh sects, [a]while the wisdom of one is that a white coat is best to serve God in, and another saith a black, another a grey, another a blue: and while one saith that God will hear your prayer in this place, another saith in that place: [b]And while one saith this place is holier, and another that place is holier, [c]and this religion is holier than that, and this saint is greater with God than that and an hundred thousand like things. Man's [d]wisdom is plain idolatry, neither is there any other idolatry than to imagine of God after man's wisdom. [e]God is not man's imagination, but that only which he saith of himself. God is nothing but his law and his promises,[184] that is to say, that which he biddeth thee do and that which he biddeth thee believe and hope. God is but his word: as Christ saith (John 8). I am that I say unto you, that is to say, that which I preach am I. My words are spirit and life. God is that only which he testifieth of himself and to imagine any other thing of God than that, is damnable idolatry. Therefore saith the 118th Psalm[185] happy are they which search the testimonies of the Lord, that is to say, that which God testifieth and witnesseth unto us. But how shall I that do when ye will not let me have his testimonies or witnesses in a tongue which I understand? Will ye resist God? Will ye forbid him to give his spirit unto the lay as well as unto you? Hath he not made the English tongue? Why forbid ye him to speak in the English tongue then, as well as in the Latin?

Finally that this threatening and forbidding the lay people to read the scripture is not for love of your souls (which they care for as the fox doth for the geese) is evident and clearer than the sun, inasmuch as they permit and suffer you to read [f]Robin Hood[186] and Bevis of Hampton,[187] Hercules,[188] Hector[189] and Troilus[190] with a thousand histories and fables of love and wantonness and of ribaldry as filthy as heart can think, to corrupt the minds of you withal, clean contrary to the doctrine of Christ and of his apostles. For Paul (Ephesians 5) saith: see that fornication

a. Coats.
b. Place.
c. One religion is holier than another.
d. Man's wisdom is idolatry.
e. What God is.
f. Read what thou wilt: yea and say what thou wilt save the truth.

24

and all uncleanness or covetousness be not once named among you, as it becometh saints: neither filthiness, neither foolish talking, nor jesting, which are not comely. For this ye know that no whoremonger or unclean person or covetous person (which is the worshipper of images) hath any inheritance in the kingdom of Christ and of God. And after, saith he, through such things cometh the wrath of God upon the children of unbelief. Now saying they permit you freely to read those things which corrupt your minds and rob you of the kingdom of God and Christ and bring the wrath of God upon you how is this forbidding for the love of your souls?

A thousand reasons more might be made (as thou mayest see in *Paraclesis* Erasmi and in his preface to the paraphrases of Matthew)[191] unto which they should be compelled to hold their peace or to give shameful answers. But I hope that these are sufficient unto them that thirst the truth. God for his mercy and truth shall well open them more: yea and other secrets of his godly wisdom, if they be diligent to cry unto him, which grace grant God. AMEN.

The prologue unto the book.

Forasmuch as our holy prelates and our ghostly religious,[1] which ought to defend God's word, speak evil of it and do all the shame they can to it, and rail on it and bear their captives in hand that it causeth insurrection and teacheth the people to disobey their heads and governors, and moveth them to rise against their princes and to make all common and to make havoc of other men's goods. Therefore have I made this little treatise that followeth containing all [a]obedience that is of God. In which (whosoever readeth it) shall easily perceive, not the contrary only and that they lie: but also the very cause of such blasphemy and what steereth them so furiously to rage and to belie the truth.

Howbeit, it is no new thing unto the word of God to be railed upon, neither is this the first time that hypocrites have ascribed to God's word the vengeance whereof they themselves were ever cause. [b]For the hypocrites with their false doctrine and idolatry have evermore laid the wrath and vengeance of God upon the people, so sore that [c]God could no longer forbear nor defer his punishment. Yet God, which is always merciful, before he would take vengeance, hath ever sent his true prophets and true preachers, to warn the people that they might repent. But the people for the most part and namely the heads and rulers through comfort and persuading of the hypocrites, have ever waxed more hard hearted than before, and have persecuted the word of God and his prophets. Then God which is also righteous, hath always poured his plagues upon them without delay. [d]Which plagues

a. The obedience of monks and friars is not here. For they are not of God but of their own feigning.
b. The hypocrites lay that to God's word which they themselves are the cause of.
c. God warneth ere he strike.
d. When God punisheth the idolatry of the hypocrites then say they that new learning is cause thereof.

the hypocrites ascribe unto God's word saying: see what mischief is come upon us since this new learning[2] come up and this new sect and this new doctrine. This seest thou (Jeremiah 44), where the people cried to go to their old idolatry again saying: since we left it, we have been in all necessity and have been consumed with war and hunger. But the prophet answered them, that their idolatry went unto the heart of God, so that he could no longer suffer the maliciousness of their own imaginations or inventions, and that the cause of all such mischiefs was because they would not hear the voice of the Lord and walk in his law, ordinances and testimonies.[3] [a]The scribes and the Pharisees laid also to Christ's charge (Luke 23) that he moved the people to sedition. And said to Pilate, we have found this fellow perverting the people and forbidding to pay tribute to Caesar, and saith that he is Christ a king. And again in the same chapter, he moveth the people (said they) teaching throughout all Jewry and began at Galilee even to this place. So likewise laid they to the Apostles' charge, as thou mayest see in the Acts.[4] Saint Cyprian also and Saint Augustine[5] and many other more made works in defence of the word of God against such blasphemies: so that thou mayest see, how that it is no new thing, but an old and accustomed thing with the hypocrites to wite[6] God's word and the true preachers of all the mischief which their lying doctrine is the very cause of.[b]

Neverthelater in very deed, after the preaching of God's word, because it is not truly received, God sendeth great trouble into the world: partly to avenge himself of the tyrants and persecutors of his word and partly to destroy those worldly people which make of God's word nothing but a cloak of their fleshly liberty. They are not all good that follow the gospel. Christ (Matthew in the thirteenth chapter) likeneth the kingdom of heaven unto a net cast in the sea that catcheth fishes both good and bad. The kingdom of heaven is the preaching of the gospel, unto which come both good and bad. But the good are few. [c]Christ calleth them therefore a little flock (Luke 12). For they are ever few that come to the gospel of a true intent seeking therein nothing but the glory and praise

a. Christ was accused of insurrection.
b. Why trouble followeth the preaching of the gospel.
c. Christ's flock a little flock.

of God and offering themselves freely and willingly to take adversity with Christ for the gospel's sake and for bearing report unto the truth, that all men may hear it. The greatest number come and ever came and followed even Christ himself for a worldly purpose. As thou mayest well see (John 6) how that almost five thousand followed Christ and would also have made him a king, because he had well fed them. Whom he rebuked saying: ye seek me not, because ye saw the miracles, but because ye ate of the bread and were filled: and drove them away from him with hard preaching.

Even so now (as ever) the most part seek ªliberty. They be glad when they hear the unsatiable covetousness of the spirituality rebuked: when they hear their falsehood and wiles uttered: when tyranny and oppression is preached against: when they hear how kings and all officers should rule christianly and brotherly and seek no other thing save the wealth[7] of their subjects: and when they hear that they have no such authority of God so to pill and poll[8] as they do and to raise up taxes and gatherings to maintain their fantasies and to make war they wot not for what cause. ᵇAnd therefore because the heads will not so rule, will they also no longer obey, but resist and rise against their evil heads. ᶜAnd one wicked destroyeth another. Yet is God's word not the cause of this neither yet the preachers. For though that Christ himself taught all obedience,[9] how that it is not lawful to resist wrong (but for the officer[10] that is appointed thereunto) and how a man must love his very enemy and pray for them that persecute him and bless them that curse him,[11] and how that all vengeance must be remitted to God,[12] and that a man must forgive, if he will be forgiven of God.[13] Yet the people for the most part received it not. They were ever ready to rise and to fight. For ever when the scribes and Pharisees went about to take Christ they were afraid of the people. Not on the holy day (said they Matthew 26), lest any rumour arise among the people. And (Matthew 21), they would have taken him, but they feared the people. And (Luke 20), Christ asked the Pharisees a question unto which they durst not answer, lest the people should have stoned them.

a. Liberty.
b. God destroyeth one wicked with another.
c. God's word is not the cause of evil.

[a]Last of all forasmuch as the very disciples and apostles of Christ after so long hearing of Christ's doctrine were yet ready to fight for Christ clean against Christ's teaching. As Peter (Matthew 26) drew his sword: but was rebuked. And (Luke 9) James and John would have had fire to come from heaven to consume the Samaritans and to avenge the injury of Christ: but were likewise rebuked. If Christ's disciples were so long carnal what wonder is it, if we be not all perfect the first day? [b]Yea inasmuch as we be taught even of very babes, to kill a Turk,[14] to slay a Jew,[15] to burn an heretic, to fight for the liberties and right of the church as they call it: yea and inasmuch as we are brought in belief if we shed the blood of our even Christian, or if the son shed the blood of his father that begat him, for the defence, not of the Pope's godhead only, but also for whatsoever cause it be, yea though it be for no cause but that his holiness commandeth it only, that we deserve as much as Christ deserved for us when he died on the cross: or if we be slain in the quarrel, that our souls go, nay fly to heaven, and be there ere our blood be cold. Inasmuch (I say) as we have sucked in such bloody imaginations into the bottom of our hearts even with our mothers' milk, and have been so long hardened therein, what wonder were it if while we be yet young in Christ, we thought that it were lawful to fight for the true word of God? Yea and though a man were thoroughly persuaded that it were not lawful to resist his king, though he would wrongfully take away life and goods: yet might he think that it were lawful to resist the hypocrites and to rise, not against his king: but with his king to deliver his king out of bondage and captivity, wherein the hypocrites hold him with wiles and falsehood, so that no man may be suffered to come at him, to tell him the truth.

[c]This seest thou, that it is the bloody doctrine of the Pope which causeth disobedience, rebellion and insurrection. For he teacheth to fight and to defend his traditions and whatsoever he dreameth with fire, water and sword and to disobey father, mother, master, lord, king and emperor: yea and to invade whatsoever land or nation that will not receive and

---

a. Christ's disciples were long weak and worldly minded.
b. The Pope's doctrine causeth: yea commandeth murder.
c. The Pope's doctrine is bloody.

admit his godhead. [a]Where the peaceable doctrine of Christ teacheth to obey and to suffer for the word of God and to remit the vengeance and the defence of the word to God which is mighty and able to defend it, [b]which also as soon as the word is once openly preached and testified or witnessed unto the world, and when he hath given them a season to repent, is ready at once to take vengeance of his enemies and shooteth arrows with heads dipped in deadly poison at them and poureth his plagues from heaven down upon them and sendeth the murrain[16] and pestilence among them, and sinketh the cities of them and maketh the earth swallow them, and compasseth them in their wiles and taketh them in their own traps and snares, and casteth them into the pits which they digged for other men, and sendeth them a dazing in the head and utterly destroyeth them with their own subtle counsel. [c]Prepare thy mind therefore unto this little treatise and read it discreetly and judge it indifferently, and when I allege any scripture, look thou on the text, whether I interpret it right which thou shalt easily perceive, by the circumstance and process of them, if thou make Christ the foundation and ground and build all on him and referrest all to him, and findest also that the exposition agreeth unto the common articles of the faith and open scriptures. And God the father of mercy which for his truth's sake raised our saviour Christ up again to justify us, give thee his spirit to judge what is righteous in his eyes and give thee strength to abide by it and to maintain it with all patience and long suffering, unto the example and edifying of his congregation and glory of his name. AMEN.

a. Christ's doctrine is peaceable.
b. God avengeth his doctrine himself.
c. How a man ought to behave himself in
reading of doctors and also in the scripture.

The obedience of all degrees[1] proved by God's word and first of children unto their elders.

God (which worketh all in all things) for a secret judgment and purpose and for his godly pleasure, provided an hour that thy father and mother should come together, to make thee through them. He was present with thee in thy mother's womb and fashioned thee and breathed life into thee, and for the great love he had unto thee, provided milk in thy mother's breasts for thee against thou were born: moved also thy father and mother and all other to love thee, to pity thee and to care for thee.

And as he made thee through them, so hath he cast thee under the power and authority of them, to obey and serve them [a]in his stead saying: honour thy father and mother (Exodus 20). Which is not to be understood in bowing the knee and putting off the cap only, but that thou love them with all thine heart and fear and dread them and wait on their commandments and seek their worship, pleasure, will and profit in all things, and give thy life for them counting them worthy of all honour, remembering that thou art their good and possession, and that thou owest unto them thine own self and all that thou art able, yea and more than thou art able to do.

[b]Understand also that whatsoever thou doest unto them (be it good or bad) thou doest unto God. When thou pleasest them thou pleasest God: when thou displeasest them thou displeasest God: when they are angry with thee, God is angry with thee, neither is it possible for thee to come unto the favour of God again (no though all the angels of heaven pray for thee) until thou have submitted thyself unto thy father and mother again.

[c]If thou obey (though it be but carnally either for fear, for vainglory

a. Our fathers and mothers are unto us in God's stead.
b. What we do to our fathers and mothers that we do to God.
c. The reward of obedience.

or profit) thy blessing shall be long life upon the earth. For he saith, honour thy father and mother, that thou mayest live long upon the earth (Exodus 20). ᵃContrarywise if thou disobey them, thy life shall be shortened upon the earth. For it followeth (Exodus 21), he that smiteth his father or mother shall be put to death for it. And he that curseth (that is to say, raileth or dishonoureth his father or mother with opprobrious words) shall be slain for it. And (Deuteronomy 21), if any man have a son stubborn and disobedient which heareth not the voice of his father and the voice of his mother, so that they have taught him nurture and he regardeth them not, then let his father and mother take him and bring him forth unto the seniors or elders of the city and unto the gate of the same place. And let them say unto the seniors of that city: this our son is stubborn and disobedient. He will not hear unto our voice: he is a rioter and a drunkard. Then let all the men of the city stone him with stones unto death so shall ye put away wickedness from among you and all Israel shall hear and shall fear.

And though that the temporal officers (to their own damnation) be negligent in punishing such disobedience (as the spiritual officers are to teach it) and wink at it or look on it through the fingers: yet shall they not escape unpunished. ᵇFor the vengeance of God shall accompany them (as thou mayest see Deuteronomy 28) with all misfortune and evil luck, and shall not depart from them until they be murdered, drowned or hanged, either until by one mischance or another they be utterly brought to nought. Yea and the world often times hangeth many a man for that they never deserved, but God hangeth them because they would not obey and hearken unto their elders: as the consciences of many will find when they come unto the gallows. There can they preach and teach other, that which they themselves would not learn in season.

ᶜThe marriage also of the children pertaineth unto their elders, as thou mayest see (1 Corinthians 7), and throughout all the scripture, by the authority of the said commandment, child obey father and mother. Which thing that heathen and gentiles have ever kept and to this day

a. The reward of disobedience.
b. God avengeth disobedience himself though the officer will not.
c. Marriage.

keep, unto the great shame and rebuke of us Christians: inasmuch as the weddings of our virgins (shame it is to speak it) are more like unto the saute[2] of a [a]bitch, than the marriage of a reasonable creature. See not we daily three or four calling one woman before the commissary or official, of which not one hath the consent of her father and mother. And yet he that hath most money, hath best right and shall have her in the despite of all her friends and in defiance of God's ordinances.

Moreover when she is given by the judge unto the one party and also married even then ofttimes shall the contrary party sue before an higher judge or another that succeedeth the same and for money divorce her again. So shamefully doth that covetousness and ambition of our prelates mock with the laws of God. I pass over with silence how many years they will prolong the sentence with cavillations[3] and subtlety, if they be well moneyed on both parties, and if a damsel promise two, how shameful counsel they will give the [b]second and also how the religious of Satan do separate unseparable matrimony. For after thou art lawfully married at the commandment of father and mother and with the consent of all thy friends [c]yet if thou wilt be disguised like unto one of them and swear obedience unto their traditions, thou mayest disobey father and mother, break the oath which thou hast sworn to God before his holy congregation and withdraw love and charity the highest of God's commandments[4] and that duty and service which thou owest unto thy wife: whereof Christ cannot dispense with thee. For Christ is not against God, but with God and came not to break God's ordinances, but to fulfil them. That is he came to overcome thee with kindness and to make thee to do of very love that thing which the law compelleth thee to do. For love only and to do service unto thy neighbour is the fulfilling of the law in the sight of God. To be a monk or a friar, thou mayest thus forsake thy wife before thou hast lain with her, but not to be a secular priest. [d]And yet after thou art professed, the Pope for money will dispense with thee, both for thy coat and all thy obedience, and make a secular priest of

a. Covetousness maketh our spirituality that they cannot see that which a Turk is ashamed of.
b. Get her with child say they, so shall thy cause be best.
c. God's commandments break they through their own tradition.
d. Money maketh merchandise.

thee: likewise as it is simony[5] to sell a benefice (as they call it), but to resign upon a pension and then to redeem the same, is no simony at all. [a]O crafty jugglers and mockers with the word of God.

The obedience of wives unto their husbands.

After that Eve was deceived of the serpent, God said unto her (Genesis 3), thy lust or appetite shall pertain unto thy husband and he shall rule thee or reign over thee. God which created the woman knoweth what is in that weak vessel (as Peter calleth her) and hath therefore put her under the obedience of her husband to rule her lusts and wanton appetites. Peter (1 Peter 3) exhorteth wives to be in subjection unto their husbands, after the example of the holy women which in old time trusted in God, and as Sara obeyed Abraham and called him lord. Which Sara before she was married, was Abraham's sister[6] and equal with him: but as soon as she was [b]married was in subjection and became without comparison inferior. For so is the nature of wedlock by the ordinance of God. It were much better that our wives followed the example of the holy women of old time in obeying their husbands, than to worship them with a *Pater Noster*, an *Ave* and a *Credo*, or to stick up candles before their images. Paul (Ephesians 5) saith: women submit yourselves unto your own husbands, as unto the Lord. For the husband is the wife's head even as Christ is the head of the congregation.[7] Therefore as the congregation is in subjection to Christ, likewise let wives be in subjection unto their husbands in all things. Let the woman therefore fear her husband, as Paul saith in the said place. For her husband is unto her in the stead of God, that she obey him and wait on his commandments. And his commandments are God's commandments. [c]If she therefore grudge[8] against him or resist him she grudgeth against God and resisteth God.

a. Jugglers.
b. Marriage altereth the degree of nature.
c. The husband is to the wife in God's stead.

The obedience of servants unto their masters.

Servants obey your carnal masters with fear and trembling in singleness of your hearts as unto Christ: not with service in the eyesight as men pleasers: but as the servants of Christ doing the will of God from the heart with good will, even as though ye served the Lord and not men (Ephesians 6). And (1 Peter 2) servants obey your masters with all fear not only if they be good and courteous but also though they be froward. For it cometh of grace, if a man for conscience toward God endure great suffering wrongfully. For what praise is it if when ye be buffeted for your faults, ye take it patiently? But and if when ye do well, ye suffer wrong and take it patiently, then is there thanks with God. Hereunto verily were ye called. For Christ also suffered for our sakes leaving us an example to follow his steps. [a]In whatsoever kind therefore thou art a servant, during the time of thy covenants, thy master is unto thee in the stead and room of God and through him feedeth thee, clotheth thee, ruleth and learneth thee: his commandments are God's commandments and thou oughtest to obey him as God, and in all things to seek his pleasure and profit. For thou art his good and possession, as his ox or his horse in so much that whosoever doth but desire thee in his heart from him without his love and licence is condemned of God, which saith (Exodus 20). See thou once covet not thy neighbour's servants.

[b]Paul the Apostle sent home Onesimus unto his master (as thou readest in the epistle of Paul to Philemon).[9] Insomuch that though the said Philemon with his servant also was converted by Paul and owed unto Paul and to the word that Paul preached, not his servant only, but also himself: yea and though that Paul was in necessity and lacked ministers to minister unto him in the bonds which he suffered for the gospel's sake: yet would he not retain the servant necessary unto the furtherance of the gospel without the consent of the master.

[c]O how sore differeth the doctrine of Christ and his apostles from

a. The master is unto the servant in God's stead.
b. Our spirituality retain man's servants not to honour God but their traditions and ceremonies only.
c. Christ's doctrine and the Pope's differ.

the doctrine of the Pope and of his apostles. [a]For if any man will obey neither father nor mother, neither lord nor master, neither king nor prince, the same needeth but only to take the mark of the beast, that is, to shave himself a monk, a friar or a priest, and is then immediately free and exempted from all service and obedience due unto man. [b]He that will obey no man (as they will not) is most acceptable unto them. The more disobedient that thou art unto God's ordinances, the more apt and meet art thou for theirs. Neither is the professing, vowing and swearing obedience unto their ordinances any other thing, than the defying, denying and forswearing obedience unto the ordinances of God.[10]

The obedience of subjects unto kings, princes and rulers.

The thirteenth Chapter of Paul (Romans):[11] Let every soul submit himself unto the authority of the higher powers. There is no power but of God. The powers that be are ordained of God. Whosoever therefore resisteth that power resisteth the ordinance of God. They that resist, shall receive to them self damnation. For rulers are not to be feared for good works but for evil. Wilt thou be without fear of the power? Do well then and so shalt thou be praised of the same. For he is the minister of God, for thy wealth. But and if thou do evil, then fear. For he beareth not a sword for nought. For he is the minister of God, to take vengeance on them that do evil. Wherefore ye must needs obey not for fear of vengeance only, but also because of conscience. Even for this cause pay ye tribute. For they are God's ministers, serving for the same purpose.

Give to every man therefore his duty: tribute to whom tribute belongeth: custom to whom custom is due: fear to whom fear belongeth: honour to whom honour pertaineth. Owe nothing to any man: but to love one another. For he that loveth another, fulfilleth the law. For these commandments: thou shalt not commit advoutry:[12] thou shalt not kill: thou shalt not steal: thou shalt not bear false witness: thou shalt not desire:

a. If thy master please thee not, shave thyself a monk a friar or a priest.
b. To obey no man is a spiritual thing.

and so forth if there be any other commandment, are all comprehended in this saying: love thine neighbour as thyself. Love hurteth not his neighbour: therefore is love the fulfilling of the law.

As a father over his children is both lord and judge forbidding that one brother avenge himself on another, but (if any cause of strife be between them) will have it brought unto himself or his assigns, to be judges and corrected: so God forbiddeth all men to avenge themselves, and taketh that authority and office of avenging unto himself saying, vengeance is mine and I will reward: (Deuteronomy 32). Which text Paul allegeth (Romans 12). For it is impossible that a man should be a righteous an equal or an indifferent[13] judge in his own cause, lusts and appetites so blind us. Moreover when thou avengest thyself, thou makest not peace, but stirrest up more debate.

God therefore hath given laws unto all nations and in all lands hath put kings, governors and rulers in his own stead, to rule the world through them. And hath commanded all causes to be brought before them, as thou readest (Exodus 22). In all causes (saith he) of injury or wrong, whether it be ox, ass, sheep or vesture, or any lost thing which another challengeth, let the cause of both parties be brought unto the gods:[14] whom the gods condemn the same shall pay double unto his neighbour. Mark, [a]the judges are called gods in the scriptures because they are in God's room and execute the commandments of God. And in another place of the said chapter Moses chargeth saying: see that thou rail not on the gods neither speak evil of the ruler of thy people. Whosoever therefore resisteth them resisteth God (for they are in the room of God) and they that resist shall receive their damnation.

Such obedience unto father and mother, master, husband, emperor, king, lords and rulers requireth God of all nations, yea of the very Turks and infidels. [b]The blessing and reward of them that keep them, is the life of this world. As thou readest (Leviticus 18), Keep my ordinances and laws, which if a man keep he shall live therein. Which text Paul rehearseth (Romans 10), proving thereby that the righteousness of the law is but worldly, and the reward thereof is the life of this world. And

a. Judges are called gods.
b. Blessing.

the [a]curse of them that breaketh them, is the loss of this life: as thou seest by the punishment appointed for them.

And whosoever keepeth the law (whether it be for fear, for vainglory or profit) though no man reward him, yet shall God [b]bless him abundantly and send him worldly prosperity, as thou readest (Deuteronomy 28). What good blessings accompany the keeping of the law, and as we see the Turks far exceed us Christian men in worldly prosperity for their just keeping of their temporal laws. [c]Likewise though no man punish the breakers of the law, yet shall God send his curses upon them till they be utterly brought to nought as thou readest most terribly even in the said place.

Neither may the inferior person avenge himself upon the superior or violently resist him for whatsoever wrong it be. If he do he is condemned in the deed doing: inasmuch as he taketh upon him that which belongeth to God only which saith [d]vengeance is mine and I will reward (Deuteronomy 22). And Christ saith (Matthew 26), All they that take the sword shall perish with the sword. Takest thou a sword to avenge thyself? So givest thou not room unto God to avenge thee but robbest him of his most high honour, in that thou wilt not let him be judge over thee.

If any man might have avenged himself upon his superior, that might [e]David most righteously have done upon King Saul which so wrongfully persecuted David, even for no other cause, than that God had anointed him king and promised him the kingdom. Yet when God had delivered Saul into the hands of David, that he might have done what he would with him as thou seest in the first book of Kings[15] the twenty-fourth chapter, how Saul came into the cave where David was. And David came to him secretly and cut off a piece of his garment. And as soon as he had done it his heart smote him because he had done so much unto his Lord. And when his men couraged him to flee him he answered, the Lord forbid it me, that I should lay mine hand on him. Neither suffered he his men to hurt him. When Saul was gone out David followed and

a. Curse.
b. God rewardeth all obedience though no man else do.
c. God avengeth all disobedience though no man else do.
d. Vengeance is God's.
e. David.

showed him the piece of his garment and said: why believest thou the words of men that say, David goeth about to do thee harm? Perceive and see that there is neither evil nor wickedness in my hand and that I have not trespassed against thee, and yet thou layest await for my life. God judge between thee and me and avenge me of that, but mine hand be not upon thee as the old proverb saith (said David) [a]out of the wicked shall wickedness proceed, but mine hand be not upon the meaning that God ever punisheth one wicked by another. And again (said David) God be judge, and judge between thee and me and behold and plead my cause, and give me judgment or right of thee.

And in the twenty-sixth chapter of the same book, when Saul persecuted David again: David came to Saul by night, as he slept and all his men, and took away his spear and a cup of water from his head. Then said Abisai David's servant, God hath delivered thee thine enemy into thine hand this day, let me now therefore nail him to the ground with my spear and give him but even one stripe and no more. David forbade him saying, Kill him not. [b]For who (said he) shall lay hands on the Lord's anointed and be not guilty? The Lord liveth or by the Lord's life[16] (said he) he dieth not except the Lord smite him or that his day be come to die or else go to battle and there perish.

[c]Why did not David slay Saul, seeing he was so wicked, not in persecuting David only, but in disobeying God's commandments and in that he had slain eighty-five of God's priests wrongfully?[17] Verily for it was not lawful. For if he had done it, he must have sinned against God. [d]For God hath made the king in every realm judge over all, and over him is there no judge. He that judgeth the king judgeth God and he that layeth hands on the king layeth hand on God, and he that resisteth the king resisteth God and damneth God's law and ordinance. If the subjects sin they must be brought to the king's judgment. [e]If the king sin he must be reserved unto the judgment, wrath and vengeance of

a. God destroyeth one wicked by another.
b. God provideth a means to take the evil out of the wary when they have fulfilled their wickedness.
c. Why David slew not Saul.
d. The king is in the room of God in this world.
e. The king must be reserved unto the vengeance of God.

God. And as it is to resist the king, so is it to resist his officer which is set or sent to execute the king's commandment.

And in the first chapter of the second book of Kings[18] David commanded the young man to be slain, which brought unto him the crown and bracelet of Saul and said to please David withal, that he himself had slain Saul. And in the fourth chapter of the same book David commanded those two to be slain which brought unto him the head of Isboseth Saul's son, by whose means yet the whole kingdom returned unto David according unto the promise of God.

And (Luke 13), when they showed Christ of the Galileans, whose blood Pilate mingled with their own sacrifice: he answered suppose ye that these Galileans were sinners above all other Galileans, because they suffered such punishment? I tell you nay: but except ye repent ye shall likewise perish. Thus was told Christ, no doubt, of such an intent as they asked him (Matthew 22), whether it were lawful to give tribute unto Caesar. [a]For they thought that it was no sin to resist an heathen prince: as few of us would think (if we were under the Turk) that it were sin to rise against him, and to rid ourselves from under his dominion, so sore have our bishops robbed us of the true doctrine of Christ.[19] But Christ condemned their deeds and also the secret thoughts of all other that consented thereunto saying: except ye repent ye shall likewise perish. As who should say, I know that ye are within in your hearts such as they were outward in their deeds, and are under the same damnation: except therefore ye repent betimes, ye shall break out at the last into like deeds, and likewise perish, as it came afterwards to pass.

Hereby seest thou that the king is in this world without law and may at his lust do right or wrong and shall give accompts, but to God only.

Another conclusion is this, that no person neither any degree may be exempt from this ordinance of God. Neither can the profession of monks and friars or anything that the Pope or bishops can lay for themselves, except them from the sword of the Emperor or kings, if they break the laws. For it is written, let every soul submit himself unto the authority of the higher powers.[20] Here is no man except, but all souls must obey. The higher powers are the temporal kings and princes

a. It is not lawful for a christian subject to resist his prince though he be an heathen man.

unto whom God hath given the sword to punish whosoever sinneth.
[a]God hath not given them swords to punish one and to let another go
free and to sin unpunished. Moreover with what face durst the spirituality,
which ought to be the light and an example of good living unto all other,
desire to sin unpunished or to be excepted from tribute, toll or custom,
that they would not bear pain with their brethren, unto the maintenance
of kings and officers ordained of God to punish sin?[21] There is no power
but of God (by power understand the authority of kings and princes).
The powers that be, are ordained of God. Whosoever therefore resisteth
power resisteth God: yea though he be Pope, bishop, monk or friar.
They that resist shall receive unto themselves damnation. Why? For
God's word is against them which will have all men under the power of
the temporal sword. For rulers are not to be feared for good works but
for evil. Hereby seest thou that they that resist the powers or seek to be
except from their authority have evil consciences and seek liberty to sin
unpunished and to be free from bearing pain with their brethren. Wilt
thou be without fear of the power? So do well and thou shalt have laud
of the same (that is to say of the ruler). With good living ought the
spirituality to rid themselves from fear of the temporal sword, and not
with craft and with blinding the kings and bringing the vengeance of
God upon them and in purchasing licence to sin unpunished.

For he is the minister of God for thy wealth:[22] to defend thee from
a thousand inconvenients, from thieves, murderers and them that would
defile thy wife, thy daughter and take from thee all that thou hast: yea
life and all, if thou did resist. [b]Furthermore though he be the greatest
tyrant in the world, yet is he unto thee a great benefit of God and a
thing wherefore thou oughtest to thank God highly. For it is better to
have somewhat than to be clean stripped out of all together: it is better
to pay the tenth than to lose all: it is better to suffer one tyrant than
many and to suffer wrong of one than of every man. Yea and it is better
to have a tyrant unto thy king than a shadow, a passive king that doth
nought himself, but suffer other to do with him what they will, and to

a. The king hath no power but to his damnation to
privilege the spirituality to sin unpunished.
b. A king is a great benefit though he be never so evil.

lead him whither they list.[23] For a tyrant though he do wrong unto the good, yet he punisheth the evil and maketh all men obey neither suffereth any man to poll but himself only. A king that is soft as silk and effeminate, that is to say turned unto the nature of a woman, what with his own lusts, which are as the longing of a woman with child, so that he cannot resist them, and what with the wily tyranny of them that ever rule him, shall be much more grievous unto the realm than a right tyrant. Read the chronicles and thou shalt find it ever so.

But and if thou do evil, then fear. [a]For he beareth not a sword for nought. For he is the minister of God,[24] to take vengeance on them that do evil. If the office of princes given them of God be to take vengeance of evil doers: that by this text and God's word, are all princes [b]damned, even as many as give liberty or licence unto the spirituality to sin unpunished, and not only to sin unpunished themselves: but also to open [c]sanctuaries, privileged places, churchyards, Saint John's hold:[25] yea and if they come too short unto all these, yet to set forth a [d]neckverse[26] to save all manner trespassers from the fear of the sword of the vengeance of God put in the hands of princes to take vengeance on all such.

God requireth the law to be kept of all men let them keep it for whatsoever purpose they will. [e]Will they not keep the law? so vouchsafeth he not that they enjoy this temporal life. Now are there three natures of men, one altogether beastly which in no wise receive the law in their hearts, but rise against princes and rulers whensoever they are able to make their party good. These are signified by them that worshipped the golden calf. For Moses brake the tables[27] of the law ere he came at them.

The second are not so beastly, but receive the law, and unto them the law cometh: but they look not Moses in the face. For his countenance is too bright[28] for them, that is, they understand not that the law is spiritual and requireth the heart. They look on the pleasure, profit and promotion that followeth the keeping of the law, and in respect of the

a. Princes are ordained to punish evildoers.
b. The damnation of princes.
c. Sanctuaries.
d. Neckverse.
e. Three natures.

reward keep they the law outwardly with works, but not in the heart. For if they might obtain like honour, glory, promotion and dignity and also avoid all inconvenients, if they broke the law, so would they also break the law and follow their lusts.

The third are spiritual and look Moses in the open face and are (as Paul saith the second to the Romans) a law unto themselves, and have the law written in their hearts by the Spirit of God. These need neither of king nor officers to drive them, neither that any man proffer them any reward for to keep the law. For they do it naturally.

The first work for fear of the sword only. The second for reward. The third work for love freely. They look on the exceeding mercy, love and kindness which God hath showed them in Christ and therefore love again and work freely. [a]Heaven they take of the free gift of God through Christ's deservings, and hope without all manner doubting that God according to his promise, will in this world also defend them and do all thing for them of his goodness that is in them. They consent unto the law that it is holy and just and that all men ought to do whatsoever God commandeth for no other cause, [b]but because God commandeth it. And their great sorrow is, because that there is no strength in their members[29] to do that which their heart lusteth to do and is athirst to do.

These of the last sort keep the law of their own accord and that in the heart, and have professed perpetual war against the lusts and appetites of the flesh, till they be utterly subdued: yet not through their own strength, but knowing and knowledging their weakness cry ever for strength to God which hath promised assistance unto all that call upon him. These follow God and are led of his Spirit. The other two are led of lusts and appetites.

[c]Lusts and appetites are diverse and many and that in one man: yea and one lust contrary to another, and the greatest lust carrieth a man all together away with him. We are also changed from one lust unto another. Otherwise[30] are we disposed when we are children, otherwise when we are young men and otherwise when we are old, otherwise over even[31]

a. Heaven cometh by Christ.
b. A Christian man seeketh no more but God's will.
c. Lusts.

and otherwise in the morning: yea sometimes altered six times in an hour. How fortuneth all this? [a]Because that the will of man followeth the wit and is subject unto the wit and as the wit erreth so doth the will, and as the wit is in captivity, so is the will, neither is it possible that the will should be free where the wit is in bondage.

That thou mayest perceive and feel[32] the thing in thine heart and not be a vain sophister disputing about words without perceiving, mark this. The root of all evil the greatest damnation and most terrible wrath and vengeance of God that we are in, is natural blindness. We are all out of the right way, every man his ways: one judgeth this best, another that to be best. Now is [b]worldly wit nothing else but craft and subtlety to obtain that which we judge falsely to be best. [c]As I err in my wit, so err I in my will. When I judge that to be evil, which in deed is good, then hate I that which is good. And when I suppose that good which is evil indeed, then love I evil. As if I be persuaded and borne in hand that my most friend is mine enemy then hate I my best friend: and if I be brought in belief that my most enemy is my friend, then love I my most enemy. Now when we say, every man hath his free will, to do what him lusteth, I say verily that men do what they lust. Notwithstanding to follow lusts is not freedom, but captivity and bondage. If God open any man's wits to make him feel in his heart, that lusts and appetites are damnable, and give him power to hate and resist them, then is he free even with the [d]freedom wherewith Christ maketh free, and hath power to do the will of God.

[e]Thou mayest hereby perceive that all that is done in the world (before the spirit of God come and giveth us light) is damnable sin,[33] and the more glorious the more damnable: so that that which the world counteth most glorious is more damnable in the sight of God, than that which the whore, the thief and the murderer do. With blind reasons of worldly wisdom mayest thou change the minds of youth and make them give

a. Free will.
b. Worldly wit.
c. The will is bound and led.
d. Freedom.
e. All is sin that springeth not of the spirit of God and all that is not done in the light of God's word.

themselves to what thou wilt either for fear, for praise or for profit: and yet doest but change them from one vice to another,[a] as the persuasions of her friends made Lucrece[34] chaste. Lucrece believed if she were a good housewife and chaste, that she should be most glorious, and that all the world would give her honour, and praise her. She sought her own glory in her chastity and not God's. When she had lost her chastity, then counted she herself most abominable in the sight of all men, and for very pain and thought which she had, not that she had displeased God, but that she had lost her honour, slew herself. Look how great her pain and sorrow was for the loss of her chastity, so great was her glory and rejoicing therein, and so much despised she them that were otherwise, and pitied them not. Which pride God more abhorreth than the whoredom of any whore. Of like pride are all the moral virtues of Aristotle, Plato and Socrates, and all the doctrine of the philosophers the very gods of our school men.

In like manner is it for the most part of our most holy religion. For they of like imagination do things which they of Bedlam may see, that they are but madness. [b]They look on the miracles which God did by the saints to move the unbelieving unto the faith and to confirm the truth of his promises in Christ, whereby all that believe are made saints: as thou seest in the last chapter of Mark. They preached (saith he) everywhere, the Lord working with them and confirming their preaching with miracles that followed. And in the fourth of the Acts the disciples prayed that God would stretch forth his hands to do miracles and wonders in the name of Jesus. And Paul (1 Corinthians 14) saith, that the miracle of speaking with divers tongues is but a sign for unbelievers and not for them that believe. These miracles turn they unto another purpose saying in [c]their blind hearts. See what miracles God hath showed for this saint, he must be verily great with God. And at once turn themselves from God's word and put their trust and confidence in the saint and his merits and make an advocate or rather a god of the saint, and of their blind imagination make a testament or bond between the saint and them, the

a. So do our spirituality in all their works.
b. True miracles are wrought to confirm the preaching and not the Godhead of the preacher.
c. Pure hypocrites are blind.

testament of Christ's blood clean forgotten. [a]They look on the saint's garments and lives or rather lies which men lie on the saints: and this wise imagine in their hearts saying: the saint for wearing such a garment and for such deeds is become so glorious in heaven. If I do likewise, so shall I be also. They see not the faith and trust which the saints had in Christ, neither the word of God which the saints preached, neither the intent of the saints, how that the saints did such things to tame their bodies and to be an example to the world, and to teach that such things are to be despised which the world most wondreth at and magnifieth. They see not also that some lands are so hot that a man can neither drink wine nor eat flesh therein: neither consider they the complexion of the saints, and a thousand like things see they not. So when they have killed their bodies and brought them in that case, that scarce with any restorative they can recover their health again yet had they lever[35] die than to eat flesh. Why? For they think, I have now this twenty, thirty or forty years eaten no flesh and have obtained I doubt not by this time as high a room as the best of them: should I now lose that? Nay I had lever die: and as Lucrece had lever have been slain if he had not been too strong for her than to have lost her glory, even so had these. They ascribe heaven unto their imaginations and mad inventions, and receive it not of the liberality of God, by the merits and deservings of Christ.[36]

[b]He now that is renewed in Christ, keepeth the law without any law written or compulsion of any ruler or officer, save by the leading of the Spirit only: but the [c]natural man is enticed and moved to keep the law carnally, with carnal reasons and worldly persuasions, as for glory, honour, riches and dignity. But the last remedy of all when all other fail, is [d]fear. Beat one and the rest will abstain for fear: as Moses ever putteth in remembrance saying: kill, stone, burn.[37] So shall thou put evil from thee, and all Israel shall hear and fear and shall no more do so. If fear help not, then will God that they be taken out of this life.

[e]Kings were ordained then, as I before said, and the sword put in

a. The religious look upon the outside only.
b. The spiritual man.
c. The natural man.
d. Fear is the last remedy.
e. Kings defend the false authority of the Pope, their office punishing of sin laid apart.

their hands to take vengeance of evil doers, that others might fear, and were not ordained to fight one against another or to rise against the Emperor to defend the false authority of the Pope that very Antichrist. ªBishops, they only can minister the temporal sword, their office the preaching of God's word laid apart, which they will neither do nor suffer any man to do, but slay with the temporal sword (which they have gotten out of the hand of all princes) them that would. The preaching of God's word is hateful and contrary unto them: Why? For it is impossible to preach Christ except thou preach against Antichrist, that is to say, them which with their false doctrine and violence of sword enforce to quench the true doctrine of Christ. And as thou canst heal no disease, except thou begin at the root: even so canst thou preach against no mischief except thou begin at the bishops. ᵇKings they are but shadows, vain names and things idle, having nothing to do in the world, but when our holy father needeth their help.

ᶜThe Pope contrary unto all conscience and against all the doctrine of Christ, which saith my kingdom is not of this world (John 18), hath usurped the right of the Emperor. And by policy of the ᵈbishops of Almany³⁸ and with corrupting the electors or choosers of the Emperor with money, bringeth to pass that such a one is ever chosen Emperor that is not able to make his party good with the Pope. To stop the Emperor that he come not at Rome, he bringeth the French king up to ᵉ Milan, and on the other side bringeth he the Venetians.³⁹ If the Venetians come too nigh, the ᶠbishops of France must bring in the French king. And the Socheners⁴⁰ are called and sent for to come and succour. And for their labour he giveth to some a rose,⁴¹ to another a ᵍCap of Maintenance.⁴² One is called ʰMost Christian King⁴³ another ⁱDefender of the

a. Bishops minister the kings' duty their own laid apart: yea they persecute their own office.
b. Kings do but wait on the Pope's pleasure.
c. The juggling of the Pope.
d. Bishops of Almany.
e. Milan.
f. Bishops of France.
g. A cap of maintenance.
h. Most Christian king.
i. Defender of the Pope's faith.

Faith,[44] another the Eldest [a]Son of the Most Holy Seat.[45] [b]He blaseth[46] also the arms of other and putteth in the holy cross, the crown of thorn or the nails and so forth. If the French king go too high, and creep up other to Bononye[47] or Naples: then must our English [c]bishops bring in our King. The craft of the bishops is to entitle one king with another's realm. He is called King of Denmark and of England, he King of England and of France. [d]Then to blind the lords and the commons, the king must challenge his right. Then must the land be taxed and every man pay, and the treasure borne out of the realm and the land beggared. How many a thousand men's lives hath it cost? And how many an hundred thousand pounds hath it carried out of the realm in our remembrance? [e]Besides how abominable an example of gathering was there? Such verily as never tyrant, since the world began, did: yea such as was never before heard or thought on neither among Jews, Saracens,[48] Turks or heathen since God created the sun to shine: that a beast should break up into the temple of God, that is to say, into the heart and consciences of men and compel them to swear every man what he was worth, to lend that should never be paid again. How many thousands forswore themselves? How many thousands set themselves above their ability, partly for fear lest they should be forsworn and partly to save their credence?[49] When the Pope hath his purpose, then is peace made, no man wotteth[50] how, and our most enemy is our most friend.

Now because the Emperor is able to obtain his right: French, English, Venetians and all must upon him. [f]O great whore of Babylon,[51] how abuseth she the princes of the world, how drunk hath she made them with her wine? How shameful licences doth she give them, to use necromancy,[52] to hold whores, to divorce themselves, to break the faith and promises that one maketh with another: that the confessors shall deliver unto the king the [g]confession of whom he will, and dispenseth

a. The eldest son of the holy seat.
b. Blasing of arms.
c. The English bishops.
d. The falsehood of bishops.
e. O a cruel and abominable example of tyranny.
Judge them by their deeds saith Christ.
f. The whore of Babylon.
g. Confession.

48

with them even of the very law of God, which Christ himself cannot do.

Against the Pope's false power.

(Matthew 26), Christ saith unto Peter, put up thy sword into his sheath. For all that lay hand upon the sword, shall perish with the sword, that is, whosoever without the commandment of the temporal officer to whom God hath given the sword layeth hand on the sword to take vengeance, the same deserveth death in the deed-doing. [a]God did not put Peter only under the temporal sword, but also Christ himself. As it appeareth in the fourth chapter to the Galatians. And Christ saith (Matthew 3), Thus becometh it us to fulfil all righteousness, that is to say, all ordinances of God. If the head be then under the temporal sword, how can the members be excepted? If Peter sinned in defending Christ against the temporal sword (whose authority and ministers the bishops then abused against Christ as ours do now) [b]who can excuse our prelates of sin which will obey no man, neither king nor Emperor? Yea who can excuse from sin, either the kings that give, either the bishops that receive such exemptions contrary to God's ordinances and Christ's doctrine?

And (Matthew 17) both Christ and also Peter pay tribute, where the meaning of Christ's question unto Peter is: if princes take tribute of strangers only and not of their children, then verily ought I to be free which am the son of God, whose servants and ministers they are and of whom they have their authority. Yet because they neither knew that neither Christ came to use that authority, but to be our servant and to bear our burden and to obey all ordinances, both in right and wrong for our sakes and to teach us: therefore said he to Saint Peter: Pay for thee and me lest we offend them. Moreover though that Christ and Peter (because they were poor)[53] might have escaped, yet would he not for fear of offending other and hurting their consciences. For he might well

a. Not Peter only but Christ also was under the temporal sword.
b. The kings sin in giving exceptions and the prelates in receiving them.

have given occasion unto the tribute-gatherers to have judged amiss both of him and his doctrine: yea and the Jews might haply have been offended thereby and have thought that it had not been lawful for them to have paid tribute unto heathen princes and idolaters, saying that he, so great a prophet, paid not. ªYea and what other thing causeth the lay so little to regard their princes, as that they see them both despised and disobeyed of the spirituality? But our prelates which care for none offending of consciences and less for God's ordinances, will pay nought but when princes must fight in our most holy father's quarrel and against Christ. Then are they the first. There also is none so poor that then hath not somewhat to give.

ᵇMark here how past all shame our school doctors are (as Rochester is in his sermon against Martin Luther)⁵⁴ which of this text of Matthew dispute that Peter because he paid tribute, is greater than the other apostles, and hath more authority and power than they, and was head unto them all, contrary unto so many clear texts, where Christ rebuketh them saying: that is an heathenish thing that one should climb above another or desire to be greater. To be great in the kingdom of heaven is to be a servant, and he that most humbleth himself and becometh a servant unto other (after the example of Christ I mean and his apostles and not of the Pope and his apostles our cardinals and bishops) the same is greatest in that kingdom.⁵⁵ If Peter in paying tribute became greatest, how cometh it, that they will pay none at all? But to pay tribute is a sign of subjection verily, and the cause why Christ paid was because he had an household, and for the same cause paid Peter also. For he had an house, a ship and nets, as thou readest in the gospel. But let us go to Paul again.⁵⁶

Wherefore ye must needs obey, not for fear of vengeance only: but also because of conscience. That is though thou be so mighty (as now many years our Pope and prelates everywhere are) that thou needest not to obey the temporal sword for fear of vengeance: yet must thou obey because of conscience. First because of thine ᶜown conscience. For

a. When the spirituality payeth tribute.
b. Shameless jugglers.
c. They make no conscience at any evil doing.

though thou be able to resist, yet shalt thou never have a good conscience, as long as God's word, law and ordinance are against thee. [a]Secondarily for thy neighbour's conscience. For though through craft and violence thou mightest escape and obtain liberty or privilege to be free from all manner duties, yet oughtest thou neither to sue or seek for any such thing, neither yet admit or accept, if it were proffered [b]lest thy freedom make thy weak brother to grudge and rebel, in that he seeth thee go empty and he himself more laden, thy part also laid on his shoulders. Seest thou not if a man favour one son more than another, or one servant more than another, how all the rest grudge, and how love, peace and unity is broken? [c]What Christianly love is in thee to thy neighbour-ward, when thou canst find in thine heart to go up and down empty by him all day long and see him overcharged, yea to fall under his burden, and yet wilt not once set to thine hand to help him? What good conscience can there be among our spirituality to gather so great treasure together and with hypocrisy of their false learning to rob almost every man of house and lands, and yet not therewith content but with all craft and wiliness to purchase so great liberties and exemptions from all manner bearing with their brethren, seeking in Christ nothing but lucre?[57] I pass over with silence how they teach princes in every land to lade new exactions and tyranny on their subjects more and more daily, neither for what [d]purpose they do it say I. God I trust shall shortly disclose their juggling and bring their falsehood to light and lay a medicine to them, to make their scabs break out. Nevertheless this I say, that they have robbed all realms, not of God's word only but also of all wealth and prosperity, and have driven peace out of all lands and withdrawn themselves from all obedience to princes and have separated themselves from the lay men, counting them viler than dogs, and have set up that great idol the whore of Babylon, Antichrist of Rome whom they call Pope, and have conspired against all commonwealths and have made

a. They care for their neighbours as the wolf doth for the sheep.

b. The evil example of the spirituality causeth the lay to believe that they are not bound to obey.

c. There is no Christian love in them.

d. What purpose even to flatter the princes that they may abuse their authority to slay whosoever believeth in Christ and to maintain the Pope.

them a several[58] kingdom, wherein it is lawful unpunished to work all abomination. In every parish have they spies[59] and in every great man's house and in every tavern and alehouse. And through ªconfessions know they all secrets, so that no man may open his mouth to rebuke whatsoever they do, but that he shall be shortly made an heretic. ᵇIn all councils is one of them, yea the most part and chief rulers of the councils are of them: But of their council is no man.

Even for this cause pay ye tribute: that is to wit, for conscience's sake, to thy neighbour, and for the cause that followeth.[60] For they are God's ministers serving for the same purpose. Because God will so have it, we must obey. We do not look (if we have Christ's Spirit in us) what is good, profitable, glorious and honourable for us, neither on our own will, but on God's will only. Give to every man therefore his duty: tribute to whom tribute belongeth: custom to whom custom is due: fear to whom fear belongeth: honour to whom honour pertaineth.

That thou mightest feel the working of the spirit of God in thee and lest the beauty of the deed should deceive thee and make thee think that the law of God which is spiritual were content and fulfilled with the outward and bodily deed it followeth: ᶜOwe nothing to any man: but to love one another. For he that loveth another fulfilleth the law. For these commandments: thou shalt not commit adultery, thou shalt not kill, thou shalt not steal, thou shalt not bear false witness, thou shalt not desire, and so forth if there be any other commandment are all comprehended or contained in this saying: love thy neighbour: therefore is love the fulfilling of the law. ᵈHere hast thou sufficient against all the sophisters,[61] work-holy[62] and justifiers[63] in the world, which so magnify their deeds. The law is spiritual and requireth the heart,[64] and is never fulfilled with the deed in the sight of God. With the deed ᵉthou fulfillest the law before the world and livest thereby, that is, thou enjoyest this present life and avoidest the wrath and vengeance, the death and punishment, which the law threateneth to them that break it. But before God thou keepest the

a. Confession.
b. Prelates know all men's secrets and no man theirs.
c. Love fulfilleth the law before God and not the outward deed.
d. Against workmen.
e. The deed fulfilleth the law before the world.

law if thou love only.[65] [a]Now what shall make us love? Verily that shall faith do. If thou behold how much God loveth thee in Christ and from what vengeance he hath delivered thee for his sake and of what kingdom he hath made thee heir, then shalt thou see cause enough to love thy very enemy without respect of reward, either in this life or in the life to come, but because that God will so have it and Christ hath deserved it: Yea thou shouldest feel in thine heart that all thy deeds to come, are abundantly recompensed already in Christ.

Thou wilt say haply, if love fulfil the law, then it justifieth. I say that wherewith a man fulfilleth the law, declareth him justified but that which giveth him wherewith to fulfil the law, justifieth him. [b]By justifying understand the forgiveness of sins and the favour of God. Now saith the text (Romans 10), the end of the law or the cause wherefore the law was made is Christ to justify all that believe. [c]That is, the law is given to utter sin, to kill the consciences, to damn our deeds, to bring to repentance and to drive unto Christ: in whom God hath promised his favour and forgiveness of sin unto all that repent and consent to the law that it is good. [d]If thou believe the promises[66] then doth God's truth justify thee, that is forgiveth thee and receiveth thee to favour for Christ's sake. In a surety whereof and to certify thine heart, he sealeth thee with the spirit (Ephesians 1 and 4). And (2 Corinthians 5) saith Paul: Which gave us his Spirit in earnest. How the Spirit is given us through Christ, read the eighth chapter of the epistle to the Romans and Galatians 3 and 2 Corinthians 4. Nevertheless the Spirit [e]and his fruits wherewith the heart is purified, as faith, hope, love, patience, longsuffering and obedience,[67] could never be seen without outward experience. For if thou were not brought sometime into cumbrance, when God only could deliver thee, thou shouldest never see thy faith, yea except thou foughtest sometime against desperation, hell, death, sin and powers of this world for thy faith's sake, thou shouldest never know true faith from a dream. Except thy brother now and then offended thee, thou couldest not know

a. Faith maketh a man love.
b. Justifying.
c. The office or duty of the law.
d. The believing of God's promise justifieth.
e. The spirit and the inward virtues are known by the outward deed.

whether thy love were godly. For a Turk is not angry, till he be hurt and offended: but if thou love him that doeth the evil, then is thy love of God: likewise if thy rulers were always kind, thou shouldest not know whether thine obedience were pure or no: but and if thou canst patiently obey evil rulers in all thing that is not to the dishonour of God: and when thou hurtest not thy neighbours, then art thou sure, that God's spirit worketh in thee and that thy faith is no dream nor any false imagination.

Therefore counselleth Paul (Romans 12) recompense to no man evil: And on your part have peace with all men. Dearly beloved avenge not yourselves: but give room unto the wrath of God. For it is written vengeance is mine and I will reward, saith the Lord. ᵃTherefore if thy enemy hunger feed him: If he thirst, give him drink. For in so doing thou shalt heap coals of fire on his head (that is thou shalt kindle love in him). Be not overcome of evil (that is let not another man's wickedness make thee wicked also). But overcome evil with good, that is, with softness, kindness and all patience win him: even as God with kindness won thee.

ᵇThe law was given in thunder, lightning, fire, smoke and the voice of a trumpet and terrible sight (Exodus 20), so that the people quoke for fear and stood afar off saying to Moses, Speak thou to us and we will hear: let not the Lord speak unto us, lest we die. No ear (if it be awaked and understandeth the meaning) is able to abide the voice of the law: except the promises of mercy be by. That thunder, except the rain of mercy be joined with it, destroyeth all and buildeth not. The law is a witness against us and testifieth that God abhorreth the sins that is in us, and us for our sins' sake.

ᶜIn like manner when God gave the people of Israel a king it thundered and rained that the people feared so sore that they cried to Samuel for to pray for them, that they should not die (1 Kings 12).⁶⁸ As the law is a terrible thing: even so is the king. For he is ordained to take vengeance and hath a sword in his hand and not peacocks' feathers. Fear him

a. Overcome thine enemy with welldoing.
b. The law.
c. The king.

therefore and look on him as thou wouldest look on a sharp sword that hanged over thy head by an hair.

[a]Heads and governors are ordained of God[69] and are even the gift of God, whether they be good or bad. And whatsoever is done unto us by them, that doeth God, be it good or bad. If they be evil [b]why are they evil? Verily for our wickedness' sake are they evil. Because that when they were good we would not receive that goodness of the hand of God and be thankful, submitting ourselves unto his laws and ordinances, but abused the goodness of God unto our sensual and beastly lusts. Therefore doth God make his scourge of them and turn them unto wild beasts contrary to the nature of their names and offices, even into lions, bears, foxes and unclean swine, to avenge himself of our unnatural and blind unkindness and of our rebellious disobedience.

In the one hundred and sixth Psalm[70] thou readest, he destroyed the rivers and dried up the springs of water and turned the fruitful land into barrenness, for the wickedness of the inhabitants therein. When the children of Israel had forgotten God in Egypt, God moved the hearts of the Egyptians to hate them and to subdue them with craft and wiliness, (Psalm 104[71] and Deuteronomy 3). Moses rehearseth saying: God was angry with me for your sakes: so that the wrath of God fell on Moses for the wickedness of the people.[72] And in the second chapter of the second book of Kings[73] God was angry with the people and moved David to number them, when Joab and the other lords wondered why he would have them numbered, and because they feared lest some evil should follow, dissuaded the king: yet it holp not. God so hardened his heart in his purpose, to have an occasion to slay the wicked people.

[c]Evil rulers then are a sign that God is angry and wroth with us. Is it not great wrath and vengeance that the father and mother should hate their children, even their flesh and their blood? Or that an husband should be unkind unto his wife or a master unto the servant that waiteth on his profit, or that lords and kings should be tyrants unto their subjects and tenants which pay them tribute, toll, custom and rent, labouring and

a. Rulers are God's gift.
b. Why the evil rulers are evil.
c. Evil rulers are a sign that God is angry with us.

toiling to find them in honour and to maintain them in their estate? Is not this a fearful judgment of God and a cruel wrath that the very prelates and shepherds of our souls which were wont to feed Christ's flock with Christ's doctrine and to walk before them in living thereafter, and to give their lives for them, to their example and edifying, and to strength their weak faiths, are now so sore changed that if they smell that one of their flock (as they now call them and no longer Christ's) do but once long or desire for the true knowledge of Christ, they will slay him, burning him with fire most cruelly? [a]What is the cause of this, and that they also teach false doctrine confirming it with lies? Verily it is the hand of God to avenge the wickedness of them that have no love nor lust unto the truth of God, when it is preached, but rejoice in unrighteousness. As thou mayest see in the second epistle of Paul to the Thessalonians, where he speaketh of the coming of Antichrist: Whose coming shall be (saith he) by the working of Satan with all miracles signs and wonders which are but lies, and in all deceivable unrighteousness among them that perish, because they received not any love to the truth to have been saved. [b]Therefore shall God send them strong delusion, to believe lies. Mark how God to avenge his truth sendeth to the unthankful false doctrine and false miracles to confirm them and to harden the hearts in the false way, that afterward it shall not be possible for them to admit the truth. As thou seest in Exodus 7 and 8 how God suffered false miracles to be showed in the sight of Pharaoh to harden his heart, that he should not believe the truth, for inasmuch as his sorcerers turned their rods into serpents and turned water into blood and made frogs by their enchantment, so thought he that Moses did all his miracles by the same craft and not by the power of God, and abode therefore in unbelief and perished in resisting God.

[c]Let us receive all things of God whether it be good or bad: let us humble ourselves under his mighty hand and submit ourselves unto his nurture and chastising and not withdraw ourselves from his correction (read Hebrews 12 for thy comfort) and let us not take the staff by the

a. Why the prelates are so wicked.

b. The cause of false miracles is: that we have no lust unto the truth.

c. The right way to come of bondage.

end or seek to avenge ourselves on his rod which is the evil rulers. [a]The child as long as he seeketh to avenge himself upon the rod hath an evil heart. For he thinketh not that the correction is right or that he hath deserved it, neither repenteth, but rejoiceth in his wickedness. And so long shall he never be without a rod: yea so long shall the rod be made sharper and sharper. If he knowledge his fault and take the correction meekly and even kiss the rod and amend himself with the learning and nurture of his father and mother then is the rod take away and burnt.

So if we resist evil rulers seeking to set ourselves at liberty, we shall no doubt bring ourselves into more cruel bondage and wrap ourselves in much more misery and wretchedness. For if the heads overcome, then lay they more weight on their backs and make their yoke sorer and tie them shorter. If they overcome their evil rulers then make they way for a more cruel nation or for some tyrant of their own nation which hath no right unto the crown. If we submit ourselves unto the chastening of God and meekly knowledge our sins for which we are scourged, and kiss the rod, and amend our living: then will God take the rod away, that is, he will give the rulers a better heart. Or if they continue their malice and persecute you for well-doing and because ye put your trust in God, then will God deliver you out of their tyranny for his truth's sake. [b]It is the same God now that was in the old time and delivered the fathers and the prophets, the apostles and other holy saints. And whatsoever he swore to them he hath sworn to us. And as he delivered them out of all temptation, cumbrance and adversity, because they consented and submitted themselves unto his will and trusted in his goodness and truth: even so will he do us if we do likewise.

Whensoever the children of Israel fell from the way which God commanded them to walk in, he gave them up under one tyrant or another. As soon as they came to the knowledge of themselves and repented crying for mercy and leaning unto the truth of his promises he sent one to deliver them, as the histories of the Bible make mention.

[c]A Christian man in respect of God is but a passive thing, a thing

a. ☞
b. God is always one always true always merciful
and excludeth no man from his promises.
c. A Christian man doth but suffer only.

that suffereth only and doeth nought, as the sick in respect of the surgeon or physician doth but suffer only. The surgeon lanceth and cutteth out the dead flesh, searcheth the wounds, thrusteth in tents,[74] seareth,[75] burneth, seweth or stitcheth and layeth corsies[76] to draw out the corruption, and last of all layeth to healing plasters and maketh whole. The physician likewise giveth purgations and drinks to drive out the disease and then with restoratives bringeth health. Now if the sick resisteth the [a]razor, the searching iron and so forth, doth he not resist his own health and is cause of his own death? So likewise is it of us, if we resist evil rulers which are the [b]rod and scourge wherewith God chastiseth us, the instruments wherewith God searcheth our wounds, and bitter drinks to drive out the sin and to make it appear, and corsies to draw out by the roots the core of the pocks[77] of the soul that fretteth inward. [c]A Christian man therefore receiveth all things of the hand of God both good and bad, both sweet and sour, both wealth and woe. If any person do me good, whether it be father mother and so forth, that receive I of God and to God give thanks. For he gave wherewith, and gave a commandment, and moved his heart so to do. Adversity also receive I of the hand of God as an wholesome medicine, though it be somewhat bitter. Temptation [d]and adversity do both kill sin and also utter it. For though a Christian man knoweth every thing how to live: yet is the flesh so weak, that he can never take up his cross himself[78] to kill and mortify the flesh. He must have another to lay it on his back. In many also sin lieth hid within and festereth and rotteth inward and is not seen: so that they think how they are good and perfect and keep the law. As the young man (Matthew 19) said he had observed all of a child and yet lied falsely in his heart, as the text following well declareth. When all is at peace and no man troubleth us, we think that we are patient and love our neighbours as ourselves: but let our neighbour hurt us in word or deed and then find we it otherwise. Then fume we and rage and set up the bristles and bend ourselves to take vengeance. If we loved with godly love for Christ's kindness' sake, we should desire no vengeance, but pity

a. ☞
b. Evil rulers are wholesome medicines.
c. A Christian man receiveth.
d. How profitable adversity is.

him and desire God to forgive and amend him knowing well that no flesh can do otherwise than sin, except that God preserve him. Thou wilt say what good doth such persecution and tyranny unto the righteous? First it maketh them feel the working of God's spirit in them and that their faith is unfeigned. [a]Secondarily I say that no man is so great a sinner, if he repent and believe, but that he is righteous in Christ and in the promises: yet if thou look on the flesh and unto the law there is no man so perfect that is not found a sinner. Nor any man so pure, that hath not somewhat to be yet purged. This shall suffice at this time as concerning obedience.

Because that God excludeth no degree from his mercy. But whosoever repenteth and believeth his promises (of whatsoever degree he be of) the same shall be partaker of his grace: therefore as I have described the obedience of them that are under power and rule, even so will I with God's help (as my duty is) declare how the rulers which God shall vouchsafe to call unto the knowledge of the truth ought to rule.[79]

The office of a father and how he should rule.

Fathers move not your children unto wrath: but bring them up in the nurture and information of the Lord (Ephesians 6 and Colossians 3). Fathers rate[80] not your children, lest they be of desperate mind, that is, lest you discourage them. For where the fathers and mothers are wayward hasty and churlish, ever brawling and chiding: there are the children anon discouraged and heartless and apt for nothing, neither can they do anything aright. [b]Bring them up in the nurture and information of the Lord. Teach them to know Christ and set God's ordinance before them saying: son or daughter, God hath created thee and made thee through us thy father and mother, and at his commandment have we so long thus kindly brought thee up and kept thee from all perils: he hath commanded thee also to obey us saying: child obey thy father and

---

a. The greatest sinner is righteous in Christ and the promises.
And the perfectest and holiest is a sinner in the law and the flesh.
b. The right bringing up of children.

mother. If thou meekly obey, so shalt thou grow both in the favour of God and man and knowledge of our Lord Christ. If thou wilt not obey us at his commandment: then are we charged to correct thee, yea and if thou repent not and amend thyself, God shall slay thee by his officers or punish thee everlastingly. [a]Nurture them not worldly and with worldly wisdom saying: thou shalt come to honour, dignity, promotion and riches, thou shalt be better than such and such, thou shalt have three or four benefices and be a great doctor or a bishop and have so many men waiting on thee and do nothing but hawk and hunt and live at pleasure, thou shalt not need to sweat, to labour or take any pain for thy living and so forth, filling them full of pride, disdain and ambition and corrupting their minds with worldly persuasions. Let the fathers and mothers mark how they themselves were disposed at all ages, and by experience of their own infirmities help their children and keep them from occasions. Let them teach their children to ask marriages of their fathers and mothers. And let their elders provide marriages for them in season: teaching them also to know, that she is not his wife which the son taketh nor he her husband which the daughter taketh without the consent and good will of their elders or them that have authority over them. If their friends will not marry them, then are they not to blame if they marry themselves. Let not the fathers and mothers always take the utmost of their authority of their children, but at a time suffer with them and bear their weaknesses as Christ doth ours.[81] Seek Christ in your children, in your wives, servants and subjects. Father, mother, son, daughter, master, servant, king and subject, be names in the worldly regiment. [b]In Christ we are all one thing, none better than other, all brethren and must all seek Christ and our brothers' profit in Christ. And he that hath the knowledge whether he be lord or king, is bound to submit himself and serve his brethren and to give himself for them, to win them to Christ.

a. The destruction and marrying of children.
b. In Christ we are all servants and he that hath knowledge is bound.

The office of an husband and how he ought to rule.

Husbands love your wives, as Christ loved the congregation, and gave himself for it, to sanctify it and cleanse it. Men ought to love their wives as their own bodies. For this cause shall a man leave father and mother and shall continue with his wife and shall be made both one flesh. See that every one of you love his wife even as his own body: All this saith Paul (Ephesians 5 and Colossians 4). He saith husbands love your wives and be not bitter unto them, and Peter in the third chapter of his first epistle saith, [a]men dwell with your wives according to knowledge (that is according to the doctrine of Christ) giving reverence unto the wife, as unto the weaker vessel (that is, help her to bear her infirmities) and as unto them that are heirs also of the grace of life, that your prayers be not let.[82] [b]In many things God hath made the men stronger than the women, not to rage upon them and to be tyrants unto them but to help them to bear their weakness. Be courteous therefore unto them and win them unto Christ and overcome them with kindness, that of love they may obey the ordinance that God hath made between man and wife.

The office of a master and how he ought to rule.

Paul (Ephesians 6) saith, ye masters do even the same things unto them (that is, be master after the example and doctrine of Christ, as he before taught the servants to obey unto their masters as unto Christ) putting away threatenings (that is, give them fair words and exhort them kindly to do their duty: yea nurture them as thine own sons with the Lord's [c]nurture, that they may see in Christ a cause why they ought lovingly to obey) and remember (saith he) that your master also is in heaven. Neither is there any respect of persons with him, that is, he is indifferent and not partial: as great in his sight is a servant as a master. And the third

a. Men ought to rule their wives by God's word.
b. Why the man is stronger than the woman.
c. Teach the servant to know Christ and after Christ's doctrine deal with him.

chapter to the Colossians saith he, ye masters do unto your servants that which is just and equal, remembering that ye also have a master in heaven. Give your servants kind words, food, raiment and learning. Be not bitter unto them, rail not on them, give them no cruel countenance: but according to the example and doctrine of Christ, deal with them. And when they labour sore cherish them again. When ye correct them [a]let God's word be by and do it with such good manner that they may see how that ye do it to amend them only, and to bring them unto the way which God biddeth us walk in, and not to avenge yourselves or to wreak your malice on them. If at a time through hastiness ye exceed measure in punishing, recompense it another way and pardon them another time.

The duty of landlords.

Let Christian landlords be content with their rent and old customs not raising the rent or fines and bringing up new customs to oppress their tenants: neither letting two or three tenantries unto one man. Let them not take in their communes neither make parks nor pastures of whole parishes. [b]For God gave the earth to men to inhabit, and not unto sheep and wild deer. Be as fathers unto your tenants: yea be unto them, as Christ was unto us, and show unto them all love, and kindness. Whatsoever business is among them, be not partial favouring one more than another. The complaints, quarrels and strife that are among them, count diseases of sick people and as a merciful physician heal them with wisdom and good counsel. Be pitiful and tenderhearted unto them and let not one of thy tenants tear out another's throat, but judge their causes indifferently and compel them to make their ditches, hedges, gates and ways. For even for such causes were ye made landlords, and for such causes paid men rent at the beginning. For if such an order were not one should slay another and all should go to waste. If thy tenant shall labour and toil all the year to pay thee thy rent and when he hath

a. Do all things with God's word.
b. God gave the earth to men.

bestowed all his labour, his neighbour's cattle shall devour his fruits, how tedious and bitter should his life be? See therefore that ye do your duties again and suffer no man to do them wrong, save the king only. If he do wrong, then must they abide God's judgment.

The duty of kings and of the judges and officers.

Let kings (if they had lever be Christian in deed then so be called) give themselves altogether to the wealth of their realms after the example of Christ: remembering that the people are God's and not theirs: ye are Christ's inheritance and possession[83] bought with his blood. The most despised person in his realm is the king's brother and fellow member with him and equal with him in the kingdom of God and of Christ. Let him therefore not think himself too good to do them service neither seek any other thing in them, than a father seeketh in his children yea than Christ sought in us. Though that the king in the temporal regiment be in the room of God and representeth God himself and is without all comparison better than his subjects: yet let him put off that and become a brother, doing and leaving undone all things in respect of the commonwealth, that all men may see that he seeketh nothing, but the profit of his subjects. When a cause that requireth execution is brought before him then only let him take the person of God on him. Then let him know no creature but hear all indifferently, whether it be a stranger or one of his own realm, and the small as well as the great and judge righteous for the judgment is the Lord's (Deuteronomy 1). In time of judgment he is no minister in the kingdom of Christ: he preacheth no gospel, but the sharp law of vengeance. Let him take the holy judges of the Old Testament for an example and namely [a]Moses which in executing the law was merciless otherwise more than a mother unto them, never avenging his own wrongs but suffering all thing, bearing every man's weakness teaching, warning, exhorting and ever caring for them and so tenderly loved them, that he desired God either to forgive them or damn him with them.

a. Moses.

[a]Let the judges also privately when they have put off the person of a judge exhort with good counsel and warn the people and help, that they come not at God's judgment: but the causes that are brought unto them, when they sit in God's stead, let them judge, and condemn the trespasser under lawful witnesses and not break up into the consciences of men, after the example of Antichrist's disciples, [b]and compel them either to forswear themselves by the almighty God and by the holy gospel of his merciful promises or to testify against themselves. Which abomination our prelates learned of [c]Caiaphas (Matthew 26) saying to Christ, I adjure or charge thee in the name of the living God, that thou tell us whether thou be Christ the son of God. [d]Let that which is secret to God only, whereof no proof can be made nor lawful witness brought, abide unto the coming of the Lord which shall open all secrets. If any malice break forth, that let them judge only. For further authority hath God not given them.

Moses [e](Deuteronomy 17) warneth judges to keep them upright and to look on no man's person, that is, that they prefer not the high before the low, the great before the small, the rich before the poor, his acquaintance, friend, kinsman, countryman or one of his own nation before a stranger, a friend or an alien; yea, or one of their own faith before an infidel: but that they look on the cause only to judge indifferently. For the room that they are in and the law that they execute are God's, which as he hath made all and is God of all and all are his sons: even so is he judge over all and will have all judged by his law indifferently and to have the right of his law, and will avenge the wrong done unto the Turk or Saracen. For though they be not under the everlasting testament of God in Christ, as few of us which are called Christian be, and even no more than to whom God hath sent his promises and poured his spirit into their hearts to believe them, and through faith graven lust in their hearts to fulfil the law of love: yet are they under the testament of the law natural which is the laws of every land made for the common wealth there and for peace and unity that one may live by another. In

a. Judges.
b. O tyranny to compel a man to accuse himself.
c. Our prelates learned of Caiaphas.
d. Secret sins pertain unto God to punish and open sins unto the king.
e. ☞

64

which laws the infidels (if they keep them) have promises of worldly things. Whosoever therefore hindereth a very infidel from the right of that law, sinneth against God and of him will God be avenged. Moreover Moses warneth them that they receive no gifts, rewards or bribes.[84] For those two points, favouring of one person more than another and receiving rewards, pervert all right and equity and is the only[85] pestilence of all judges.

And the kings warneth he that they have not too many wives, [a]lest their hearts turn away: and that they read all way in the law of God, to learn to fear him, lest their hearts be lift up above their brethren.[86] Which two points, women and pride, the despising of their subjects, which are in very deed their own brethren, are the common pestilence of all princes. Read the stories and see.

The sheriffs, baily-errants,[87] constables and such like officers may let no man that hurteth his neighbour escape, but that they bring them before the judges, except they in the mean time agree with their neighbours and make them amends.

Let kings defend their subjects from the wrongs of other nations, but pick no quarrels for every trifle, no let not our most holy father make them no more so drunk with [b]vain names, with caps of maintenance and like baubles, as it were popetry[88] for children, to beggar their realms and to murder their people, for defending of our holy father's tyranny. [c]If a lawful peace that standeth with God's word be made between prince and prince and the name of God taken to record and the body of our Saviour broken between them, upon the bond which they have made, that peace or bond can our holy father not dispense with, neither loose it with all the keys he hath: no verily Christ cannot break it. For he came not to break[89] the law but to fulfil it (Matthew 5).

If any man have broken the law or a good ordinance and repent and come to the right way again, then hath Christ power to forgive him: but licence to break the law can he not give, much more his disciples and vicars (as they call themselves) cannot do it. The [d]keys whereof they so

a. ☞
b. Vain names.
c. The holy father looseth peace and unity, truce, truth and all honesty.
d. What the keys are and why they are so called.

greatly boast themselves are no carnal things but spiritual, and nothing else save knowledge of the law and of the promises or gospel: if any man for lack of spiritual feeling desire authority of men, let him read the old doctors. If any man desire authority of scripture, Christ saith (Luke 11): woe be to you lawyers for ye have taken away the key of knowledge: ye enter not in yourselves and they that come in ye forbid. That is, they had blinded the scripture whose knowledge (as it were a key) letteth into God, with glosses and traditions. Likewise findest thou (Matthew 23). ^aAs Peter answered in the name of all so Christ promised him the keys in the person of all (Matthew 16). And in the twentieth of ^bJohn he paid them saying receive the Holy Ghost: whosoever's sins ye remit they are remitted or forgiven, and whosoever's sins ye retain they are retained or holden. ^cWith preaching the promises loose they as many as repent and believe. And for that John saith receive the Holy Ghost, Luke in his last chapter saith then opened he their wits, that they might understand the scriptures, and said unto them: thus it is written: And thus it behoved Christ to suffer and to rise again the third day. And that ^drepentance and remission of sins should be preached in his name among all nations. At preaching of the law repent men, and at the preaching of the promises do they believe and are saved. ^ePeter in the second of the Acts practised his keys and by preaching the law brought the people into the knowledge of themselves and bound their consciences, so that they were pricked in their hearts and said unto Peter and to the other apostles, what shall we do? Then brought they forth the key of the sweet promises saying: repent[90] and be baptized every one of you in the name of Jesus Christ for the remission of sins, and ye shall receive the gift of the Holy Ghost. For the promise was made unto you and unto your children and to all that are afar even as many as the Lord shall call. Of like examples is the Acts full and Peter's epistles, and Paul's epistles and all the scripture, ^fneither hath our holy father any other

a. The keys are promised.
b. The keys are paid.
c. To bind and loose.
d. Repentance and forgiveness come by preaching.
e. Peter practiseth his keys.
f. The Pope's authority: is to preach God's word only.

authority of Christ or by the reason of his predecessor Peter than to preach God's word. As Christ compareth the understanding of scripture unto a key, so compareth he it to a net and unto leaven and unto many other things for certain properties. [a]I marvel therefore that they boast not themselves of their net and leaven, as well as of their keys, for they are all one thing. But as Christ biddeth us beware of the leaven of the Pharisees,[91] so beware of their counterfeited keys and of their false net (which are their traditions and ceremonies, their hypocrisy and false doctrine) wherewith they catch, not souls unto Christ, but authority and riches unto themselves.

[b]Let Christian kings therefore keep their faith and truth and all lawful promises and bonds, not one with another only, but even with the Turk or whatsoever infidel it be. For so it is right before God as the scriptures and examples of the Bible testify. Whosoever vow an unlawful vow, promise an unlawful promise, swear an unlawful oath, sinneth against God: [c]and ought therefore to break it. He needeth not to sue to Rome for a licence. For he hath God's word, and not a licence only: but also a commandment to break it. They therefore that are sworn to be true unto cardinals and bishops, that is to say false unto God the king and the realm, may break their oaths lawfully without grudge of conscience by the authority of God's word. In making them they sinned, but in repenting and breaking them they please God highly and receive forgiveness in Christ.

Let kings take their duty of their subjects and that that is necessary unto the defence of the realm. Let them rule their realms themselves with the help of lay men that are sage, wise, learned and expert. Is it not a shame above all shames and a monstrous thing that no man should be found able to govern a worldly kingdom save [d]bishops and prelates that have forsaken the world and are taken out of the world and appointed to preach the kingdom of God? Christ saith that his kingdom is not of this world (John 18). And (Luke 12) unto the young man that desired him to bid his brother to give him part of the inheritance, he answered

a. Beware of the net and of the leaven and of the counterfeit keys of our holy father.
b. Not with an heretic saith the Pope.
c. Unlawful vows or oaths are men commanded to break.
d. Bishops.

who made me [a]judge or a divider among you? No man that layeth his hand on the plough and looketh back is apt for the kingdom of heaven (Luke 9). No man can serve two masters but he must despise the one (Matthew 6).

To preach God's word is too much for half a man. And to minister a temporal kingdom is too much for half a man also. Either other requireth an whole man. One therefore cannot well do both. He that avengeth himself on every trifle is not meet to preach the patience of Christ, how that a man ought to forgive and to suffer all things. He that is overwhelmed with all manner riches and doth but seek more daily, is not meet to preach poverty. He that will obey no man is not meet to preach how we ought to obey all men. Peter saith (Acts 6), It is not meet that we should leave the word of God and serve at the tables. Paul saith in the ninth chapter of the first Corinthians, God sent me but to preach. A terrible saying verily for popes, cardinals, and bishops. If he had said woe be to me if I fight not and move princes unto war. Or if I increase not Saint Peter's [b]patrimony[92] (as they call it) it had been a more easy saying for them.

[c]Christ forbiddeth his disciples and that oft (as thou mayest see Matthew 18 and also 20, Mark 9 and also 10, Luke 9 and also 22 even at his last supper) not only to climb above lords, kings and emperors in worldly rule, but also to exalt themselves one above another in the kingdom of God. But in vain: for the Pope would not hear it: though he had commanded it ten thousand times, [d]God's word should rule only and not bishops' decrees or the Pope's pleasure. That ought they to preach purely and spiritually and to fashion their lives thereafter and with all example of godly living and long suffering, to draw all to Christ: and not to expound the scriptures carnally and worldly saying: God spake this to Peter and I am his successor, therefore this authority is mine only: and then bring in the tyranny of their fleshly wisdom, *in presentia maioris cessat potestas minoris*[93] that is in the presence of the greater the less hath no power. There is no brotherhood where such philosophy is taught.

a. Behold the face of the Pope and of the bishops in this glass.
b. Peter's patrimony.
c. The Pope's authority is improved.
d. Bishops have captived God's word with their own decrees.

Such philosophy and so to abuse the scriptures and to mock with God's word is after the manner of the [a]Bishop of Rochester's[94] divinity. For he in his sermon of the condemnation of Martin Luther[95] proveth by a shadow[96] of the Old Testament, that is by Moses and Aaron[97] that Satan and Antichrist, our most holy father the Pope, is Christ's vicar and head of Christ's congregation.

Moses (saith he) signifieth Christ, and Aaron the Pope. And yet the Epistle unto the Hebrews proveth that the high priest[98] of the old law signifieth Christ, and his offering and his going in once in the year into the inner temple signifies the offering wherewith Christ offered himself and Christ's going in unto the father to be an everlasting mediator or intercessor for us. Nevertheless Rochester proveth the contrary by a shadow: by a shadow verily. [b]For in shadows they walk without all shame, and the light will they not come at but enforce to stop and quench it with all craft and falsehood, lest their abominable juggling should be seen. If any man look in the light of the New Testament, he shall clearly see, that that shadow may not be so understood.

Understand therefore that one thing in the scripture representeth divers things. A serpent figureth Christ in one place and the devil in another.[99] And a lion doth likewise.[100] Christ by leaven[101] signifieth God's word in one place, and in another signifieth thereby the trad-itions of the Pharisees which soured and altered God's word for their advantage. Now Moses verily in the said place representeth Christ,[102] [c]and Aaron which was not yet high priest, represented, not Peter only or his successor, as my Lord of Rochester would have it (for Peter was too little to bear Christ's message unto all the world), but signifieth every disciple of Christ and every true preacher of God's word. For Moses put in Aaron's mouth what he should say, and Aaron was Moses' prophet and spake, not his own message (as the Pope and bishops do) but that which Moses had received of God and delivered unto him (Exodus 4 and also 7). So ought every preacher to preach God's word purely and neither to add nor diminish. A true messenger

a. Rochester.
b. They walk in shadows.
c. Aaron is every true preacher.

must do his message truly and say neither more nor less than he is commanded. [a]Aaron when he is high priest and offereth and purgeth the people of their worldly sin which they had fallen in, in touching uncleanly things and in eating meats forbidden (as we sin in handling the chalice and the altar stone and are purged with the bishop's blessing) representeth Christ, which purgeth us from all sin in the sight of God, as the epistle unto the Hebrews maketh mention.[103] When Moses was gone up into the mount and Aaron left behind and made the golden calf,[104] there Aaron representeth all false preachers and namely our most holy father the Pope, which in like manner maketh us believe in a bull,[105] as the Bishop of Rochester full well allegeth the place in his sermon.

[b]If the Pope be signified by Aaron and Christ by Moses, why is not the Pope as well content with Christ's law and doctrine as Aaron was with Moses? What is the cause that our bishops preach the Pope and not Christ saying the Apostles preached not Peter, but Christ? Paul (2 Corinthians 4) saith of himself and of his fellow Apostles: [c]we preach not ourselves, but Christ Jesus the Lord: and preach ourselves your servants for Jesus' sake. And (1 Corinthians 3), Let no man rejoice in men. For all things are yours, whether it be Paul, or Apollos, or Peter:[106] whether it be the world, or life or death, whether they be present things or things to come: all are yours and ye are Christ's and Christ is God's. He leaveth out ye are Peter's or ye are the Pope's. And in the chapter following he saith. Let men thuswise esteem us, even the ministers of Christ, etc. And (2 Corinthians 11) Paul was jealous over his Corinthians, because they fell from Christ, to whom he had married them, and clave unto the authority of men (for even then false prophets sought authority in the name of the high Apostles). I am, saith he, jealous over you with godly jealousy. For I coupled you to one man, to make you a chaste virgin to Christ: but I fear lest as the serpent deceived Eve through his subtlety, even so your wits should be corrupt from the singleness that is in Christ. And it followeth: if he that cometh to you preached another Jesus, or if ye receive another spirit or another gospel, then might ye

a. Aaron representeth Christ.
b. Aaron addeth nothing to Moses' law.
c. The Apostles preached not Peter but Christ.

well have suffered him to have authority above me. But I suppose (saith he) that I was not behind the high Apostles: meaning in preaching Jesus and his gospel and in ministering the spirit. And in the said eleventh chapter he proveth by the doctrine of Christ, that he is greater than the high Apostles. For Christ saith, to be great in the kingdom of God, is to do service[107] and take pain for other. Upon which rule [a]Paul disputeth saying: if they be the ministers of Christ I am more: In labours more abundant, in stripes above measure, in prison more plenteously, in death often and so forth. [b]If Paul preached Christ more than Peter and suffered more for his congregation, then is he greater than Peter by the testimony of Christ.[108] And in the twelfth he saith, In nothing was I inferior unto the high Apostles. [c]Though I be nothing, yet the tokens of an Apostle were wrought among you with all patience, with signs and wonders and mighty deeds. So proved he his authority and not with a bull from Peter sealed with cold lead, other[109] with shadows of the Old Testament falsely expounded.

[d]Moreover the Apostles were sent immediately of Christ and of Christ received they their authority, as Paul boasteth himself everywhere. Christ (saith he) sent me to preach the gospel (1 Corinthians 1). And I received of the Lord that which I delivered unto you (1 Corinthians 11). And (Galatians 1), I certify you brethren that the gospel which was preached of me, was not after the manner of men (that is to wit carnal or fleshly) neither received I it of man, neither was it taught me: but I received it by the revelation of Jesus Christ. And (Galatians 2), he that was mighty in Peter in the Apostleship over the circumcision, was mighty in me among the gentiles. And (1 Timothy 1), readest thou likewise. And (John 20) Christ sent them forth indifferently and gave them like power. As my father sent me (saith he) so send I you: that is to preach and to suffer, as I have done, and not to conquer empires and kingdoms and to subdue all temporal power under you with disguised hypocrisy. He gave them the Holy Ghost to bind and loose indifferently, as thou seest,

a. Paul is greater than the high Apostles.
b. Paul is greater than Peter.
c. Paul proved his Apostleship with preaching and suffering:
the bishops prove their Apostleship with bulls and shadows.
d. The Apostles were sent of Christ with like authority.

and afterward he sent forth Paul with like authority, as thou seest in the Acts. And in the last of Matthew saith he: all power is given me in heaven and in earth: go therefore and teach all nations baptizing them in the name of the Father and of the Son and of the Holy Ghost, teaching them to observe whatsoever I commanded you. The authority [a]that Christ gave them was to preach, yet not what they would imagine, but what he had commanded. Lo saith he, I am with you all ways, even unto the end of the world. He said not I go my way, and lo here is Peter in my stead: But sent them every man to a sundry country, whithersoever the spirit carried them, and went with them himself. And as he wrought with Peter where he went, so wrought he with the other where they went, as Paul boasteth of himself unto the Galatians. [b]Seeing now that we have Christ's doctrine and Christ's holy promises, and seeing that Christ is ever present with us his own self, how cometh it that Christ may not reign[110] immediately over us, as well as the Pope which cometh never at us. Seeing also that the office of an Apostle is to preach only, how can the Pope challenge with right, any authority where he preacheth not? How cometh it also that Rochester will not let us be called one congregation by the reason of one God, one Christ, one Spirit, one gospel, one faith, one hope, and one baptism,[111] as well as because of one Pope?

[c]If any natural beast with his worldly wisdom strive that one is greater than another, because that in congregations one is sent of another, as we see in the Acts, I answer that Peter sent no man, but was sent himself, and John was sent, and Paul, Silas and Barnabas[112] were sent. Howbeit such manner sendings are not worldly, as princes send their ambassadors, no nor as friars send their limiters to gather their brotherhoods,[113] which must obey whether they will or will not. Here all thing is free and willingly. And the Holy Ghost bringeth them together which maketh their wills free and ready to bestow themselves upon their neighbours' profit. And they that come, offer themselves and all that they have or can do, to serve the Lord and their brethren. And every man, as he is

a. The authority that Christ gave
was to preach Christ's word.
b. ☞
c. ☞

found apt and meet to serve his neighbour, so is he sent or put in office. And of the Holy Ghost are they sent with the consent of their brethren and with their own consent also. And God's word ruleth in that congregation, unto which word every man confirmeth his will. And Christ which is all way present is the head. ^aBut as our bishops hear not Christ's voice, so see they him not present: and therefore make them a god on the earth, of the ^bkind (I suppose) of Aaron's calf. For he bringeth forth no other fruit but bulls.

Forasmuch also as Christ is as great as Peter, why is not his seat as great as Peter's? Had the head of the empire been at Jerusalem, there had been no mention made of Peter. It is verily, as Paul saith in the eleventh chapter of the second Epistle to the Corinthians: The false Apostles are deceitful workers, and fashion themselves like unto the Apostles of Christ. That is the shaven ^cnation[114] preached Christ falsely, yea under the name of Christ preached themselves and reign in Christ's stead: have also taken away the key of knowledge and have wrapped the people in ignorance and have taught them to believe in themselves, in their traditions and false ceremonies: ^dso that Christ is but a vain name. And after they had put Christ out of his room, they gave themselves to the Emperor and kings and so long ministered their business till they have also put them out of their rooms and have got their authorities from them and reign also in their stead:^e so that the Emperor and kings are but vain names and shadows, as Christ is, having nothing to do in the world. Thus reign they in the stead of God and man and have all power under them and do what they list.

^fLet us see another point of our great clerk.[115] A little after the beginning of his sermon, intending to prove that which is clearer than the sun and serveth no more for his purpose than *Ite missa est*[116] serveth to prove that our lady was born without original sin: he allegeth a saying that Martin Luther saith, which is this: If we affirm that any one Epistle

a. Why bishops make them a god on earth.
b. Aaron made a calf. And the Pope maketh bulls.
c. The shaven nation hath put Christ out of his room and all kings and the emperors.
d. Christ is but a vain name.
e. Proper ministers.
f. Rochester is proved both ignorant and malicious.

of Paul or any one place of his Epistles pertaineth not unto the universal church, that is, to all the congregation of them that believe in Christ, we take away all Saint Paul's authority.[117] Whereupon saith Rochester: If it be thus of the words of Saint Paul much rather it is true of the gospels of Christ and of every place of them. O malicious blindness. First note his blindness. He understandeth by this word gospel no more but the four evangelists Matthew, Mark, Luke and John and thinketh not that the Acts of the Apostles and the Epistles of Peter, of Paul and of John and of other like are also the gospel. [a]Paul calleth his preaching the gospel (Romans 2, and 1 Corinthians 4, and Galatians 1, and 1 Timothy 1). The gospel is everywhere one, though it be preached of divers[118] and [b]signifieth glad tidings, that is to wit, an open preaching of Christ and the holy testament and gracious promises that God hath made in Christ's blood to all that repent and believe. Now is there more gospel in one epistle of Paul, that is to say, Christ is more clearly preached and more promises rehearsed in one epistle of Paul, than in the three first Evangelists, Matthew, Mark and Luke.

Consider also his maliciousness, how wickedly and how craftily he taketh away the authority of Paul. It is much rather true of the gospels and of every place in them than of Paul. [c]If that which the four Evangelists wrote be truer than that which Paul wrote, then is it not one gospel that they preached, neither one Spirit that taught them. If it be one gospel and one Spirit, how is one truer than the other? [d]Paul proveth his authority to the Galatians[119] and to the Corinthians,[120] because that he received his gospel by revelation of Christ and not of man, and because that when he communed with Peter and the high Apostles of his gospel and preaching, they could improve nothing, neither teach him anything: and because also that as many were converted and as great miracles[121] showed by his preaching as at the preaching of the high Apostles, and therefore will be of no less authority, than Peter and other high Apostles. Nor have his gospel of less reputation than theirs.

a. The epistles of Paul are the gospel.
b. What gospel signifieth.
c. One gospel one Spirit one truth.
d. The authority of Paul and of his gospel.

[a]Finally that thou mayest know Rochester forever and all the remnant by him, what they are within the skin, mark how he playeth Bo Peep[122] with the scripture. He allegeth the beginning to the tenth chapter of the Hebrews: *Umbram habens lex futurorum bonorum*, the law hath but a shadow of things to come. And immediately expoundeth the figure clean contrary unto the chapter following and to all the holy epistle, making Aaron a figure of the Pope whom the epistle maketh a figure of Christ.[123]

He allegeth half a text of Paul (1 Timothy 4), in the later days some shall depart from the faith giving heed unto spirits of error and devilish doctrine:[124] but it followeth in the text, giving attendance or heed unto the devilish doctrine of them which speak false through hypocrisy and have their consciences marked with a hot iron, forbidding to marry and commanding to abstain from meats which God hath created to be received with giving thanks. Which two things whoever did, save the [b]Pope Rochester's god, making sin in the creatures which God hath created for man's use to be received with thanks. The kingdom of heaven is not meat and drink, saith Paul, but righteousness, peace and joy in the Holy Ghost. For whosoever in these things serveth Christ pleaseth God and is allowed of men (Romans 14). Had Rochester therefore not a conscience marked with the hot iron of malice, so that he cannot consent unto the will of God and glory of Christ, he would not have so alleged the text which is contrary to none save themselves.

He allegeth another text of Paul in the second chapter of his second epistle to the Thessalonians. *Erit disessio primum*, that is saith Rochester, before the coming of Antichrist there shall be a notable departing from the faith.[125] And Paul saith: The Lord cometh not except there come a departing first. Paul's meaning is that the last day cometh not so shortly, but that Antichrist shall come first and destroy the faith and sit in the temple of God and make all men worship him and believe in him (as the Pope doth) and then shall God's word come to light again (as it doth at this time) and destroy him and utter his juggling and then cometh Christ unto judgment. What say ye of this crafty conveyer? Would he spare, suppose ye, to allege and to wrest other doctors pestilently, which

a. Rochester playeth Bo Peep.
b. Never man forbade to marry save the Pope.

feareth not for to juggle with the Holy Scripture of God expounding that unto Antichrist which Paul speaketh of Christ? No be thou sure. But even after this mannerwise pervert they the whole scripture and all doctors wresting them unto their abominable purpose clean contrary to the meaning of the text and to the circumstances that go before and after. [a]Which devilish falsehood lest the lay men should perceive, is the very cause why that they will not suffer the scripture to be had in the English tongue, neither any work to be made, that should bring the people to knowledge of the truth.

He allegeth for the Pope's authority Saint Cyprian,[126] Saint Augustine,[127] Ambrose,[128] Jerome[129] and Origen:[130] of which never one knew of any authority that one bishop should have above another. And Saint Gregory[131] allegeth he which would receive no such authority above his brethren when it was proffered him. As the manner is to call [b]Tully[132] chief of orators for his singular eloquence, and Aristotle chief of philosophers and Virgil chief of poets for their singular learning, and not for any authority that they had over other: so was it the manner to call Peter chief of the Apostles for his singular activity and boldness, and not that he should be lord over his brethren contrary to his own doctrine. Yet compare that chief Apostle unto Paul, and his is found a great way inferior. This I say not that I would that any man should make a god of Paul, contrary unto his own learning. Notwithstanding yet, this manner of speaking is left unto us of our elders that when we say the Apostle saith so, we understand Paul for his excellency above other Apostles. I would he would tell you how Jerome, Augustine, Bede,[133] Origen and other doctors expound this text: Upon this rock I will build my congregation: and how they interpret the keys also. Thereto, *Pasce, pasce, pasce*[134] which Rochester leaveth without any English signifieth not Poll, shear[135] and shave. Upon which the text behold the faithful exposition of Bede.

[c]Note also how craftily he would enfeoff[136] the Apostles of Christ with their wicked traditions and false ceremonies which they themselves have feigned, alleging Paul (2 Thessalonians 2).[137] I answer that Paul

a. The cause why they will not have the scripture in English.
b. Tully chief of orators.
c. Rochester allegeth Paul for his blind ceremonies contrary to Paul's doctrine.

taught by mouth such things as he wrote in his Epistles. And his traditions were the gospel of Christ and honest manners and living and such a good order as becometh the doctrine of Christ. As that a woman obey her husband,[138] have her head covered,[139] keep silence[140] and go womanly and Christianly apparelled:[141] that children[142] and servants[143] be in subjection: and that the young obey their elders,[144] that no man eat[145] but he that laboureth and worketh, and that men make an earnest thing of God's word and of his holy sacraments and to watch, fast[146] and pray and such like, as the scripture commandeth.[147] Which things he that would break were no Christian man. But we may well complain and cry to God for help, that it is not [a]lawful for[148] the Pope's tyranny, to teach the people what prayer is, what fasting is and wherefore it serveth. There were also certain customs always which were not commanded in pain of hell or everlasting damnation, as to watch all night,[149] and to kiss one another:[150] which as soon as the people abused them they brake them. For which cause the bishops might break many things now in like manner. Paul also in many things which God had made free, gave pure and faithful counsel without tangling of any man's conscience and without all manner commanding under [b]pain of cursing, pain of excommunication, pain of heresy, pain of burning, pain of deadly sin, pain of hell and pain of damnation. As thou mayest see (1 Corinthians 7) where he counselleth the unmarried, the widows and virgins that it is good so to abide, if they have the gift of chastity. Not to win heaven thereby (for neither circumcision neither uncircumcision is anything at all, but the keeping of the commandments is all together): But that they might be without trouble, and might also the better wait on God's word and freelier serve their brethren. And saith (as a faithful servant) that he had none [c]authority of the Lord to give them any commandment. But that the Apostles gave us any blind ceremonies whereof we should not know the reason, that I deny and also defy, as a thing clean contrary unto the learning of Paul everywhere.

[d]For Paul commandeth that no man once speak in the church, that

a. It is not lawful for us to tell what prayer is what fasting is or wherefore it serveth.
b. Pain of cursing damnation and so forth.
c. If Paul had none authority: then had Peter none. Where had then the Pope this authority?
d. Rochester is improved.

is, in the congregation, but in a tongue that all men understand, except that there be an interpreter[151] by. He commandeth to labour for knowledge, understanding, and feeling and to beware of superstition and persuasions of worldly wisdom, philosophy, and of hypocrisy and ceremonies, and of all manner disguising, and to walk in the plain and open truth. Ye were once darkness (saith he) but now are ye light in the Lord, walk therefore as the children of light (Ephesians 5). How doth Paul also wish them increase of grace in every epistle? How crieth he to God to augment their knowledge, that they should be no more children wavering with every wind of doctrine,[152] but would vouchsafe to make them full men in Christ and in the understanding of the mysteries of secrets of Christ:[153] so that it should not be possible for any man to deceive them with any enticing reasons of worldly wisdom, or to beguile them with blind ceremonies or to lead them out of the way with superstitiousness of disguised hypocrisy, unto which full [a]knowledge are the spiritual officers[154] ordained to bring them (Ephesians 4). So far it is away that Christ's Apostles should give them traditions of blind ceremonies without signification or of which no man should know the reason as Rochester which loveth shadows and darkness lieth on them: God stop his blasphemous mouth.

[b]Consider also how studiously Rochester allegeth Origen, both for his Pope and also to establish his blind ceremonies withal which Origen of all heretics is condemned to be the greatest. He is an ancient doctor saith he, yea and to whom in this point great faith is to be given: yea verily Aristotle and Plato and even very [c]Robin Hood is to be believed in such a point, that so greatly maintaineth our holy father's authority and all his disguisings.

Last of all as once a crafty thief when he was espied and followed, cried unto the people: Stop the thief, stop the thief: And as many to begin withal cast first in another man's teeth that which he feareth should lead to his own charge: even so Rochester layeth to Martin Luther's charge the slaying and murdering[155] of Christian men, because they will not believe in his doctrine, which thing Rochester and his brethren have

a. Wherefore the spiritual officers are ordained.
b. Rochester allegeth heretics for his purpose for lack of scripture.
c. Robin Hood is of authority enough to prove the Pope withal.

not ceased to do now certain hundred years, with such malice that when they be dead, they rage, burning the bodies, of which some they themselves of likelihood killed before secretly.[156] And because that all the world knoweth that Martin Luther slayeth no man but killeth only with the spiritual sword the word of God such cankered consciences as Rochester hath. Neither persecuteth, but suffereth persecution: yet Rochester with a goodly argument proveth that he would do it if he could. [a]And mark I pray you what an orator he is and how vehemently he persuadeth it. Martin Luther hath burned the Pope's decretals:[157] a manifest sign, saith he, that he would have burnt the Pope's holiness also, if he had had him.[158] A like argument (which I suppose to be rather[159] true) I make. Rochester and his holy brethren have burnt Christ's testament:[160] an evident sign verily that they would have burnt Christ himself also if they had had him.

[b]I had almost verily left out the chiefest point of all. Rochester both abominable and shameless: yea and stark mad of pure malice, and so adased[161] in the brains, of spirit that he cannot overcome the truth that he saith not or rather careth not what he saith: in the end of his first destruction,[162] I would say instruction as he calleth it, intending to prove that we are justified through holy works, allegeth[163] half a text of Paul of the fifth to the Galatians (as his manner is to juggle and convey craftily) *fides per dilectionem operans*[c] Which text he this wise Englisheth: faith which is wrought by love, and maketh a verb passive of a verb deponent.[164] Rochester will have love to go before and faith to spring out of love. Thus Antichrist turneth the roots of the tree upward. I must first love a bitter medicine (after Rochester's doctrine) and then believe that it is wholesome. When by natural reason, I first hate a bitter medicine, until I be brought in belief of the physician that it is wholesome and that the bitterness shall heal me, and then afterward love it of that belief. Doth the child love the father first and then believe that he is his son or heir or rather because he knoweth that he is his son or heir and beloved, therefore loveth again? John saith in the third of his first

a. Rochester is an orator.
b. Rochester is clean beside himself.
c. If Rochester be such a juggler. What suppose ye of the rest? Let Rochester be an example therefore to judge them all.

Epistle: [a]See what love the father hath showed upon us, that we should be called his sons. Because we are sons therefore love we. Now by faith are we sons as John saith in the first chapter of his gospel. He gave them power to be the sons of God in that they believed on his name. And Paul saith, in the third Chapter of his epistle to the Galatians, we are all the sons of God by the faith which is in Jesus Christ. And John in the said chapter of his epistle saith: Hereby perceive we love, that he gave his life for us. We could see no love nor cause to love again, except that we believed that he died for us and that we were saved through his death. And in the chapter following saith John: Herein is love: not that we loved God: but that he loved us and sent his Son to make agreement for our sins. So God sent not his Son for any love that we had to him: but of the love, that he had to us sent he his Son, that we might see love and love again. Paul likewise in the eighth chapter to the Romans, after that he hath declared the infinite love of God to us-ward in that he spared not his own Son but gave him for us, crieth out saying: Who shall separate us from the love of God? Shall persecution, shall a sword, etc.? No, saith he, I am sure that no creature shall separate us from the love of God that is in Christ Jesus our Lord: as who should say, we see so great love in God to us-ward in Christ's death, that though all misfortune should fall on us, we cannot but love again. Now how know we that God loveth us? Verily by faith. [b]So therefore, though Rochester be a beast faithless, yet ought natural reason to have taught him, that love springeth out of faith and knowledge and not faith and knowledge out of love. But let us see the text. Paul saith thus:[165] In Christ Jesu, neither circumcision is anything worth, nor incircumcision: but faith which worketh through love or which through love is strong or mighty in working and not which is wrought by love as the juggler saith.

Faith that loveth God's commandments justifieth a man. If thou believe God's promises in Christ and love his commandments then art thou safe. If thou love the commandment then art thou sure that thy faith is unfeigned and that God's spirit is in thee.

a. Faith is the root and love springeth of faith.
b. Though Rochester have not the spirit to judge spiritual things yet ought reason to have kept him from so shameful lying. But God hath blinded him to bring that falsehood to light.

How faith justifieth before God in the heart and how love springeth of faith and compelleth us to work, and how the works justify before the world and testify what we are and certify us that our faith is unfeigned and that the right Spirit of God is in us, see in my book of the justifying of faith[166] and there shalt thou see all things abundantly. Also of the ᵃcontroversy between Paul and James see there. Neverthelater, when Rochester saith, if faith only justified, then both the devils and also sinners that lie still in sin should be saved,[167] his argument is not worth a straw. For neither the devils ᵇnor yet sinners that continue in sin of purpose and delectation, have any such faith as Paul speaketh of. For Paul's faith is to believe God's promises. Faith saith he (Romans 10) cometh by hearing and hearing cometh by the word of God. And how shall they hear without a preacher, and how shall they preach except they be sent? As it is written (saith he) how beautiful are the feet that bring glad tidings of peace and bring glad tidings of good things. Now when sent God any messengers unto the devils to preach them peace or any good thing? The devil hath no promise: he is therefore excluded from Paul's faith. ᶜThe devil believeth that Christ died, but not that he died for his sins. Neither doth any that consenteth in the heart to continue in sin, believe that Christ died for him. ᵈFor to believe that Christ died for us, is to see our horrible damnation and how we were appointed unto eternal pains and to feel and to be sure that we are delivered therefrom through Christ in that we have power to hate our sins and to love God's commandments. All such repent and have their hearts loosed out of captivity and bondage of sin and are therefore justified through faith in Christ. Wicked sinners have no faith but imaginations and opinions about Christ as our schoolmen have in their principles, about which they brawl so fast one with another. It is another thing to believe that the king is rich and that he is rich unto me, and that my part is therein: and that he will not spare a penny of his riches at my need, when I believe that the king is rich I am not moved. But when I believe he is rich for me and that he will never fail me at my

a. The controversy between James and Paul.

b. Why devils have none of Paul's faith nor sinners that repent not.

c. A man may believe that Christ died and many other things and not believe in Christ.

d. What it is to believe in Christ.

need, then love I and of love am ready to work unto the utmost of my power. But let us return at the last unto our purpose again.

[a]What is the cause that lay men cannot now rule, as well as in time past, and as the Turks yet do? Verily because that Antichrist with the mist of his juggling hath beguiled our eyes and hath cast a superstitious fear upon the world of Christian men, and hath taught them to dread, not God and his word, but himself and his word: not God's law and ordinances, princes and officers which God hath set to rule the world, but his own law and ordinances, traditions and ceremonies and disguised disciples, which he hath set everywhere to deceive the world and to expel the light of God's word, that his darkness may have room. For we see by daily experience of certain hundred years long, that he which feareth neither God nor his word, neither regardeth father, mother, master, or Christ himself, which rebelleth against God's ordinances, riseth against the kings and resisteth his officers, [b]dare not once lay hands on one of the Pope's anointed: no though he slay his father before his face or do violence unto his brother or defile his sister, wife or mother. Like honour give we unto his traditions and ceremonies. What devotion have we when we are blessed (as they call it) with the chalice, or when the bishop lifteth up his holy hand over us? Who dare handle the chalice, touch the altar stone or put his hand in the font or his finger unto the holy oil? What reverence give we unto holy water, holy fire, holy bread, holy salt, hallowed bells, holy wax, holy boughs, holy candles and holy ashes?[168] And last of all unto the holy candle commit we our souls at our last departing. Yea and of the very clout[169] which the bishop or his chaplain that standeth by, knitteth about children's necks at confirmation, what lay person durst be so bold as to unloose the knot? Thou wilt say do not such things bring the Holy Ghost and put away sin and drive away spirits? I say that a steadfast faith or belief in Christ and in the promises that God hath sworn to give us for his sake, bringeth the Holy Ghost as all the scriptures make mention, and as Paul saith (Acts 19): have ye received the Holy Ghost through faith or believing? Faith is the rock whereon Christ buildeth his congregation, against which

a. Why lay men cannot rule.
b. Men fear the Pope's oil more than God's commandment.

saith Christ (Matthew 16): Hell gates shall not prevail. [a]As soon as thou believest in Christ, the Holy Ghost cometh, sin falleth away and devils flee: when we cast holy water at the devil or [b]ring the bells, he fleeth, as men do from young children, and maketh with us, to bring us from the true faith that is in God's word unto a superstitious and a false belief of our own imagination. If thou haddest faith and threwest an unhallowed stone at his head, he would earnestly flee and without mocking, yea though thou threwest nothing at all, he would not yet abide.

[c]Though at the beginning miracles were showed through such ceremonies to move the infidels to believe the word of God, as thou readest how the Apostles anointed the sick with oil and healed them, and Paul sent his pertelet or jerkin[170] to the sick and healed them also: Yet was it not the ceremony that did the miracle, but faith of the preacher and the truth of God which had promised to confirm and establish his gospel with such miracles. Therefore as soon as the gift of miracles ceased, ought the ceremony to have ceased also: or else if they will needs have ceremony to signify some promise or benefit of God (which I pray not but would have God's word preached every Sunday, for which intent Sundays and holy days were ordained) [d]then let them tell the people what it meaneth: and not set up a bald and a naked ceremony without signification, to make the people believe therein and to quench the faith that ought to be given unto the word of God.

[e]What helpeth it also that the priest when he goeth to mass disguiseth himself with a great part of the passion of Christ and playeth out the rest under silence with signs and proffers,[171] with nodding, becking and mowing,[172] as it were jackanapes,[173] when neither he himself neither any man else wotteth what he meaneth? Not at all verily, but hurteth and that exceedingly. Forasmuch as it not only destroyeth the [f]faith and quencheth the love that should be given unto the commandments, and maketh the people unthankful, in that it bringeth them into such

a. Faith driveth the devils away.
b. Why do not the bishops make him flee from shooting of guns.
c. Ceremonies did not the miracle but faith.
d. Let them tell what the ceremony meaneth.
e. The priest disguiseth himself with the passion of Christ.
f. Dumb ceremonies quench faith and love and make the infidels mock us.

superstition, that they think that they have done abundantly enough for God, yea and deserved above measure, if they be present once in a day at such mummying.[174] But also maketh the infidels to mock us and abhor us, in that they see nothing but such apes' play among us, whereof no man can give a reason.

[a]All this cometh to pass to fulfil the prophecy which Christ prophesied (Mark 13 and Luke 21) that there shall come in his name which shall say that they themselves are Christ. That do verily the Pope and our holy orders of religion. For they under the name of Christ preach themselves their own word and their own traditions, and teach the people to believe in them.

The Pope giveth pardons of his full power, of the treasure of the church and of the merits of saints. The friars likewise make their benefactors (which only they call their brethren and sisters) partakers of their masses, fasting, watchings, prayings and woolward-goings.[175] [b]Yea and when a novice of the Observants[176] is professed, the father asketh him, will ye keep these rules of holy Saint Francis? And he saith yea: will ye so in deed saith he? The other answereth: yea forsooth father. Then saith the father, and I promise you again everlasting life. O blasphemy. If eternal life be due unto the pilled[177] traditions of lousy friars, where is the testament become that God made unto us in Christ's blood? Christ saith (Matthew 24 and Mark 13) that there shall come pseudochristi. [c]Which though I, for a consideration have translated false christs keeping the Greek word: yet signifieth it in the English false anointed and ought so to be translated. There shall come (saith Christ) false anointed and false prophets and shall do miracles and wonders, so greatly that, if it were possible, the very elect or chosen should be brought out of the way. Compare the Pope's doctrine unto the word of God and thou shalt find that there hath been and yet is a great going out of the way, and that evil men and deceivers (as Paul prophesied 2 Timothy 3) have prevailed and waxed worse and worse, beguiling other as they are beguiled themselves. Thou tremblest and quakest saying: shall God

a. The prophecy of Christ is fulfilled.
b. The testament of the Observants.
c. False anointed.

let us go so sore out of the right way? [a]I answer it is Christ that warneth us, which as he knew all that should follow, so prophesied he before and is a true prophet, and his prophecy must needs be fulfilled.

God anointed his son Jesus with the Holy Ghost, and therefore called him Christ, which is as much to say as anointed. Outwardly he disguised him not but made him like other men and sent him into the world to bless us and to offer himself for us a [b]sacrifice of a sweet savour, to kill the stench of our sins, that God henceforth should smell them no more, nor think on them any more: and to make full and sufficient[178] satisfaction or amends for all them that repent, believing the truth of God and submitting themselves unto his ordinances both for they sin that they do, have done and shall do. For sin we through fragility never so oft, yet as soon as we repent and come into the right way again and unto the testament which God hath made in Christ's blood, our sins vanish away as smoke in the wind and as darkness as the coming of light or as thou cast a little blood or milk into the main sea. [c]Insomuch that whosoever goeth about to make satisfaction for his sins to God-ward, saying in his heart, this much have I sinned, this much will I do again, or this wise will I live to make amends withal, or this will I do to get heaven withal, the same is an infidel, faithless and damned in his deed doing, and hath lost his part in Christ's blood: because he is disobedient unto God's testament, and setteth up another of his own imagination, unto which he will compel God to obey. If we love God we have a commandment to love our neighbour also, as saith John in his epistle.[179] [d]And if we have offended him, to make him amends, or if we have not wherewith, to ask him forgiveness, and to do and suffer all things for his sake, to win him to God and to nourish peace and unity: but to God-ward Christ is an everlasting satisfaction and ever sufficient.

[e]Christ when he had fulfilled his course, anointed his Apostles and disciples with the same Spirit and sent them forth without all manner

a. Christ's prophecy be it never so terrible must be yet fulfilled.
b. Christ was neither shaven nor shorn nor anointed with oil.
c. He that doth ought to make satisfaction or to get heaven hath lost his part of Christ's blood.
d. To our neighbour make we amends.
e. The Apostles were neither shaven nor shorn nor anointed with oil.

disguising like other men also, to preach the atonement and peace which Christ had made between God and man. The Apostles likewise disguised no man, but chose men anointed with the same Spirit: one to preach the word of God, whom we call after the Greek tongue a [a]bishop or a priest, that is, in English, an overseer and an elder.[180] How he was anointed thou readest (1 Timothy 3). [b]A bishop or an overseer must be faultless, the husband of one wife (many Jews and also gentiles that were converted unto the faith had at that time divers wives, yet were not compelled to put any of them away: which Paul, because of example, would not have preachers: forasmuch as in Christ we return again unto the first ordinance of God, that one man and one woman should go together). He must be sober, of honest behaviour, honestly apparelled, harborous[181] (that is, ready to lodge strangers), apt to teach, no drunkard, no [c]fighter, not given to filthy lucre: but gentle, abhorring fighting, abhorring covetousness and one that ruleth his own household honestly, having children under obedience with all honesty. For if a man cannot rule his own house, how can he care for the congregation of God? He may not be young in the faith or as a man would say a novice, lest he be swayed and fall into the judgment of the evil speaker,[182] that is, he may not be unlearned in the secrets of the faith. For such are at once stubborn and headstrong and set not a little by themselves. But alas, we have above twenty thousand that know no more scripture than is written in their portesses[183] and among them is he exceeding well learned that can turn to his service.[184] He must be well reported of them that are without, lest he fall into rebuke and into the snare of the evil speaker, that is, lest the infidels which yet believe not should be hurt by him and driven from the faith, if a man that were defamed were made head and overseer of the congregation.

[d]He must have a wife for two causes.[185] One, that it may thereby be known who is meet for the room. He is unapt for so chargeable an office which had never household to rule. Another cause is, that chastity is an exceeding seldom gift, and unchastity exceeding perilous for that

a. Bishop: an overseer.
b. The true anointing of a priest.
c. This oil is not among our bishops.
d. Priests ought to have wives and why.

degree.[186] Inasmuch as that people look as well unto the living as unto the preaching, and are hurt at once if the living disagree, and fall from the faith and believe not the word.

[a]This overseer because he was taken from his own business and labour, to preach God's word unto the parish, hath right by the authority of his office, to calling an honest living of the parish, as thou mayest see in the Evangelists and also in Paul. For who will have a servant and will not give him meat, drink and raiment and all things necessary? How [b]they would pay him, whether in money or assign him so much rent or in tithes, as the guise is now in many countries, was at their liberty.

Likewise in every congregation chose they another after the same example and even so anointed, as it is to see in the said chapter of Paul[187] and Acts 6. [c]Whom after the Greek word we call deacon, that is to say in English, a servant or a minister whose office was to help and assist the priest and to gather up his duty and to gather for the poor of the parish, which were destitute of friends and could not work: [d]common beggars to run from door to door were not then suffered. On the saints' days namely such as had suffered death, [e]for the word's sake came men together into the church, and the priest preached unto them and exhorted them to cleave fast unto the word and to be strong in the faith and to fight against the powers of the world, with suffering for their faith's sake after the example of the saints. [f]And taught them not to believe in the saints and to trust in their merits and to make gods of them: but took the saints for an example only and prayed God to give them like faith and trust in his word and like strength and power to suffer therefore and to give them so sure hope of the life to come, as thou mayest see in the collects of Saint Laurence[188] and of Saint Stephen[189] in Our Lady matins.[190] And in such days, as we now offer, so gave they every man his portion according to his ability and as God put in his heart, to the maintenance of the priest, deacon and other common ministers and of

a. What the priests' duty is to do: and what to have.
b. Men are not bound to pay the priest in tithes by God's law.
c. Deacon what it signifieth and what is his office.
d. No beggars.
e. How holy days and offerings came up.
f. Saints were not yet gods.

the poor and to find learned men to teach, and so forth. And all was put in the hands of the deacon, as thou mayest see in the life of Saint Laurence and in the histories.[191] [a]And for such purposes gave men lands afterward to ease the parishes, and made hospitals and also places to teach their children and to bring them up and to nurture them in God's word, which lands our monks now devour.

Antichrist.[192]

[b]Antichrist of another manner hath sent forth his disciples, those false anointed of which Christ warneth us before that they should come and show miracles and wonders, even to bring the very elect out of the way, if it were possible. [c]He anointeth them after the manner of the Jews and shaveth them and shoreth[193] them after the manner of the heathen priests which served the idols. He sendeth them forth not with false oil only, but with false [d]names also. For compare their names unto their deeds and thou shalt find them false. He sendeth them forth as Paul prophesied of them (2 Thessalonians 2) with lying signs and wonders. [e]What sign is the anointing? that they be full of the Holy Ghost. Compare them to the signs of the Holy Ghost which Paul reckoneth, and thou shalt find it a false sign. A bishop must be faultless, the husband of one wife.[194] [f]Nay saith the Pope, the husband of no wife, but the holder of as many whores as he liketh. God commandeth all degrees, if they burn and cannot live chaste, to marry.[195] The Pope saith if thou burn take a [g]dispensation for a concubine and put her away, when thou art old, or else as our lawyers say, *si non caste tamen caute*, [h]that is, if ye live not chaste, see ye carry clean and play the knave secretly. Harborous, yea to whores

a. Why lands were given unto the spiritual officers before we fell from the faith.
b. False anointed.
c. Shaving is borrowed of the heathen and oiling of the Jews.
d. False names.
e. Lying signs.
f. No wife but an whore.
g. Take a dispensation.
h. Knaveate.

and bawds, for a poor man shall as soon break his neck as his fast with them, but of the scraps and with the dogs, when dinner is done. Apt to teach and as Peter saith (1 Peter 2) ready always to give an answer to everyone that asketh you a reason of the hope that ye have and that with meekness. Which thing is signified by the [a]boots[196] which doctors of divinity are created in, because they should be ready always to go through thick and thin, to preach God's word, and by the bishops' two-horned [b]mitre, which betokeneth the absolute and perfect knowledge that they ought to have in the New Testament and the Old. Be not these false signs? For they beat only and teach not. Yea, saith the Pope, if they will not be ruled[c] cite them to appear and [d]pose them sharply, what they hold of the Pope's power, of his pardons, of his bulls, of Purgatory, of the ceremonies, of confession and such like creatures of our most holy fathers. If they miss in any point, [e]make heretics of them and [f]burn them. If they be of mine anointed and bear my mark, disgress[197] them, I would say disgraduate[198] them and (after the example of noble Antiochus 2 Maccabees 7) pare the crowns and the fingers[199] of them and torment them craftily and for very pain make them deny the truth. But now say our bishops, because the truth is come too far abroad and the lay people begin to smell our wiles, it is best to oppress them with craft secretly and tame them in prison. Yea, let us find the means to have them in the king's prison and to make treason of such doctrine. Yea, we must stir up some war one where or another to bring the people into another imagination. If they be gentle men abjure them secretly.

[g]Curse them four times in the year.[200] [h]Make them afraid of everything and namely[201] to touch mine anointed, and make them to fear the sentence of the church, suspensions, excommunications and curses. Be

a. Boots.
b. Mitres.
c. Cite them.
d. Pose them.
e. Make them heretics.
f. Burn them.
g. Curse them.
h. Fear them.

thee right or wrong, bear them in hand that they are to be feared yet.[202] Preach me and mine authority, and how terrible a thing my curse is, and how black it maketh their souls. On the holy days which were ordained to preach God's word, set up long ceremonies, long matins, long masses and long evensongs, and all in ªLatin that they understand not, and ᵇroll them in darkness, that ye may lead them whither ye will. And lest such things should be too tedious, ᶜsing some, say some, pipe some, ᵈring the bells and ᵉlull them and ᶠrock them asleep. And yet Paul (1 Corinthians 14) forbiddeth to speak in the church or congregation save in the tongue that all understand. For the lay man thereby is not edified or taught. How shall the lay man say amen (saith Paul) to the blessing or thanksgiving, when he wotteth not what thou sayest. He wotteth not whether thou bless or curse.

What then, saith the Pope, what care I for Paul? ᵍI command by the virtue of obedience to read the gospel in Latin.ʰ Let them not pray but in Latin no, not their *Pater Noster.* If any be sick, go also and say them a gospel and all in Latin: yea to the very corn and fruits of the field in the procession week,[203] preach the gospel in Latin. Make the people believe, that it shall grow the better. It is verily as good to preach it to swine as to men, if thou preach it in a tongue they understand not. How shall I prepare myself to God's commandments? How shall I be thankful to Christ for his kindness?[204] How shall I believe the truth and promises which God hath sworn, while thou tellest them unto me in a tongue which I understand not? ⁱWhat then saith my Lord of Canterbury to a priest that would have had the New Testament gone forth in English? What (saith he) wouldst thou that the lay people should wete[205] what we do?

a. All in Latin.
b. Roll them.
c. Sing.
d. Ring.
e. Lull them.
f. Rock them asleep.
g. Pray in Latin.
h. Say them a gospel.
i. What quod my Lord of Canterbury.

No fighter,[206] which I suppose is signified by the [a]cross that is borne before the high prelates and borne before them in procession. Is that also not a false sign? What realm can be in [b]peace for such turmoilers? What so little a parish is it, but they will pick one quarrel or another with them other, for some surplice, chrisom[207] or mortuary,[208] other for one trifle or other, and cite them to the Arches?[209] Traitors they are to all creatures and have a secret conspiration between themselves. [c]One craft they have, to make many kingdoms and small, and to nourish old titles or quarrels that they may ever move them to war at their pleasure. And if much land by any chance, fall to one man, ever to cast a bone[210] in the way, that he shall never be able to obtain it, as we now see in the Emperor. Why? For as long as the kings be small, if God would open the eyes of any to set a reformation in his realm, then should the Pope [d]interdict his land, and send in other princes to conquer it.

Not given to filthy lucre, but abhorring covetousness. And as Peter saith (1 Peter 5) taking the oversight of them, not as though ye were compelled thereunto: but willingly. Not for desire of filthy lucre but of a good mind: not as though ye were lords over the parishes (over the parishes quoth he). [e]O Peter, Peter thou wast too long a fisher, thou wast never brought up at the Arches, neither was Master of the Rolls,[211] nor yet Chancellor of England.[212] They[213] are not content to reign over king and Emperor and the whole earth: but calling authority also in heaven and in hell. It is not enough for them to reign over all that are quick,[214] but have created them a Purgatory,[215] to reign also over the dead and to have one kingdom more than God himself hath. [f]But that ye be an example to the flock (saith Peter) and when the chief shepherds shall appear ye shall receive an incorruptible crown of glory. This abhorring of covetousness is signified as I suppose by shaving and [g]shearing of

a. Cross.
b. Turmoilers.
c. The craft of prelates.
d. Interdict.
e. Peter went never to school at the Arches.
f. The Pope hath one kingdom more than God himself.
g. Shearing what it signifieth.

the hair, that they have no superfluity. But is not this also a false sign? Yea verily it is to them a remembrance to shear and shave, to heap benefice upon benefice, promotion upon promotion, dignity upon dignity, bishopric upon bishopric, with pluralities,[216] unions[217] and ᵃtot quots.[218]

First by the authority of the gospel, they that preach the word of God in every parish and other necessary ministers have right to challenge an honest living like unto one of the brethren, and therewith ought to be content. ᵇBishops and priests that preach not or that preach ought save God's word, are none of Christ's nor of his anointing: but servants of the beast whose mark they bear,[219] whose word they preach, whose law they maintain clean against God's law, and with their false sophistry give him greater power than God ever gave to his son Christ.

But they as unsatiable beasts not unmindful why they were shaven and shorn, because they will stand at no man's grace or be in any man's danger, have gotten into their own hands, first the ᶜtithe or tenth of all the realm: Then I suppose within a little or all together the third foot[220] of all the ᵈtemporal lands.

Mark well how many parsonages or vicarages are there in the realm which at the least have a ploughland[221] apiece. Then note the lands of bishops, abbots, priors, nuns, knights of Saint John's,[222] cathedral churches, colleges, chantries and ᵉfreechapels.[223] For though the house fall in decay and the ordinance of the founder be lost, yet will not they lose the lands. What cometh once in, may never more out. They make a freechapel of it, so that he which enjoyeth it shall do nought therefore. Besides all this, how many chaplains do gentlemen find at their own cost in their houses? How many sing for souls by testaments?[224] Then the proving of ᶠtestaments, the pressing of goods (the bishop of Canterbury's prerogative). Is that not much through the realm in a year? Four ᵍoffering

a. *Tot quot.*
b. Bishops that preach not.
c. Tithes.
d. Temporal lands.
e. Freechapel.
f. Testaments.
g. Offering days.

days[225] and [a]privy[226] tithes? There is no servant, but that he shall pay somewhat of his wages. None shall receive the body of Christ at Easter, be he never so poor a beggar or never so young a lad or maid, but they must pay somewhat for it. Then [b]mortuaries for forgotten tithes (as they say). And yet what person or vicar is there that will forget to have a pigeon house to peck up somewhat both at sowing time and at harvest when corn is ripe? They will forget nothing. No man shall die in their debt, or if any man do, he shall pay it when he is dead. They will lose nothing. Why? It is God's, it is not theirs. It is Saint Cuthbert's rents,[227] Saint Alban's lands,[228] Saint Edmund's right,[229] Saint Peter's patrimony[230] say they, and none of ours. [c]Item[231] if a man die in another man's parish, besides that he must pay at home a mortuary for forgotten tithes, he must there [d]pay also the best that he there hath. Whether it be an horse of twenty pound or how good soever he be, either a chain of gold of an hundred mark or five hundred pound, if it so chance. It is much verily for so little pain-taking in confessions and in ministering the sacraments. Then [e]beadrolls.[232] Item chrisom,[233] churchings, banns, weddings, offering at weddings, offering at buryings, offering to images, offering of wax and lights which come to their vantage, besides the superstitious waste of wax in torches and tapers throughout the land. Then brotherhoods[234] and pardoners.[235] What get they also by [f]confessions? Yea and many enjoin penance to give a certain, for to have so many masses said, and desire to provide a chaplain and themselves. Soul masses,[236] diriges,[237] month minds, years' minds,[238] All Souls day and trentals.[239] The mother church and the high altar must have somewhat in every testament. Offerings at priests' [g]first masses. Item no man is [h]professed, of whatsoever religion it be, but he must bring somewhat. The hallowing or rather [i]conjuring[240] of churches, chapels, altars, superaltars,

a. Privy tithes.
b. Mortuaries.
c. If ye die from home.
d. Thou must pay ere thou pass.
e. Petty pillage.
f. Confession.
g. First masses.
h. Professings.
i. Conjurations.

chalice vestments and bells. Then book, bell, candlestick, organs, chalice, vestments, copes, altar cloths, surplices: towels, basins, ewers, ship,[241] censer and all manner ornaments must be found them freely, they will not give a mite thereunto. Last of all what swarms of begging friars are there? [a]The parson sheareth, the [b]vicar shaveth, the [c]parish priest polleth, the [d]friar scrapeth and the pardoner pareth.[242] We lack but a butcher to pull off the skin.

What get they in their [e]spiritual law (as they call it) in a year, at the Arches and in every diocese? What get the commissaries[243] and officials with their summoners[244] and apparitors[245] by bawdry[246] in a year? [f]Shall ye not find curates enough which, to flatter the commissaries and officials withal, that they may go quit themselves, shall open unto them the confessions of the richest of their parishes? Whom they cite privily and lay to their charges secretly. If they desire to know their accusers, nay say they, the matter is known well enough and to more than ye are ware of. [g]Come lay your hand on the book, if ye forswear yourself, we shall bring proofs, we will handle you, we will make an example of you. O how terrible are they. Come and swear (say they) that ye will be obedient unto our injunctions. And by that craft wring they their purses and make them drop as long as there is a penny in them. In three or four years shall they in those offices get enough to pay for a bishop's bulls.[247] What other thing are these in a realm save horseleeches and even very maggots, cankers[248] and caterpillars, which devour no more but all that is green, and those wolves which Paul prophesied should come and should not spare the flock (Acts twentieth chapter)? And which Christ said should come in lambs' skins[249] and bade us beware of them and judge them by their works.

[h]Though as I before have sufficiently proved, a Christian man must

a. Parson.
b. Vicar.
c. Parish priest.
d. Friars.
e. Spiritual law.
f. A proper commodity of confession.
g. Lay your hand on the book.
h. No man may avenge save the king and he is bound by his office.

suffer all things, be it never so great unright, as long as it is not against God's commandment, neither is it lawful for him to cast any burden off his back by his own authority till God pull it off which laid it on for our deservings, yet ought the kings everywhere to defend their realms from such oppression, if they were Christian, which is seldom seen and is an hard thing verily, though not impossible. For alas they be [a]captives or ever they be kings, yea all most ere they be born. No man may be suffered about them but flatterers and such as are first sworn true unto our most holy fathers the bishops that is to say false to God and man.

If any of the nobles of the realm be true to the king and so bold that he dare counsel him that which should be to his honour and for the wealth of the realm, they will wait a season[250] for him (as men say), they will provide a ghostly[251] father for him. God bring their wickedness to light. There is no mischief whereof they are not the root, nor blood shed, but through their cause other[252] by their counsel or in that they preach not true obedience and teach not the people to fear God. If any faithful servant be in all the court, he shall have twenty spies waiting upon him, he shall be cast out of the court, or (as the saying is) conveyed to Calais, and made a captain, or an ambassador, he shall be kept far enough from the king's presence.

[b]The kings ought I say to remember that they are in God's stead and ordained of God not for themselves, but for the wealth of their subjects. Let them remember that their subjects are their brethren, their flesh and blood, members of their own body and ever their own selves in Christ. Therefore ought they to pity them and to rid them from such wily tyranny which increaseth more and more daily. And though that the kings by the falsehood of the bishops and abbots be sworn to defend such liberties; yet ought they not to keep their [c]oaths, but to break them. Forasmuch as they are unright and clean against God's ordinance, and even but cruel oppression, contrary unto brotherly love and charity. [d]Moreover the spiritual officer ought to punish no sin, but and if any

a. Kings are in captivity.
b. The duty of kings.
c. Unlawful oaths ought to be broken and may without dispensation.
d. The king only ought to punish sin, I mean that is broken forth: the heart must remain to God.

sin break out the king is ordained to punish it and they not: but to preach and exhort them to fear God and that they sin not.

And let the kings put down some of their tyranny, and turn some unto a commonwealth. If the tenth part of such tyranny were given the king yearly and laid up in the shire towns against the realm had need, what would it grow to in certain years? Moreover one king, one law, is God's ordinance in every realm. Therefore ought not the king to suffer them to have a several law by themselves and to draw his subjects thither. It is not meet, will they say, that a spiritual man should be judged of a worldly or a temporal man. [a]O abomination: see how they divide and separate themselves. If the lay man be of the world, so is he not of God. If he believe in Christ, then is he a member of Christ,[253] Christ's brother,[254] Christ's flesh, Christ's blood,[255] Christ's spouse, coheir with Christ[256] and hath his Spirit in earnest[257] and is also spiritual. If they would rob us of the spirit of God, why should they fear to rob us of worldly goods? Because thou art put in office to preach God's word, art thou therefore no more one of thy brethren? Is the mayor of London no more one of the city, because he is the chief officer? Is the king no more of the realm because he is head thereof? [b]The king is in the room of God, and his law is God's law and nothing but the law of nature and natural equity which God graved in the hearts of men. Yet Antichrist is too good to be judged by the law of God: he must have a new of his own making. It were meet verily that they went to no law at all. No more needed they, if they would study to preach God's word truly and be content with sufficient and to be like one of their brethren.

If any question arose about the faith or of the scripture, [c]that let them judge by the manifest and open scriptures, not excluding the lay men. For there are many found among the lay men which are as wise as the officers. Or else when the officer dieth, how could we put another in the room? Wilt thou so teach twenty, thirty, forty or fifty years, that no man shall have knowledge or judgment in God's word save thou only? [d]Is it not a shame that we Christians come so oft to church in vain,

a. The spirit pertaineth unto the shaven only.
b. The king's law is God's law.
c. How men ought to judge question of the scripture.
d. We come often to school. But are never taught.

when he of four score years old knoweth no more than he that was born yesterday?

[a]Moreover when the spiritual officers have excommunicate any man or have condemned any opinion for heresy: Let not the king nor temporal officers punish and slay by and by[258] at their commandment. But let them look on God's word, and compare their judgment unto the scripture and see whether it be right or no, and not believe them at the first chop:[259] whatsoever they say namely[260] in things that pertain unto their own authorities and power. For no man is a right judge in his own cause. Why doth Christ command the scripture to be preached unto all creatures, but that it pertaineth unto all men to know them? Christ referreth himself unto the scriptures (John 5). And in the eleventh chapter of Matthew, unto the question of John Baptist's disciples he answered: The blind see, the lepers are cleansed, the dead arise again etc. meaning that if I do the works which are prophesied that Christ should do when he cometh, why doubt ye whether I be he or no as who should say, ask the scripture whether I be Christ or no and not myself? How happeneth it then that our prelates will not come to the light also, that we may see whether their works be wrought in God or no? Why fear they to let the lay men see what they do? Why make they all their examinations in darkness? [b]Why examine they not their causes of heresy openly, as the lay men do their felons and murderers? Wherefore did Christ and his Apostles also warn us so diligently of Antichrist and of false prophets that should come? Because that we should slumber or sleep careless, or rather that we should look in the light of the scripture with all diligence to spy them when they came, and not to suffer ourselves to be deceived and led out of the way. John biddeth judge the spirits.[261] Whereby shall we judge them but by the scripture? How shalt thou know, whether the prophet be true or false or whether he speak God's word or of his own head if thou wilt not see the scriptures? [c]Why said David in the second Psalm be learned ye that judge the earth lest the Lord be angry with you and ye perish from the right way?

a. Kings ought to see what they do and not to believe the bishops namely seeing their living is so sore suspect.
b. ☞
c. Be learned ye that judge the earth.

A terrible warning verily: yea and look on the stories well and thou shalt find very few kings since the beginning of the world that have not perished from the right way, and that because they would not be learned.

[a]The Emperor and kings are nothing nowadays but even hangmen unto the Pope and bishops, to kill whosoever they condemn, without any more ado, as Pilate was unto the scribes and Pharisees and the high bishops, to hang Christ. For as those prelates answered Pilate (when he asked what he had done) if he were not an evil doer[262] we would not have brought him unto thee. As who should say, we are too holy to do anything amiss, thou mayest believe us well enough: yea and his blood on our heads,[263] said they, kill him hardly,[264] we will bear the charge, our souls for thine: we have also a law[265] by which he ought to die, for he calleth himself God's son. Even so say our prelates, he ought to die by our laws, he speaketh against the church. And your grace is sworn to defend the liberties and ordinances of the church and to maintain our most holy father's authority: our souls for yours, ye shall do a meritorious deed therein. Nevertheless as Pilate escaped not the judgment of God, even so is it to be feared lest our temporal powers shall not. Wherefore [b]be learned ye that judge the earth lest the Lord be angry with you and ye perish from the right way.[266]

[c]Who slew the prophets? Who slew Christ? Who slew his Apostles? Who the martyrs and all the righteous that ever were slain? The kings and the temporal sword at the request of the false prophets. They deserved such murder to do and to have their part with the hypocrites because they would not be learned and see the truth themselves. [d]Wherefore suffered the prophets? Because they rebuked the hypocrites which beguiled the world and namely princes and rulers and taught them to put their trust in things of vanity[267] and not in God's word. [e]And taught them to do such deeds of mercy as were profitable unto no man but unto the false prophets themselves only, making merchandise of God's word. [f]Wherefore slew

a. The kings are become Antichrist's hangmen.
b. Be learned ye that judge the earth.
c. Who slew the prophets?
d. Why were the prophets slain?
e. What deeds of mercy teach the hypocrites?
f. Why slew they Christ.

they Christ? Even for rebuking the hypocrites: because he said, woe be to you scribes and Pharisees, hypocrites, for ye shut up the kingdom of heaven before men (Matthew 23) that is, as it is written (Luke 11), Ye have taken away the [a]key of knowledge. The law of God which is the key wherewith men bind, and the promises[268] which are the keys wherewith men loose, have our hypocrites also taken away. They will suffer no man to know God's word but burn it and make heresy of it:[269] yea and because the people begin to smell their falsehood they make it [b] treason to the king and breaking of the king's peace to have so much as their *Pater Noster* in English. [c]And instead of God's law, they bind with their own law. And instead of God's promises they loose and justify with pardons and ceremonies which they themselves have imagined for their own profit. [d]They preach it were better for thee to eat flesh on Good Friday than to hate thy neighbour: but let any man eat flesh but on a Saturday or break any other tradition of theirs, and he shall be bound and not loosed, till he have paid the uttermost farthing,[270] other with shame most vile or death most cruel, but hate thy neighbour as much as thou wilt and thou shalt have no rebuke of them, yea rob him, murder him, and then come to them and welcome. They have a sanctuary for thee, to save thee, yea and a neckverse,[271] if thou canst but read a little Latin though it be never so sorely, so that thou be ready to receive the beast's mark. They care for no understanding, it is enough, if thou canst roll up[272] a pair of matins or an evensong and mumble a few ceremonies. And because they be rebuked, this they rage. [e]Be learned therefore ye that judge the world lest God be angry with you and ye perish from the right way.

Woe be to you scribes and Pharisees, hypocrites, saith Christ (Matthew 23), for ye [f]devour widows' houses under a colour of long prayer. Our hypocrites rob not the widows only: but knight, squire, lord, duke, king and emperor and even the whole world under the same colour: teaching

a. The keys.
b. Christ is a traitor and a breaker of the king's peace.
c. How the hypocrites bind and loose.
d. ☞
e. Be learned ye that judge the earth.
f. For rebuking this was Christ slain. And for the same cause are we persecuted.

the people to trust in their prayers and not in Christ for whose sake God hath forgiven all the sin of the whole world, unto as many as repent and believe.[273] [a]They fear[274] them with Purgatory and promise to pray perpetually, lest the lands should ever return home again unto the right heirs. What hast thou bought with robbing thy heirs or with giving the hypocrites that which thou robbest of other men? Perpetual prayer? Yea, perpetual pain. For they appoint thee no time of deliverance, their prayers are so mighty. The Pope for money can empty Purgatory when he will. It is verily Purgatory. [b]For it purgeth and maketh clean riddance: yea it is hell. For it devoureth all things. His fatherhood[275] sendeth them to heaven with [c]*scala celi*:[276] that is, with a ladder, to scale the walls. [d]For by the door Christ,[277] will they not let them come in. That door have they stopped up, and that because ye should buy ladders of them. [e]For some they pray daily which gave them perpetuities and yet make saints of them receiving offerings in their names and teaching other to pray to them. [f]None of them also which taketh upon them to save other with their prayers trusteth to be saved thereby themselves, but hire other to pray for them.

[g]Moses taketh record of God that he took not of any of the people so much as an ass, neither vexed any of them (Numbers 16). Samuel in the first book of Kings[278] the twelfth chapter, asked all Israel whether he had taken any man's ox or ass or had vexed any man or had taken any gift or reward of any man. And all the people testified nay, yet these two both taught the people and also prayed for them as much as our prelates do. Peter (1 Peter 5) exhorts the elders to take the oversight of Christ's flock not for filthy lucre: but of a goodwill even for love. Paul (Acts 20) taketh the priests or elders to record, that he had taught repentance and faith and all the counsel of God. And yet had desired no man's gold, silver, or vesture: but fed himself with the labour of his

a. They be not a little afraid of Purgatory that make perpetuities.
b. Why it is called Purgatory.
c. *Scala celi.*
d. The door is stopped up ye must climb and scale the walls.
e. Some are prayed for and prayed to also.
f. The craft that helpeth other helpeth not his own master.
g. Prayer was not sold in the old time.

hands. And yet these two taught and prayed for the people as much as our prelates do, with whom it goeth after the common saying, no penny no *Pater Noster*. Which prelates yet as they teach not but beat, only for wot they not what prayer meaneth.

Moreover the law of love[279] which Christ left among us, is to give and not to receive. [a]What prayer is it then that thus robbeth all the world contrary to that great commandment which is the end of all commandments and in which all other are contained? If men should continue to buy prayer four or five hundred years more, as they have done, there would not be a foot of ground in Christendom neither any worldly thing which they that will be called spiritual only should not possess. And thus all should be called spiritual.

Woe be to you lawyers, for ye lade men with burdens which they are not able to bear, and ye yourselves touch not the packs with one of your fingers saith Christ (Luke 11). Our [b]lawyers verily have laden us a thousand times more. What spiritual kindred have they made in baptism, to let[280] matrimony, besides that they have added certain degrees unto the law natural for the same purpose?[281] What an unbearable burden of chastity do they violently thrust on other men's backs, and how easily bear they it themselves? How sore a burden? How cruel an hangman? How grievous a torment? [c]Yea and how painful an hell is this ear-confession unto men's consciences? For the people are brought in belief that without that they cannot be saved. Insomuch that some fast certain days in the year and pray certain superstitious prayers all their lives long; that they may not die without confession. In peril of death, if the priest be not by, the shipmen shrive[282] themselves unto the mast. If any be present, they run then every man into his ear but to God's promises flee they not: for they know them not. If any man have a death's wound, he crieth immediately for a priest. If a man die without shrift many take it for a sign of damnation. Many by reason of that false belief die in desperation. Many for shame keep back their confessions twenty, thirty

a. Their prayer breaketh the great commandment
of God. It is time that it were tied up therefore.
b. The burden of our spiritual lawyers.
c. Confession tormenteth the conscience, robbeth the
pure of money and the soul of faith.

years and think all the while that they be damned. I knew a poor woman with child which longed, and being overcome of her passion, ate flesh on a Friday, which thing she durst not confess in the space of eighteen years, and thought all that while that she had been damned, and yet sinned she not at all. Is not this a sore burden that so weigheth down the soul unto the bottom of hell? What should I say? A great book were not sufficient to rehearse the snares which they have laid to rob men both of their goods and also of the trust which they should have in God's word.[283]

The scribes and Pharisees do all their works to be seen of men. They set abroad their phylacteries and make long borders on their garments and love to sit uppermost at feasts and to have the chief seats in the synagogues, that is in the congregations or councils, and to be called rabbi, that is to say master, saith Christ (Matthew 23). Behold the deeds of our spirituality, and how many thousand factions are among them to be known by. Which as none is like another so loveth none another. [a]For every one of them supposeth that all other poll too fast and make too many captives: yet to resist Christ, are they all agreed lest they should be all compelled to deliver up their prisoners to him. Behold the monsters how they are disguised, with mitres, crosses and hats, with crosses, pillars, and poleaxes, and with three crowns.[284] What names [b]have they? My lord prior, my lord abbot, my lord bishop, my lord archbishop, cardinal and legate: if it please your fatherhood, if it please your lordship, if it please your grace, if it like your holiness and innumerable such like. [c] Behold how they are esteemed, and how high they be crept up above all, not into worldly seats only: but into the seat of God the hearts of men, where they sit above God himself. For both they and whatsoever they make of their own heads is more feared and dread, than God and his commandments. In them and their deservings put we more trust than in Christ and his merits. To their promises give we more faith, than to the promises which God hath sworn in Christ's blood.

The hypocrites say unto the kings and lords, these heretics would

a. Badges or baubles to be known by.
b. Glorious names.
c. How are they esteemed.

have us down first, and then you, to make all common. [a]Nay ye hypocrites and right heretics approved by open scripture, the kings and lords are down already and that so low that they cannot go lower. Ye tread them under your feet and lead them captive and have made them your bond servants to wait on your filthy lusts and to avenge your malice on every man contrary unto the right of God's word. Ye have not only robbed them of their land, authority, honour and due obedience which ye owe unto them, but also of their wits, so that they are not without understanding in God's word only but even in worldly matters that pertain unto their offices, they are more than children. Ye bear them in hand what ye will, and have brought them even in case like unto them which when they dance naked in nets,[285] believe they are invisible. We would have them up again and restored unto the room and authority which God hath given them, and whereof ye have robbed them. And your inward falsehood we do but utter only with the light of God's word, that your hypocrisy might be seen. Be learned therefore ye that judge the world lest God be angry with you and ye perish from the right way.

Woe be to you scribes and Pharisees, hypocrites. For ye make clean the utter side of the cup and of the platter, but within they are full of bribery and excess saith Christ (Matthew 23). [b]Is that which our hypocrites eat and drink and all their riotous excess any other thing save robbery and that which they have falsely gotten with their lying doctrine? Be learned therefore ye that judge the world and compel them to make retribution again.

Ye blind guides saith Christ, ye strain out a gnat and swallow a camel (Matthew 23). Do not our blind guides also stumble at a straw and leap over a block, making narrow [c]consciences at trifles, and at matters of weight none at all. If any of them happen to swallow his spittle or any of the water wherewith he washeth his mouth,[286] ere he go to mass, or touch the sacrament with his nose[287] or if the ass[288] forget to breathe on him[289] or happen to handle it with any of his fingers which are not

a. Kings are down: they cannot go lower.
b. Our hypocrites live by theft.
c. Consciences that are so narrow about traditions have wide mouths about God's commandments.

anointed, or say *Alleluia* instead of *Laus tibi domine* or *Ite missa est* instead of *Benedicamus domino* or pour too much wine in the chalice, or read the gospel without light,[290] or make not his crosses aright, how trembleth he? How feareth he? What an horrible sin is committed? I cry God mercy, saith he, and you my ghostly father. But to hold an whore or another man's wife, to buy a benefice, or set one realm at variance with another and to cause twenty thousand men to die on a day is but a trifle and a pastime with them.

[a]The Jews boasteth themselves of Abraham. And Christ said unto them (John 8), If ye were Abraham's children ye would do the deeds of Abraham. Our hypocrites boast themselves of the authority of Peter and of Paul and the other Apostles, clean contrary unto the deeds and doctrine of Peter, Paul and of all the other Apostles. Which both obeyed all worldly authority and power usurping none to themselves, and taught all other to fear the kings and rulers and obey them in all things not contrary to the commandment of God, and not to resist them, though they took away life and goods wrongfully, but patiently to abide God's vengeance. This did our spirituality never yet, nor taught it. [b]They taught not to fear God in his commandments, but to fear them in their traditions. In so much that the evil people which fear not to resist a good king and to rise against him, dare not lay hands on one of them, neither for defiling of wife daughter or very mother. [c]When all men lose life and lands, they remain all ways sure and in safety, and ever win somewhat. For whosoever conquereth other men's lands unrightfully ever gives them part with them. To them is all things lawful. In all councils and parliaments are they the chief. [d]Without them may no king be crowned, neither until he be sworn to their liberties. All secrets know they, even the very thoughts of men's hearts. By them all things are ministered. No king nor realm may through their falsehood live in peace. To believe they teach, not in Christ but in them and their disguised hypocrisy. And of them compel they all men to buy redemption and forgiveness of sins.

a. As the Jews are the children of Abraham so are
the bishops the successors of the Apostles.
b. The spirituality have taught to fear their traditions.
c. They win somewhat always.
d. ☞

The people's sin they eat and thereof wax fat. The wickeder the people are, the more prosperous is their commonwealth. If kings and great men do amiss they must build abbeys and colleges: mean men build chantries:[291] the poor find trentals and brotherhoods[292] and begging friars. Their own heirs do men disherit to endote[293] them. All kings are compelled to submit themselves to them. Read the story of King John,[294] and of other kings. They will have their causes avenged, though whole realms should therefore perish. Take from them their disguising, so are they not spiritual. Compare that they have taught us unto the scripture, so are we without faith.

Christ saith (John fifth chapter), How can ye believe which receive glory one of another? [a]If they that seek to be glorious, can have no faith, then are our prelates faithless verily. And (John 7) he saith, he that speaketh of himself, seeketh his own glory. If to seek glory and honour be a sure token, that man speaketh of his own self and doeth his own message and not his master's: then is the doctrine of our prelates of themself and not of God. [b]Be learned therefore ye that judge the earth lest God be angry with you and ye perish from the right way.

Be learned lest the hypocrites bring the wrath of God upon your heads and compel you to shed innocent blood: as they have compelled your predecessors to slay the prophets, to kill Christ and his Apostles and all the righteous that since were slain. [c]God's word pertaineth unto all men as it pertaineth unto all servants to know their masters' will and pleasure, and to all subjects to know the laws of their prince. Let not the hypocrites do all thing [d]secretly. [e]What reason is it that mine enemy should put me in prison at his pleasure and there diet[295] me and handle me as he lusteth, and judge me himself and that secretly, and condemn me by a law of his own making, and then deliver me to Pilate to murder me?[296] Let God's word try every man's doctrine and whomsoever God's word proveth unclean let him be taken for a leper. [f]One scripture will

a. They that seek honour have no faith
neither can they do God's message.
b. Be learned.
c. God's word ought all men to know.
d. They do all secretly.
e. ☞
f. God's word ought to judge.

help to declare another. [a]And the circumstances, that is to say, the places that go before and after, will give light unto the middle text. And the open and manifest scriptures will ever improve the false and wrong exposition of the darker sentences. Let the temporal power to whom God hath given the sword to take vengeance, look or ever that they leap, and see what they do. Let the causes be disputed before them, and let him that is accused have room to answer for himself. [b]The powers to whom God hath committed the sword shall give accounts for every drop of blood that is shed on the earth. Then shall their ignorance not excuse them nor the saying of the hypocrites help them: my soul for yours, your grace shall do a meritorious deed, your grace ought not to hear them, it is an old heresy condemned by the church. The king ought to look in the scripture and see whether it were truly condemned or no, if he will punish it. If the king or his officer for him, will slay me, so ought the king or his officer to judge me. The king cannot, but unto his damnation, lend his sword to kill whom he judgeth not by his own laws. Let him that is accused stand on the one side and the accuser on the other side and let the king's judge sit and judge the cause, if the king will kill and not be a murderer before God.

[c]Hereof may ye see, not only that our persecution is for the same cause that Christ's was, and that we say nothing that Christ said not, but also that all persecution is only for rebuking of hypocrisy, that is to say, of man's righteousness and of holy deeds which man hath imagined to please God and to be saved by, without God's word, and beside the testament that God hath made in Christ. If Christ had not rebuked the Pharisees because they taught the people, believe in their traditions and holiness and offerings that came to their vantage, and that they taught the widows[297] and them that had their friends dead to believe in their prayers and that through their prayers the dead should be saved, and through that means robbed them both of their goods and also of the testament and promises that God had made, to all that repented, in Christ to come, he might have been uncrucified unto this day.

a. The right way to understand the scripture.
b. The kings have a judge before whom my soul for yours helpeth not.
c. Preach what thou wilt but rebuke not hypocrisy.

If Saint Paul also had not preached against circumcision,[298] that it justified not and that vows, offering and ceremonies justified not, and that righteousness and forgiveness of sins came not by any deserving of our deeds but by faith[299] or believing the promises of God and by the deserving and merits of Christ only, he might have lived unto this hour. Likewise if we preached but against paid covetousness, lechery, extortion, usury, simony and against the evil living both of the spirituality as well as the temporality and against enclosings of parks, raising of rent and fines, and of the carrying out of wool out of the realm, we might endure long enough. But touch the scab of hypocrisy or popeholiness[300] and go about to utter their false doctrine wherewith they reign as gods in the heart and consciences of men and rob them, not of lands, goods and authority only, but also of the testament of God and salvation that is in Christ: then helpeth thee neither God's word, nor yet if thou didst miracles, but that thou art, not an heretic only and hast the devil within thee, but also a breaker of the King's peace and a traitor. But let us return unto our lying signs again.

[a]What signifieth that the prelates are so bloody and clothed in red? That they be ready every hour to suffer martyrdom for the testimony of God's word. Is that also not a false sign? When no man dare for them once open his mouth to ask a question of God's word because they are ready to burn him.

[b]What signify the poleaxes that are borne before high legates *a latere*?[301] Whatsoever false sign they make of them I care not: but of this I am sure, that as the old hypocrites when they had slain Christ, set poleaxes to keep him in his sepulchre that he should not rise again: even so have our hypocrites buried the testament that God made unto us in Christ's blood, and to keep it down, that it rise not again, is all their study: whereof these poleaxes are the very sign.

Is not that shepherd's hook the bishop's crose[302] a false sign? Is not that white rochet[303] that the bishops and canons wear so like a nun and so effeminately, a false sign? What other things are their sandals, gloves, mitres and all the whole pomp of their disguising, than false signs in

a. The prelates are clothed in red.
b. Poleaxes.

which Paul prophesied that they should come? And as Christ warned us to beware of wolves in lambs' skins and bade us look rather unto their fruits[304] [a]and deeds than to wonder at their disguisings. Run throughout all our holy religions, and thou shalt find them likewise all clothed in falsehood.

Of the sacraments.

Forasmuch as we be come to signs, we will speak a word or two of the signs which God hath ordained: that is to say, of the sacraments which Christ left amongst us for our comfort, that we may walk in light and in truth and in feeling of the power of God. For he that walketh in the day stumbleth not, when contrarywise he that walketh in the night stumbleth (John 11). And they that walk in darkness wot not whither they go (John 12).

[b]This word sacrament is as much to say as an holy sign, and representeth all way some promise of God: as in the Old Testament God ordained that the rainbow[305] should represent and signify unto all men an oath that God swore to Noah and to all men after him, that he would no more drown the world through water.

The sacrament of the body and blood of Christ.

So the sacrament of the body and blood of Christ hath a promise annexed which the priest should declare in the English tongue: This is my body that is broken for you. This is my blood that is shed for many unto the forgiveness of sins. This do in remembrance of me saith Christ (Luke 12 and 1 Corinthians 11). [c]If when thou seest the sacrament or eateth his body or drinkest his blood, thou have this promise fast in thine heart (that his body was slain and his blood shed for thy sins) and believest

---

a. Judge the tree by his fruit and not by his leaves.
b. Sacraments are signs of God's promises.
c. The promise which the sacrament preacheth justifieth only.

it, so art thou saved and justified thereby. If not, so helpeth it thee not, though thou hearest a thousand masses in a day or though thou doest nothing else all thy life long, than eat his body or drink his blood: nor more than it should help thee in a dead thirst, to behold a bush at a tavern door,[306] if thou knewest not thereby that there were wine within to be sold.

Baptism.

Baptism hath also his word and promise which the priest ought to teach the people and christen them in the English tongue, and not to play the popinjay[307] with *credo* say ye, *volo* say ye and *baptismum*[308] say ye, for there ought to be no mumming in such a matter. The priest before he baptiseth asketh saying: believest thou in God the Father Almighty, and in his Son Jesus Christ, and in the Holy Ghost, and that the congregation of Christ is holy? And they say yea. Then the priest upon this faith baptiseth the child in the name of the Father, and of the Son, and of the Holy Ghost, for the forgiveness of sins, as Peter saith (Acts 2).

The washing without the word helpeth not: but through the word it purifieth and cleanseth us. As thou readest (Ephesians 5) how Christ cleanseth the congregation in the fountain of water through the word. The word is the promise that God hath made. [a]Now as a preacher in preaching the word of God saveth the hearers that believe, so doth the washing in that it preacheth and representeth unto us the promise that God hath made unto us in Christ. The washing preacheth unto us, that we are cleansed[309] with Christ's bloodshedding which was an offering and a satisfaction for the sin of all that repent and believe, consenting and submitting themselves unto the will of God. The plunging into the water signifieth that we die and are buried with Christ as concerning the old life of sin which is Adam.[310] And the pulling out again signifieth that we rise again with Christ in a new life full of the Holy Ghost which shall teach us and guide us and work the will of God in us as thou seest (Romans 6).

a. How the sacraments justify.

Of wedlock.

Matrimony or wedlock is a state or a degree ordained of God and an office wherein the husband serveth the wife and the wife the husband. It was ordained for a remedy and to increase the world, and for the man to help the woman and the woman the man with all love and kindness, and not to signify any promise that ever I heard or read of in the scripture. [a]Therefore ought it not to be called a sacrament. It hath a promise that we sin not in that state, if a man receive his wife as a gift given to him of God, and the wife her husband likewise: as all manner meats and drinks have a promise that we sin not, if we use them measurably with thanksgiving. If they call matrimony a sacrament because the scripture useth the similitude of matrimony to express the marriage[311] or wedlock that is between us and Christ (for as a woman though she be never so poor, yet when she is married, is as rich as her husband: even so we when we repent and believe the promises of God in Christ, though we be never so poor sinners, yet are as rich as Christ, all his merits are ours with all that he hath): If for that cause they call it a sacrament, so will I mustard seed, leaven, a net, keys, bread, water[312] and a thousand other things which Christ and the prophets and all the scripture use, to express the kingdom of heaven and God's word with all. They praise wedlock with their mouth, and say it is an holy [b]thing, as it is verily: but had lever[313] be sanctified with an whore, than to come within that sanctuary.

Of order.[314]

Subdeacon, deacon, priest, bishop, cardinal, patriarch and pope, be names of offices and services or should be, and not sacraments. There is no promise coupled therewith. If they minister their offices truly, it is a sign that Christ's Spirit is in them, if not, that the devil is in them. Are these all sacraments, or which one of them? Or what thing in them is

a. Matrimony was not ordained to signify any promise.
b. If wedlock be holy why had they lever have whores than wives?

that holy sign or sacrament? The shaving or the anointing? What also is the promise that is signified thereby? But what words printeth in them that ᵃcharacter, that spiritual seal? O dreamers and natural beasts without the seal of the spirit of God: but sealed with the mark of the beast and with cankered consciences.

There is a word called in Latin ᵇ*sacerdos*, in Greek *hierus*, in Hebrew *cohan*, that is a minister, an officer, a sacrificer or a priest, as Aaron was a priest and sacrificed for the people and was a mediator between God and them. And in English should it have had some other name than priest: but Antichrist hath deceived us with unknown and strange terms, to bring us into confusion and superstitious blindness. Of that manner[315] is Christ a priest forever[316] and all we priests[317] through him and need no more of any such priest on earth to be a mean for us unto God. For Christ hath brought us all in into the inner temple within the veil[318] or forehanging, and unto the mercy stool[319] of God. And hath coupled us unto God, where we offer every man for himself the desires and petitions of his heart, and sacrifice and kill the lusts and appetites of his flesh with prayer, fasting and all manner godly living.

Another word is there in Greek called ᶜ*presbyter*, in Latin *senior*, in English an elder[320] and is nothing but an officer to teach, and not to be a mediator between God and us. ᵈThese need no anointing of man. They of the Old Testament were anointed with oil, to signify the anointing of Christ and of us through Christ with the Holy Ghost. This wise is no man priest but he that is chosen, save as in time of necessity every person christeneth, so may every man teach his wife and household and the wife her children. So in time of need if I see my brother sin I may between him and me rebuke him and damn his deed by the law of God. And may also comfort them that are in despair with the promises of God, and save them if they believe.

ᵉBy a priest then in the New Testament understand nothing but an elder to teach the younger and to bring them unto the full knowledge

a. Character.
b. *Sacerdos.*
c. *Presbyter.*
d. Priests now ought not to be anointed with oil.
e. The office of a priest.

and understanding of Christ and to minister[321] the sacraments which Christ ordained, which is also nothing but to preach Christ's promises. And by them that give all their study to quench the light of truth and to hold the people in darkness understand the disciples of Satan and messengers of Antichrist, whatsoever names they have or whatsoever they call themselves. And as concerning that our spirituality (as they will be called) make themselves [a]holier than the lay people and take so great lands and goods to pray for them, and promise them pardons and forgiveness of sins, or absolution, without preaching of Christ's promises, is falsehood and the working of Antichrist and (as I have said) the ravening of those wolves which Paul (Acts 20) prophesied should come after his departing not sparing the flock. Their doctrine is that merchandise whereof Peter speaketh, saying: through covetousness shall they with feigned words make merchandise of you (2 Peter 2). And their reasons wherewith they prove their doctrine are (as saith Paul, 1 Timothy 6) [b] superstitious disputings, arguings or brawlings of men with corrupt minds and destitute of truth, which think that lucre is godliness. But Christ saith (Matthew 7) by their fruits shall thou know them, that is by their filthy covetousness and shameless ambition and drunken desire of honour, contrary unto the example and doctrine of Christ and of his Apostles. Christ said to Peter, the last chapter of John, feed my sheep, and not shear thy flock. And Peter saith (1 Peter 5), not being lords over the parishes: but these shear and are become lords. Paul saith (2 Corinthians 2) not that we be lords over your faith: but these will be lords and compel us to believe whatsoever they lust, without any witness of scripture, yea clean contrary to the scripture, when the open text rebuketh it. Paul saith, it is better to give than receive (Acts 20). But these do nothing in the world but lay snares to catch and receive whatsoever cometh, as it were the gaping mouth of hell. And (2 Corinthians 12), I seek not yours but you: but these seek not you to Christ but yours to themselves, and therefore lest their deeds should be rebuked will not come at the light.

a. They will be holier but their deeds be not holy at all.
b. Compare their deeds to the doctrine and deeds of
Christ and of his Apostles and judge these fruits.

Nevertheless the truth is, that we are all equally beloved in Christ, and God hath sworn to all indifferently.[322] According therefore as every man believeth God's promises, longeth for them and is diligent to pray unto God to fulfil them so is his prayer heard, and as good is the prayer of a cobbler, as of a cardinal, and of a butcher, as of a bishop, and the blessing of a baker that knoweth the truth, is as good as the blessing of our most holy father the Pope. And by blessing [a]understand not the wagging of the Pope's or the bishop's hand over thine head, but prayer as when we say God make thee a good man, Christ put his Spirit in thee or give thee grace and power to walk in the truth and to follow his commandments etc. As Rebecca's friends blessed her when she departed (Genesis 24), saying, thou art our sister: grow unto thousand thousands and thy seed possess the gates of their enemies. And as Isaac blessed Jacob (Genesis 27) saying, God give thee of the dew of heaven and of the fatness of the earth abundance of corn, wine and oil etc. And (Genesis 28), Almighty God bless thee and make thee grow, and multiply thee, that thou mayest be a great multitude of people and give to thee and to thy seed after thee the blessings of Abraham, that thou mayest possess the land wherein thou art a stranger which he promised to thy grandfather and such like.

Last of all one singular doubt they have, what maketh the priest, that anointing or putting on of the hands, or what other ceremony or what words? About which they brawl and scold one ready to tear out another's throat. One saith this and another that, but cannot agree. Neither can any of them make so strong a reason which another cannot improve. For they are all out of the way and without the Spirit of God to judge spiritual things. Howbeit to this I answer, that when Christ called twelve[323] up into the mountain and chose them, then immediately without any anointing or ceremony were they his Apostles, that is to wit, ministers chosen to be sent to preach his testament unto all the whole world. And after the resurrection[324] when he had opened their wits and given them knowledge to understand the secrets of his testament and how to bind and loose[325] and what he would have them to do in all things, then he sent them forth with a commandment to preach and bind the unbelieving

a. What blessing meaneth.

that continue in sin, and to loose the believing that repent. [a]And that commandment or charge made them bishops, priests, popes and all things. If they say that Christ made them priests at his Maundy or Last Supper when he said, do this in remembrance of me,[326] I answer, though the Apostles wist[327] not then what he meant, yet I will not strive nor say that against. Neverthelater the commandment and the charge which he gave them made them priests.

And, Acts the first, when Matthias was chosen by lot, it is not to be doubted but that the Apostles, after their common manner, prayed for him that God would give him grace to minister his office truly and put their hands on him, and exhorted him and gave him charge to be diligent and faithful and then was he as great as the best. And (Acts 6), when the disciples that believed had chosen six deacons to minister to the widows, the Apostles prayed and put their hands on them and admitted them without more ado. [b]Their putting on of hands was not after the manner of the dumb blessing of our holy bishops with two fingers: but they spake unto them and told them their duty and gave them a charge and warned them to be faithful in the Lord's business: as we choose temporal officers and read their duty to them and they promise to be faithful ministers and then are admitted. Neither is there any other manner or ceremony at all required in making of our spiritual officers, than to choose an able person and then to rehearse him his duty and give him his charge and so to put him in his room. And as for that other solemn doubt, as they call it whether [c]Judas was a priest or no, I care not what he then was: but of this I am sure, that he is now not only priest, but also bishop, cardinal and pope.

a. The commandment maketh priests.
b. Putting on of hands.
c. What Judas is now.

Of penance.

Penance is a word of their own forging to deceive us withal, as many other are. In the scripture we find *penitentia*, repentance. *Agite penitentiam*, do penance: *peniteat vos*, let it repent you. *Metanoiete* in Greek, forthink[328] ye, or let it forthink you. [a]Of repentance they have made penance, to blind the people and to make them think that they must take pain and do some holy deeds to make satisfaction for their sins, namely such as they enjoin them. [b]As thou mayest see in the chronicles,[329] when great kings and tyrants (which with violence of sword conquered other kings' lands and slew all that came to hand) came to themselves and had conscience of their wicked deeds, then the bishop coupled them, not to Christ: but unto the Pope and preached the Pope unto them, and made them to submit themselves and also their realms unto the holy father the Pope and to take penance, as they call it, that is to say, such injunctions as the Pope and bishops would command them to do, to build abbeys, to endote them with livelihood, to be prayed for forever: and to give them exemptions and privilege and licence to do what they lust unpunished.

[c]Repentance goeth before faith and prepareth the way to Christ and to the promises. For Christ cometh not, but unto them that see their sins in the law and repent. Repentance that is to say, this mourning and sorrow of the heart, lasteth all our lives long. For we find ourselves all our lives long too weak for God's law, and therefore sorrow and mourn longing for strength. Repentance is no sacrament, as faith, hope, love, and knowledging of a man's sins are not to be called sacraments. For they are spiritual and invisible. Now must a sacrament be an outward sign that may be seen, to signify, to represent and to put a man in remembrance of some spiritual promise which cannot be seen but by faith only. Repentance and all the good deeds which accompany repentance to slay the lusts of the flesh are signified by [d]baptism. For Paul saith (Romans 6 as it is above rehearsed), Remember ye not (saith

a. A point of practice.
b. ☞
c. Repentance.
d. Repentance is signified by baptism.

he) that all we which are baptized in the name of Christ Jesus, are baptized to die with him. We are buried with him in baptism for to die, that is, to kill the lusts and the rebellion which remaineth in the flesh. And after that he saith, ye are dead as concerning sin but live unto God, through Jesus Christ our Lord. [a]If thou look on the profession of our hearts and on the spirit and forgiveness which we have received through Christ's merits, we are full dead: but if thou look on the rebellion of the flesh we do but begin to die and to be baptized that is, to drown and quench the lusts, and are full baptized at the last minute of death. And as concerning the working of the spirit we begin to live and grow every day more and more both in knowledge and also in godly living, according as the lusts abate. As a child receiveth the full soul at the first day, yet groweth daily in the operations and works thereof.

Of confession.

[b]Confession is divers.[330] One followeth true faith inseparably. And is the confessing and knowledging with the mouth, wherein we put our trust and confidence. As when we say our credo: confessing that we trust in God the Father Almighty and in his truth and promises: and in his son Jesus our Lord and in his merits and deservings: and in the Holy Ghost, and in his power, assistance and guiding. This confession is necessary unto all men that will be saved. For Christ saith (Matthew 10), He that denieth me before men him will I deny before my father that is in heaven. And of this confession saith the holy Apostle Paul in the tenth chapter,[331] The belief of the heart justifieth: and to knowledge[332] with the mouth maketh a man safe. This is a wonderful text for our philosophers or rather sophisters, our worldly wise, enemies to the wisdom of God, our deep and profound wells without water, our clouds without moisture of rain, that is to say, natural souls without the spirit of God and feeling of godly things. To justify and to make safe are both one thing. And to confess with the mouth is a good work and the fruit of a true faith, as all other works are.

a. ☞
b. One confession is to knowledge
wherein thou restest thy trust.

If thou repent and believe the promises then God's truth justifieth thee, that is, forgiveth thee thy sins and sealeth thee with his Holy Spirit and maketh thee heir of everlasting life through Christ's deservings. Now if thou have true faith so seest thou the exceeding and infinite love and mercy which God hath showed thee freely in Christ: then must thou needs love again: [a]and love cannot but compel thee to work and boldly to confess and knowledge thy Lord Christ and the trust which thou hast in his word. And this knowledge maketh thee safe, that is, declareth that thou art safe already and certifieth thine heart and maketh thee feel[333] that thy faith is right and that God's spirit is in thee, as all other good works do. For if when it cometh unto the point, thou have no lust to work nor power to confess, how couldest thou presume to think that God's Spirit were in thee?

[b]Another confession is there which goeth before faith and accompanieth repentance. For whosoever repenteth doth knowledge his sins in his heart. And whosoever doth knowledge his sins receiveth forgiveness (as saith John in the first of his first epistle): If we knowledge our sins he is faithful and just to forgive us our sins and to cleanse us from all unrighteousness, that is, because he hath promised, he must for his truth's sake do it. This confession is necessary all our lives long, as is repentance. And as thou understandest of repentance, so understand of this confession, for it is likewise included in the sacrament of baptism. For always repent and always knowledge or confess our sins unto God, and yet despair not: but remember that we are washed in Christ's blood, which thing our baptism doth represent and signify unto us.

[c]Shrift in the ear is verily a work of Satan and that the falsest that ever was wrought and that most hath devoured the faith. It began among the Greeks and was not as it is now, to reckon all a man's sins in the priest's ear: but to ask counsel of such doubts as men had, as thou mayest see in Saint Jerome[334] and in other authors. Neither went they to priests only which were very few at that time, no more than preached the word of God (for this so great vantage in so many masses-saying

a. If when tyrants oppose thee thou have the power to confess then art thou sure that thou art safe.
b. Another confession is to knowledge thy sins in thine heart unto God.
c. Shrift.

was not yet found): but went indifferently, where they saw a good and a learned man. [a]And for because of a little knavery which a deacon at Constantinople played through confession with one of the chief wives of the city it was laid down again.[335] But we are Antichrist's possession: the more knavery we see grow therefore daily, the more we establish it. A Christian man is a spiritual thing and hath God's word in his heart and God's spirit to certify him of all thing. He is not bound to come to any ear. And as for the reasons which they make, [they] are but persuasions of man's wisdom. First, as pertaining unto the keys and manner of binding and loosing, is enough above rehearsed and in other places. Thou mayest also see how the Apostles used them in the Acts[336] and in Paul's epistles,[337] how at the preaching of faith the spirit came and certified their hearts that they were justified through believing the promises.

[b]When a man feeleth that his heart consenteth unto the law of God, and feeleth himself meek, patient, courteous and merciful to his neighbour, altered and fashioned like unto Christ, why should he doubt but that God hath forgiven him and chosen him and put his spirit in him, though he never cram his sin into the priest's ear?

[c]One blind reason have they saying, How shall the priest unbind, loose and forgive the sin which he knoweth not? How did the Apostles? The scripture forsake they and run unto their blind reasons and draw the scripture unto a carnal purpose. When I have told thee in thine ear all that I have done my life long, in order and with all circumstances after the shamefullest manner, what canst thou do more, than preach me the promises saying: If thou repent and believe, God's truth shall save thee for Christ's sake. Thou seest not mine heart, thou knowest not whether I repent or no, neither whether I consent to the law, that it is holy righteous and good. Moreover whether I believe the promises or no, is also unknown to thee. If thou preach the law and the promises (as the Apostles did) so should they that God hath chosen repent and believe and be saved: even now as well as then. Howbeit Antichrist must know all secrets to establish his kingdom and to work his mysteries withal.

> a. Shrift was put down for knavery among the
> Greeks. But is established thereby among us.
> b. How a man shall know that his sins are forgiven.
> c. Blind reason is their guide and not God's spirit.

They bring also for them the story of the ten lepers which is written in the seventeenth chapter of Luke. [a]Here mark their falsehood and learn to know them forever. The fourteenth Sunday after the feast of the Trinity, the beginning of the seventh lesson, is the said gospel, and the eighth and the ninth lessons with the rest of the seventh is the exposition of Bede upon the said gospel. Where, saith Bede,[338] of all that Christ healed of whatsoever disease it were, he sent none unto the priests, but the lepers. And by the lepers interpreteth followers of false doctrine only, which the spiritual officers, and the learned men of the congregation ought to examine, and rebuke their learning with God's word and to warn the congregation to beware of them. Which, if they were afterward healed by the grace of Christ, ought to come before the congregation and there openly confess their true faith.

But all other vices (saith he) doth God heal within in the conscience. Though they this wise read at matins, yet at high mass, if they have any sermon at all, they lie clean contrary unto this open truth. Nother[339] are they ashamed at all. For why? they walk all together in darkness.

Of contrition.

Contrition and repentance are both one and nothing else but a sorrowful and a mourning heart. And because that God hath promised mercy unto a contrite heart, that is, to a sorrowful and repenting heart, they to beguile God's word and to establish their wicked tradition, have feigned that new word attrition[340] saying: thou canst not know whether thy sorrow or repentance be [b]contrition or attrition, except thou be shriven. When thou art shriven, then it is true contrition. O foxy Pharisee, that is thy leaven, of which Christ so diligently had us beware (Matthew 6). And the very prophecy of Peter, through covetousness with feigned words shall they make merchandise of you (2 Peter 2). With such glosses corrupt they God's word, to sit in the consciences of the people, to lead them captive, and to make a prey of them: buying and selling their sins,

a. Learn to know them for they are verily lepers in their hearts.
b. Attrition is of the leaven of the Pharisees.

to satisfy their unsatiable covetousness. Nevertheless the truth is, when any man hath trespassed against God: If he repent and knowledge his trespass, God promiseth him forgiveness without ear shrift.

If he that hath offended his neighbour repent and knowledge his fault asking forgiveness, if his neighbour forgive him, God forgiveth him also, by his holy promise (Matthew 18). Likewise if he that sinneth openly, when he is openly rebuked, repent and turn, then if the congregation forgive him God forgiveth him. And so forth: whosoever repenteth and when he is rebuked knowledgeth his fault is forgiven.

He also that doubteth or hath his conscience tangled, ought to open his mind unto some faithful brother that is learned, and he shall give him faithful counsel to help him with all.

[a]To whom a man trespasseth unto him he ought to confess. But to confess myself unto thee O Antichrist, whom I have not offended, I am not bound.

They of the old law had no confession in the ear. Neither the Apostles nor they that followed many hundred years after knew of any such whispering. Whereby then was their attrition turned unto contrition? Yea why are we which Christ came to loose more bound than the Jews? Yea and why are we more bound without scripture? For Christ came not to make us more bound, but to loose us and to make a thousand things no sin which before were sin and are now become sin again. He left no other law with us but the law of love. He loosed us not from Moses to bind us unto Antichrist's ear. God hath not tied Christ unto Antichrist's ear neither hath poured all his mercy in thither, for it hath no record in the Old Testament, that Antichrist's ear should be *propriatorium*,[341] that is to wit God's mercy stool, and that God should creep into so narrow a hole, so that he could nowhere else be found. [b]Neither did God write his laws neither yet his holy promises in Antichrist's ear: but hath graved them with his holy spirit in the hearts of them that believe, that they might have them all ways ready at hand to be saved thereby.

a. Whom a man offendeth to him must he confess.
b. It hath no record in the scripture that God should
creep in and hide himself in Antichrist's ear.

Satisfaction.

As pertaining unto satisfaction, this wise understand, that he that loveth God hath a commandment (as Saint John saith in the fourth chapter of his first epistle) to love his neighbour also, whom if thou have offended thou must make him amends or satisfaction or at the least way if thou be not able, ask him forgiveness, and if he will have mercy of God, he is bound to forgive thee. [a]If he will not: yet God forgiveth thee, if thou thus submit thyself. But unto God-ward Christ is a perpetual and an everlasting satisfaction forever more.

As oft as thou fallest through frailty repent and come again and thou art safe and welcome, as thou mayest see by the similitude of the riotous son (Luke 15). If thou be lopen out of sanctuary come in again. If thou be fallen from the way of truth come thereto again and thou art safe, if thou be gone astray come to the fold again and the shepherd[342] Christ shall save thee, yea and the angels[343] of heaven shall rejoice at thy coming, so far it is off that any man shall beat thee or chide thee. If any Pharisee envy thee, grudge[344] at thee or rail upon thee, thy father shall make answer for thee, as thou seest in the fore-rehearsed likeness or parable. Whosoever therefore is gone out of the way by whatsoever chance it be, let him come to his baptism again and unto the profession thereof and he shall be safe.

[b]For though that the washing of baptism be past, yet the power thereof, that is to say, the word of God which baptism preacheth, lasteth ever and saveth forever. As Paul is past and gone, nevertheless the word that Paul preached lasteth ever and saveth ever as many as come thereto with a repenting heart and a steadfast faith.

Hereby seest thou that when they make penance of repentance and call it a sacrament and divide it into contrition, confession and satisfaction they speak of their own heads and lie falsely.

a. Christ is an everlasting satisfaction.
b. Baptism lasteth ever.

Absolution.

Their absolution also justifieth no man from sin. For with the heart do men believe to be justified withal, saith Paul (Romans 10). That is through faith and believing the promises, are we justified, as I have sufficiently proved in other places with the scripture. Faith (saith Paul in the same place) cometh by hearing, that is to say, by hearing the preacher that is sent from God and preacheth God's promises. Now when thou absolvest in Latin the unlearned heareth not. For how, saith Paul (1 Corinthians 14), when thou blessest in an unknown tongue, shall the unlearned say Amen unto thy thanksgiving? For he wotteth not what thou seest. So likewise the lay[345] wotteth not whether thou loose or bind, or whether thou bless or curse. In like manner is it if the lay understand Latin or though the priest absolve in English. For in his absolution he rehearseth no promise of God: but speaketh his own words saying: I by the authority of Peter and Paul absolve or loose thee from all thy sins. Thou sayest so, which art but a lying man and never more than now verily.

Thou sayest I forgive thee thy sins, and the scripture saith (John the first) that Christ only forgiveth and taketh away the sins of the world. And Paul and Peter and all the Apostles preach that all is forgiven in Christ and for Christ's sake. God's word only looseth, and thou in preaching that mightest loose also and else not.

Whosoever hath ears let him hear[346] and let him that hath eyes, see. If any man love to be blind, his blindness on his own head and not on mine.

[a]They allege for themselves the saying of Christ to Peter (Matthew 16), whatsoever thou bindest on earth, it shall be bound, and whatsoever thou loosest, it shall be loosed, and so forth. Lo say they, whatsoever we bind and whatsoever we loose here is nothing excepted. And another text lay they of Christ in the last of Matthew: All power is given to me saith Christ, in heaven and in earth: go therefore and preach etc. [b]Preaching

---

a. Of binding and loosing and of the Pope's authority or power.
b. The Pope challengeth power not over man only but over God also.

leaveth the Pope out, and saith lo all power is given me in heaven and in earth. And thereupon taketh upon him temporal power above king and emperor, and maketh laws and bindeth them. And like power taketh he over God's laws and dispenseth with them at his lust, making no sin of that which God maketh sin and maketh sin where God maketh none: yea and wipeth out God's law clean and maketh at his pleasure, and with him is lawful what he lusteth. He bindeth where God looseth and looseth where God bindeth. He blesseth where God curseth and curseth where God blesseth. ªHe taketh authority also to bind and loose in Purgatory. That permit I unto him for it is a creation of his own making.³⁴⁷ He also bindeth the angels. ᵇFor we read of popes that have commanded the angels to set divers out of Purgatory. Howbeit I am not yet certified whether they obeyed or no.

ᶜUnderstand therefore that to bind and to loose, is to preach the law of God and the gospel or promises, as thou mayest see in the third chapter of the second epistle to the Corinthians, where Paul calleth the preaching of the law the ministration of death and damnation, and the preaching of the promises the ministering of the spirit and of righteousness. For when the law is preached all men are found sinners and therefore damned: and when the gospel and glad tidings are preached, then are all that repent and believe, found righteous in Christ. And so expound it all the old doctors. Saint ᵈJerome³⁴⁸ saith upon this text, whatsoever thou bindest: the bishops and priests saith he, for lack of understanding, take a little presumption of the Pharisees upon them. And think that they have authority to bind innocents and to loose the wicked, which thing our Pope and bishops do. ᵉFor they say the curse is to be feared, be it right or wrong. Though thou have not deserved, yet if the Pope curse thee thou art in peril of thy soul as they lie: yea and though he be never so wrongfully cursed, he must be fain to buy absolution. ᶠBut Saint Jerome saith as the priest of the old law made the

a. Purgatory is the Pope's creature he may
therefore be bold there.
b. The Pope bindeth the angels.
c. The true binding and loosing.
d. Saint Jerome against bishops and priests.
e. The curse is to be feared.
f. The right manner of loosing.

lepers clean or unclean, so bindeth and unbindeth the priest of the new law.[a]

The priest here made no man a leper neither cleansed any man, but God: and the priest judged only by Moses' law who was clean and who was unclean, when they were brought unto him.

So here we have the law of God to judge what is sin and what is not, and who is bound and who is not. Moreover if any man have sinned,[349] yet if he repent and believe the promise, we are sure by God's word that he is loosed and forgiven in Christ. Other authority than thiswise to preach have the priests not. Christ's Apostles had no other themselves as it appeareth throughout all the New Testament. Therefore it is manifest that they have not.

[b]Saint Paul saith (1 Corinthians 15), When we say all things are under Christ, he is to be excepted that put all under him. God the Father is not under Christ, but above Christ and Christ's head (1 Corinthians 6). Christ saith (John 13), I have not spoken of mine own head but my Father which sent me gave a commandment what I should say, and what I should speak. [c]Whatsoever I speak therefore, even as my Father bade me so I speak. If Christ had a law what he should do, how happeneth it, that the Pope so runneth at large lawless though that all power[350] were given unto Christ in heaven and earth. Yet had he no power over his father nor yet to reign temporally over temporal princes: but a commandment to obey them. How hath the Pope then such temporal authority over king and emperor? How hath he authority above God's laws and to command the angels, the saints and God himself?

Christ's [d]authority which he gave to his disciples, was to preach the law and to bring sinners to repentance, and then to preach unto them the promises which the father had made unto all men for his sake. And the same to preach only sent he his Apostles. [e]As a king sendeth forth his judges and giveth them his authority saying: What ye do that do I. I

a. ☞

b. Christ understood this text, all power is given in heaven and in earth, and also used it far otherwise than the Pope.

c. ☞

d. What authority Christ gave his Apostles.

e. The right binding and loosing.

give you my full power. Yet meaneth he not by that full power, that they should destroy any town or city, or oppress any man or do what they list or should reign over the lords and dukes of his realm and over his own self. But giveth them a law with them and authority to bind and loose as farforth as the law stretcheth and maketh mention: that is, to punish the evil, that do wrong, and to avenge the poor that suffer wrong. And so far as the law stretcheth, will the king defend his judge against all men. And as the temporal judges bind and loose temporally, so do the priests spiritually and no other ways. ªHowbeit by falsehood and subtlety the Pope reigneth under Christ, as cardinals and bishops do under kings lawless.

ᵇThe Pope (say they) absolveth or looseth *a pena et a culpa*,³⁵¹ that is from the fault or trespass and from the pain due unto the trespass. God, if a man repent, forgiveth the offence only, and not the pain also, say they: so turneth the everlasting pain unto a temporal pain, and appointeth seven years in Purgatory for every deadly sin. ᶜBut the Pope for money forgiveth both, and hath more power than God and is more merciful than God. This do I, saith the Pope of my full power and of the treasure³⁵² of the church, of deservings of martyrs, confessors³⁵³ and merits of Christ.

ᵈFirst the merits³⁵⁴ of the saints did not save themselves but were saved by Christ's merits only.

Secondarily God hath promised Christ's ᵉmerits unto all that repent: so that whosoever repenteth is immediately heir of all Christ's merits and beloved of God as Christ is. ᶠHow then came this foul monster to be lord over Christ's merits, so that he hath power to sell that which God giveth freely? O dreamers, yea O devils and O venomous scorpions what poison have ye in your tails? O pestilent leaven that so turneth the sweet bread of Christ's doctrine into the bitterness of gall.

a. How the Pope reigneth under Christ.
b. *A pena et a culpa* is a proper dream.
c. The Pope is more mighty and more merciful for money than God is for the death of his only son.
d. The merits of saints.
e. The merits of Christ.
f. The Pope selleth that which God giveth freely.

aThe friars run in the same spirit and teach saying: do good deeds and redeem the pains that abide you in Purgatory yea give us somewhat to do good works for you. bAnd thus is sin become the profitablest merchandise in the world. O the cruel wrath of God upon us because we love not the truth.

For this is the damnation and judgment of God to send a false prophet unto him that will not hear the truth. I know you saith Christ (John 5) that ye have not the love of God in you. cI am come in my Father's name and ye receive me not, if another shall come in his own name, him shall ye receive. Thus doth God avenge himself on the malicious hearts which have no love to his truth.

dAll the promises of God have they either wiped clean out or thus leavened them with open lies to establish their confession with all. eAnd to keep up from knowledge of the truth, they do all things in Latin.

They pray in Latin, they christen in Latin, they bless in Latin, they give absolution in Latin: only curse they in the English tongue.[355] Wherein they take upon them greater authority than ever God gave them. For in their curses as they call them, with book bell and candle, they command fGod and Christ and the angels and all saints to curse them: curse them God (say they) Father, Son and Holy Ghost, curse them Virgin Mary, etc. O ye abominable! Who gave you authority to command God to curse? God commandeth you to bless and ye command him to curse. Bless them that persecute you: bless but curse not saith Saint Paul (Romans 12). What tyranny will these not use over men, which presume and take upon them to be lords over God and to command him? If God shall curse any man, who shall bless and make him better? No man can amend himself, except God pour his Spirit unto him. Have we not a commandment to love our neighbour as our self? How can I love him and curse him also? James saith,[356] it is not possible that blessing and cursing should come both out of one mouth. Christ commandeth

a. Friars.
b. Sin is the best merchandise that is.
c. Christ prophesied of Antichrist and told why he should come.
d. The promises are either put out or leavened and why.
e. All is in Latin.
f. The Pope commandeth God to curse.

(Matthew 5) saying: love your enemies. Bless them that curse you. Do good to them that hate you. Pray for them that do you wrong and persecute you, that ye may be the children of your heavenly Father.

[a]In the marches of Wales[357] it is the manner if any man have an ox or a cow stolen, he cometh to the curate and desireth him to curse the stealer. And he commandeth the parish to give him every man God's curse and his. God's curse and mine have he, saith every man in the parish. O merciful God what is blasphemy, if this be not blasphemy and shaming of the doctrine of Christ?

Understand therefore, the power of excommunication is this. If any man sin openly and amendeth not when he is warned: then ought he to be rebuked openly before all the parish. And the priest ought to prove by the scripture, that all such have no part with Christ. For Christ serveth not but for them that love the law of God and consent that it is good holy and righteous. And repent sorrowing and mourning for power and strength to fulfil it. And all the parish ought to be warned, to avoid the company of all such, and to take them as heathen people. This is not done that he should perish, but to save him, to make him ashamed and to kill the lusts of the flesh, that the spirit might come unto the knowledge of the truth. And we ought to pity him and to have compassion on him and with all diligence to pray unto God for him, to give him grace to repent and to come to the right way again, and not to use such tyranny over God and man, commanding God to curse. And if he repent we ought with all mercy to receive him in again. This mayest thou see Matthew 18 and 1 Corinthians 5 and 2 Corinthians 2.

Confirmation.

If confirmation have a promise, then it justifieth, as far as the promise extendeth. If it have no promise, then is it not of God as the bishops be not. [b]The Apostles and ministers of God preach God's word, and God's signs or sacraments signify God's word also and put us in

a. A custom that is used in the marches of Wales.
b. God's sacraments preach God's promises.

remembrance of the promises which God hath made unto us in Christ. [a]Contrarywise Antichrist's bishops preach not and their sacraments speak not, but as the disguised bishops mum,[358] so are their superstitious sacraments dumb. After that the bishops had left preaching, then feigned they this dumb ceremony of confirmation to have somewhat at the least way, whereby they might reign over their diocese. [b]They reserved unto themselves also the christening of bells and conjuring or hallowing of churches and churchyards, and of altars of superaltars, and hallowing of chalices and so forth, whatsoever is of honour or profit. Which confirmation and the other conjurations also they have now committed to their [c]suffragans:[359] because they themselves have no leisure to minister such things, for their lusts and pleasures and abundance of all things, and for the cumbrance that they have in the king's masters and business of the realm. [d]One keepeth the privy seal, another the great seal,[360] the third is confessor, that is to say, a privy traitor and a secret Judas: he is president of the prince's council, he an ambassador, another sort are of the king's secret council. Woe is unto the realms where they are of the council. As profitable are they verily unto the realms with their council, as the wolves unto the sheep or the foxes unto the geese.

[e]They will say that the Holy Ghost is given through such ceremonies.[361] If God had so promised, so should it be: but Paul saith (Galatians in the third chapter) that the spirit is received through preaching of the faith. And Acts in the tenth chapter, while Peter preached the faith, the Holy Ghost fell on Cornelius and on his household. How shall we say then to that which they will lay against us, in the eighth chapter of the Acts of the Apostles, [f]where Peter and John put their hands on the Samaritans and the Holy Ghost came? I say that by putting or with putting or as they put their hands on them, the Holy Ghost came. Nevertheless the putting on of the hands did neither help nor hinder. For the text saith they prayed for them that they might receive the Holy Ghost.

a. The Pope's sacraments are dumb.
b. Christening of bells.
c. Why suffragans are ordained.
d. The bishops divide all among them.
e. Ceremonies bring not the Holy Ghost.
f. Putting on of hands.

God had made the Apostles a promise, that he would with such miracles confirm their preaching and move others to the faith (Mark the last). The Apostles therefore believed and prayed God to fulfil his promise, and God for his truth's sake even so did. So was it the ªprayer of faith that brought the Holy Ghost, as thou mayest see also in the last of James. If any man be sick, saith James, call the elders of the congregation, and let them pray over him, anointing him with oil in the name of the Lord, and the prayer of faith shall heal the sick.[362] Where a promise is, there is faith bold to pray, and God true to give her her petition. Putting on of the hands is an indifferent thing. For the Holy Ghost came by preaching of the faith, and miracles were done at the prayer of faith as well without putting on of hands as with, as thou seest in many places. Putting on of the hands was the manner of that nation, as it was to rend their clothes, and to put on sack, and to sprinkle themselves with ashes and earth, when they heard of or saw any sorrowful thing, as it was Paul's manner to stretch out his hand[363] when he preached. And as it is our manner to hold up our hands, when we pray, and as some kiss their thumb nail and put it to their eyes, and as we put our hands on children's heads, when we bless them saying: Christ bless thee my son, and God make thee a good man: which gestures neither help nor hinder. This mayest thou well see by the thirteenth of the Acts, where the Holy Ghost commanded to separate Paul and Barnabas, to go and preach. Then the other fasted and prayed and put their hands on their heads and sent them forth. They received not the Holy Ghost then, by putting on of hands, but the other as they put their hands on their heads prayed for them, that God would go with them and strength them, and couraged them also, bidding them to be strong in God, and warned them to be faithful and diligent in the work of God and so forth.

a. Prayer of faith doeth the miracles.

Anoiling.[364]

Last of all cometh the anoiling without promise, and therefore without the Spirit and without profit, but all together unfruitful and superstitious. The sacraments which they have imagined are all without promise, and therefore help not. For whatsoever is not of faith is sin (Romans 14). Now without a promise can there be no faith. [a]The sacraments which Christ himself ordained, which have also promises and would save us if we knew them and believed them, them minister they in the Latin tongue. So are they also become as unfruitful as the other. [b]Yea, they make us believe that the work self without the promise saveth us, which doctrine they learned of Aristotle. And thus are we become an hundred times worse than the wicked Jews which believed that the very work of their sacrifice justified them. Against which Paul fighteth in every [c]epistle, proving that nothing helpeth save the promises which God hath sworn in Christ. Ask the people what they understand by their baptism or washing. And thou shalt see that they believe, how that the very plunging into the water saveth them: of the promises they know not, nor what is signified thereby. [d]Baptism is called volowing in many places of England, because the priest saith volo[365] say ye. The child was well volowed (say they) yea and our vicar is as fair a volower as ever a priest within this twenty miles.

Behold how narrowly the people look on the ceremony. If ought be left out, or if the child be not altogether dipped in the water, or if, because the child is sick, the priest dare not plunge him into the water, but pour water on his head, how tremble they! How quake they! How say ye sir John,[366] say they, is this child christened enough? Hath it his full christendom? They believe verily that the child is not christened: [e]yea I have known priests that have gone unto the orders again supposing that they were not priests, because that the bishop left one of his

a. The Latin tongue destroyeth the faith.
b. That the work without the promise saveth is unproved.
c. The people believe in the work without the promise.
d. Volowing.
e. ☞

ceremonies undone. That they call confirmation, the people call bishoping. They think that if the bishop butter the child in the forehead that it is safe. ^aThey think that the work maketh safe, and likewise suppose they of an oiling. Now is this false doctrine verily. For James saith in the first chapter of his Epistle: Of his good will begat he us with the word of life, that is, with the word of promise.[367] In which are we made God's sons and heirs of the goodness of God before any good works. For we cannot work God's will till we be his sons and know his will and have his spirit to teach us. And Saint Paul saith in the fifth chapter of his epistle to the Ephesians: Christ cleansed the congregation in the fountain of water through the word. And Peter saith in the first of his first epistle: Ye are born anew, not of mortal seed, but of immortal seed, by the word of God which liveth and lasteth ever. Paul in every epistle warneth us that we put no trust in works, and to beware of persuasions or arguments of man's wisdom, of superstitiousness, of ceremonies of popeholiness and of all manner disguising. And exhorteth us to cleave fast unto the naked and pure word of God. The promise of God is the anchor that saveth us in all temptations. If all the world be against us, God's word is stronger than the world. If the world kill us, that shall make us alive again. If it be possible for the world[368] to cast us into hell from thence yet shall God's word bring us again. Hereby seest thou that it is not the work but the promise that justifieth us through faith. Now where no promise is there can no faith be and therefore no justifying though there be never so glorious works. The sacrament of Christ's body after this wise preach they: ^bThou must believe that it is no more bread, but the very body[369] of Christ, flesh, blood and bone, even as he went here on earth, save his coat.[370] For that is here yet, I wot not in how many places. I pray thee what helpeth all this? Here is no promise. The devils know that Christ died on a Friday and the Jews also. What are they holp thereby? We have a promise that Christ and his body and his blood and all that he did and suffered, is a sacrifice, a ransom and a full satisfaction for our sins: that God for his sake will think no more on them, if we have power to repent and believe.

a. The work saveth not but the word that is to say the promise.
b. In all things they leave out the promises.

Holyworkmen[371] think that God rejoiceth in the deed self without any further respect. They think also that God as a cruel tyrant, rejoiceth and hath delectation in our pain taking without any further respect. And therefore many of them martyr themselves without cause, after the example of Baal's priests which (3 Kings 18)[372] cut themselves to please their God withal and as the old heathen pagans sacrificed their children in the fire unto their gods. The monks of the Charterhouse[373] think that the very eating of fish in itself pleaseth God and refer not the eating unto the chastening of the body. For when they have slain their bodies with cold phlegm of fisheating: yet then will they eat no flesh and slay themselves before their days. We also when we offer our sons or daughters and compel or persuade them to vow and profess chastity, think that the very pain and that rage and burning which they suffer in abstaining from a make[374] pleaseth God, and so refer not our chastity unto our neighbours' profit. For when we see thousands fall to innumerable diseases thereof and to die before their days: yea though we see them break the commandments of God daily and also of very impatience work abominations against nature too shameful to be spoken of: yet will we not let them marry, but compel them to continue still with violence. And thus teach our divines as it appeareth by their arguments. He that taketh most pain, say they, is greatest and so forth.

The people are thoroughly brought in belief that the deed in itself without any further respect saveth them if they be so long at church or say so many *Pater Nosters* and read so much in a tongue which they understand not or go so much a pilgrimage and take so much pain or fast such a superstitious fast, or observe such a superstitious observance neither profitable to himself nor to his neighbour: but done of a good intent only, say they, to please God with all: yea to kiss the pax[375] they think it a meritorious deed, when to love their neighbour and to forgive him, which thing is signified thereby, they study not to do, nor have power to do, nor think that they are bound to do it, if they be offended by him. So sore have our false prophets brought the people out of their wits and have wrapped them in darkness and have rocked them asleep in blindness and ignorancy. Now is all such doctrine false doctrine, and all such faith false faith. For the deed pleaseth not, but as farforth as it is applied unto our neighbours' profit or the taming of our bodies to keep the commandment.

Now must the body be tame only, and that with the remedies that God hath ordained, and not killed. Thou must not forswear the natural remedy which God hath ordained and bring thyself into such case that shouldest either break God's commandment or kill thyself or burn night and day without rest so that thou canst not once think a godly thought: neither is it lawful to forsake thy neighbour and to withdraw thyself from serving him and to get them to a den[376] and live idly profitable to no man, but robbing all men, first of faith and then of goods and land and of all he hath with making him believe in the hypocrisy of thy superstitious prayers and popeholy deeds. The prayer of faith and the deeds thereof that spring of love are accepted before God. The prayer is good according to the proportion of faith and the deed according to the measure of love. Now he that bideth in the world, as monks call it, hath more faith than the cloisterer. For he hangeth on God in all things. He must trust God to send him good speed, good luck, favour, help, a good master, a good neighbour, a good servant, a good wife, a good chapman[377] merchant to send his merchandise safe to land and a thousand like. He loveth also more, which appeareth in that he doth service all ways unto his neighbour. To pray one for another are we equally bound and to pray is a thing that we may always do, whatsoever we have in hand, and that to do may no man hire[378] another: Christ's blood hath hired us all ready. Thus in the deed delighteth God as farforth as we do it either to serve our neighbour withal, as I have said, or to tame the flesh, that we may fulfil the commandment from the bottom of the heart.[379]

And as for our pain taking God rejoiceth not therein as a tyrant: but pitieth us and as it were mourneth with us and is all way ready and at hand to help us, if we call, as a merciful father and a kind mother. Neverthelater he suffereth us to fall into many temptations and much adversity: yea himself layeth the cross of tribulation on our backs, not that he rejoiceth in our sorrow, but to drive sin out of the flesh which can none otherwise be cured: as the physician and surgeon do many things which are painful to the sick, not that they rejoice in the pains of the poor wretches: but to persecute and to drive out the diseases which can no other wise be healed.

When the people believe therefore if they do so much work or suffer so much pain or go so much a pilgrimage, that they are safe, is a false faith. For a Christian man is not saved by works, but by faith in the promises before all good works, though that the works (when we work God's commandment with a good will and not works of our own imagination) declare that we are safe and that the spirit of him that hath made us safe is in us: yea and as God through preaching of faith doth purge and justify the heart, even so through working of deeds doth he purge and justify the members, making us perfect both in body and likeness of Christ.

[a]Neither needeth a Christian man to run hither or thither, to Rome, to Jerusalem, or Saint James[380] or any other pilgrimage far or near, to be saved thereby, or to purchase forgiveness of his sins. [b]For a Christian man's health and salvation is within him: even in his mouth (Romans 10). The word is nigh, even in thy mouth and in thine heart that is the word of faith which we preach saith Paul. If we believe the promises with our hearts and confess them with our mouths, we are safe. This is our health within us. But how shall they believe that they hear not. And how shall they hear without a preacher? saith Paul (Romans 10). For look on the promises of God: and so are all our preachers dumb. Or if they preach them they so sauce them and leaven them that no stomach can brook them nor find any savour in them. For they paint us such an ear [c]confession as is impossible to be kept, and more impossible that it should stand with the promises and testament of God. And they join[381] them penance, as they call it, to fast, to go pilgrimages and give so much to make satisfaction withal. They preach their masses, their merits, their pardons, their ceremonies and put the promise clean out of possession. The word of health and salvation is nigh thee, in thy mouth and thine heart saith Paul. [d]Nay say they, thy salvation is in our faithful ear. That is their hold, thereby know they all secrets, thereby mock they all men and all men's wives and beguile knight and squire, lord and king, and betray all realms. [e]The bishops with the Pope have a certain conspiration

a. A Christian man needeth not to go a pilgrimage to be saved thereby.
b. Salvation is within us.
c. Confession.
d. ☞
e. Bishops work their treason through confession.

and secret treason against the whole world. And by confession know they what kings and emperors think. If ought be against them, do they never so evil, then move they their captives to war and to fight and give them pardons to slay whom they will have taken out of the way. They have with falsehood taken from all kings and emperors their right and duties, which now they call their freedoms liberties and privileges and have perverted the ordinances that God left in the world, and have made every ªking swear to defend their falsehood against their own selves. So that now if any man preach God's word truly and show the freedom and liberty of the soul which we have in Christ, or intend to restore the kings again unto their duties and right and to the room and authority[382] which they have of God, and of shadows to make them kings in deed, and to put the world in his order again: then the kings deliver their swords and authority unto the hypocrites to slay him. So drunk are they with the wine of the whore.[383]

ᵇThe text that followeth in Paul will they haply lay to my charge and others. How shall they preach except they be sent? saith Paul in the said tenth to the Romans. We, will they say, are the Pope, cardinals and bishops: all authority is ours. The scripture pertaineth unto us and is our possession. And we have a law, that whosoever presume to preach without the authority of the bishops is excommunicate in the deed doing. Whence therefore hast thou thine authority? will they say. The old Pharisees had the scripture in captivity likewise, and asked Christ by what authority doest thou these things? As who should say: We are Pharisees and thou art none of our order nor hast authority of us. Christ asked them another question and so will I do our hypocrites. Who sent you? God. Nay he that is send of God, speaketh God's word (John 3). ᶜNow speak ye not God's word, nor anything save your own laws made clean contrary unto God's word. Christ's Apostles preached Christ and not themselves. He that is of the truth, preacheth the truth. Now ye preach nothing but lies, and therefore are of the devil the father of all lies[384] and of him are ye sent. And as for mine authority or who sent

a. Kings be sworn to the bishops and not the bishops unto the kings.
b. How shall they preach except they be sent is expounded.
c. How to know who is sent of God and who is not.

me: I report me unto my works as Christ (John the fifth and also tenth chapter). If God's word bear record that I say truth, why should any man doubt, but that God, the father of truth and of light hath sent me as the father of lies and of darkness hath sent you, and that the spirit of truth and of light is with me, as the spirit of lies and of darkness is with you. By this means thou wilt that every man be a preacher, will they say. [a]Nay verily. For God will that not and therefore will I it not, no more than [b]I would that every man of London were mayor of London, or every man of the realm king thereof. God is not the author of dissension and strife, but of unity and peace and of good order. I will therefore that where a congregation is gathered together in Christ one be chosen after the rule of Paul, and that he only preach, and else no man openly: but that every man teach his household after the same doctrine. But if the preacher preach false: then whosoever's heart God moveth, to the same it shall be lawful to rebuke and improve the false teacher with the clear and manifest scripture, and that same is no doubt a true prophet sent of God. For the scripture is God's and theirs that believe and not the false prophets'.

Sacrament is then as much to say as an holy sign.[385] And the sacraments which Christ ordained preach God's word unto us and therefore justify and minister the spirit to them that believe, as Paul through preaching the gospel was a minister of righteousness and of the spirit unto all that believed his preaching. Dumb ceremonies are no sacraments, but superstitiousness. Christ's sacraments preach the faith of Christ as his Apostles did and thereby justify. Antichrist's dumb ceremonies preach not the faith that is in Christ, as his Apostles our bishops and cardinals do not. But as Antichrist's bishops are ordained to kill whosoever preach the true faith of Christ so are his ceremonies ordained to quench the faith which Christ's sacraments preach. [c]And hereby mayest thou know the difference between Christ's signs or sacraments and Antichrist's signs or ceremonies, that Christ's signs speak and Antichrist's be dumb.

Hereby seest thou what is to be thought of all other ceremonies, as

a. No man may preach but he that is called and sent of God.
b. ☞
c. The difference between true sacraments and false.

hallowed water, bread, salt, boughs, bells, wax, ashes and so forth, and all other disguisings and apesplay and of all manner conjurations, as the conjuring of church and churchyards and of altar stones and such like. Where no promise of God is, there can be no faith nor justifying, nor forgiveness of sins. For it is more than madness to look for anything of God save that he hath promised. How far he hath promised so far is he bound to them that believe and further not. [a]To have a faith therefore or a trust in anything, where God hath not promised, is plain idolatry and a worshipping of thine own imagination instead of God. Let us see the pith of a ceremony or two to judge the rest by. In conjuring of holy water they pray, that whosoever be sprinkled therewith may receive health as well of body as of soul, and likewise in making holy bread and so forth in the conjurations of other ceremonies. Now we see by daily experience that half their prayer is unheard. For no man receiveth health of body thereby. No more of likelihood do they of soul. Yea we see also by experience that no man receiveth health of soul thereby. For no man by sprinkling himself with holy water and with eating holy bread, is more merciful than before, or forgiveth wrong, or becometh at one with his enemy, or is more patient and less covetous and so forth. Which are the sure tokens of the soul's health.

[b]They preach also that the wagging of the bishop's hand over us blesseth us and putteth away our sins. Are these works not against Christ? How can they do more shame unto Christ's blood? For if the wagging of the bishop's hand over me be so precious a thing in the sight of God that I am thereby blessed, how then am I full blessed with all spiritual blessing in Christ, as Paul saith (Ephesians 1)? Or if my sins be full done away in Christ, how remaineth there any to be done away by such fantasies? The Apostles knew no ways to put away sin or to bless us but by preaching Christ. [c]Paul saith (Galatians 2), If righteousness come by the law, then Christ died in vain. So dispute I here. If blessing come by the wagging of the misshape's[386] hand, then died Christ in vain and his death blessed us not. And a little afore, saith Paul, if while we

---

a. A faith without God's promise is idolatry.
b. The bishop's blessing.
c. How the Apostles blessed us.

seek to be justified by Christ we be found yet sinners (so that we must be justified by the law or ceremonies) is not Christ then minister of sin? So dispute I here. If while we seek to be blessed in Christ we are yet unblessed and must be blessed by the wagging of the bishop's hand, what have we then of Christ but curse? Thou wilt say, when we come first to the faith, then Christ forgiveth us and blesseth us. But the sins which we afterward commit are forgiven us through such things. I answer: If any man repent truly and come to the faith and put his trust in Christ, then as oft as he sinneth of frailty, at the sigh of the heart is his sin put away in Christ's blood. For Christ's blood purgeth ever and blesseth ever.

For John saith in the second of his first epistle: This I write unto you that ye sin not. And though any man sin (meaning of frailty and so repent) yet have we an advocate with the father, Jesus Christ which is righteous, and he it is that obtaineth grace for our sins[387] and (Hebrews 7) it is written: But this man (meaning Christ) because he lasteth or abideth ever, hath an everlasting priesthood. Therefore is he able also ever to save them that come to God through him, seeing he ever liveth to make intercession for us. The bishops therefore ought to bless us in preaching Christ and not to deceive us and bring the curse of God upon us with wagging their hands over us. To preach is their duty only and not to offer their feet to be kissed or testicles or stones to be groped.[388] We feel also by experience that after the Pope's, bishop's or cardinal's blessing we are no otherwise disposed in our souls than before.

[a]Let this be sufficient as concerning the sacraments and ceremonies, with this protestation, that if any can say better or improve this with God's word, no man shall be better content therewith than I. For I seek nothing but the truth and to walk in the light.[389] I submit therefore this word and all other that I have made or shall make (if God will that I shall more make) unto the judgments, not of them that furiously burn all truth, but of them which are ready with God's word to correct, if anything be said amiss, and to further God's word.

[b]I will talk a word or two after the worldly wisdom with them and

a. The protestation of the author.
b. Confession robbeth the sacraments and make them fruitless.

make an end of this matter. If the sacraments justify, as they say, I understand by justifying forgiveness of sins. Then do they wrong unto the sacraments, inasmuch as they rob the most part of them through confession of their effect and of the cause wherefore they were ordained. For no man may receive the body of Christ, no man may marry, no man may be oiled or aneled as they call it, no man may receive orders, except he be first shriven. Now when the sins be forgiven by shrift aforehand, there is nought left for the sacraments to do. They will answer, that at the least way they increase grace, and not the sacraments only, but also hearing of mass, matins and evensong, and receiving of holy water, holy bread and of the bishop's blessing and so forth by all the ceremonies. [a]By grace I understand the favour of God and also the gifts and working of his spirit in us, as love, kindness, patience, obedience, mercifulness, despising of worldly things, peace, concord and such like. [b]If after thou hast heard so many masses, matins and evensong, and after thou hast received the holy bread, holy water and the bishop's blessing or a cardinal's (or the Pope's, if thou wilt), thou be more kind to thy neighbour and love him better than before, if thou be more obedient unto thy superiors, more merciful, more ready to forgive wrong done unto thee, more despisest the world and more athirst after spiritual things: if after that a priest hath take orders he be less covetous than before: if a wife after so many and oft pilgrimages be more chaste, more obedient unto her husband, more kind to her maids and other servants: if gentlemen, knights, lords, and kings and emperors, after they have said so often daily service with their [c390]chaplains, know more of Christ than before and can better skill to rule their tenants, subjects and realm Christianly than before and be content with their duties, then do such things increase grace: if not, it is a lie. Whether it be so or no I report me to experience. If they have any other interpretation of justifying or grace I pray them to teach it me. For I would gladly learn it. Now let us go to our purpose again.

a. What grace is.
b. How to know what justifieth and what not or what bringeth grace and what not.
c. With their chaplains quod he God give grace their chaplain at the last make them not so mad to say service along while they.

Of miracles and worshipping saints.[391]

Antichrist shall not only come with lying signs and disguised with falsehood but also with lying miracles and wonders, saith Paul in the said place (2 Thessalonians 2). [a]All the true miracles which are of God, are showed (as I above rehearsed) to move us to hear God's word and to establish our faith therein and to confirm the truth of God's promises, that we might without all doubting believe them. For God's word through faith bringeth the spirit into our hearts and also life, as Christ saith (John 6): the words which I speak are spirit and life. The word also purgeth us and cleanseth us, as Christ saith (John 15). Ye are clean by the means of the word. Paul saith (1 Timothy 2), One God, one mediator (that is to say, advocate, intercessory, or an atonemaker) between God and man then man and Christ Jesus which gave himself a ransom for all men Peter saith of Christ (Acts 4). Neither is there health in any other: neither yet also any other name given unto men wherein we must be saved. So now Christ is our peace, our redemption, our ransom for our sins, our righteousness, satisfaction: and all the promises of God are yea and Amen in him (2 Corinthians 1). And we for the great and infinite love which God hath to us in Christ, love him again, love also his laws and love one another: And the deeds which we henceforth do, do we not to make satisfaction or to obtain heaven: but to succour our neighbour to tame the flesh that we may wax perfect and strong men in Christ and to be thankful to God again for his mercy, and to glorify his name.

[b]Contrarywise the miracles of Antichrist are done to pull thee from the word of God and from believing his promises and from Christ, and to put thy trust in a man or a ceremony wherein God's word is not. As soon as God's word is believed, the faith spread abroad, then cease the miracles of God. But the miracles of Antichrist, because they are wrought by the devil, to quench the faith, grow daily more and more: neither shall cease until the world's end among them that believe not God's word and promises. Seest thou not how God loosed and sent forth all

a. True miracles draw to Christ.
b. False miracles drive from Christ.

the devils in the old world among the heathen or gentiles? And how the devils wrought miracles and spake to them in every image? Even so shall the devil work falsehood by one craft or another until the world's end among them that believe not God's word. For the judgment and damnation of him that hath no lust to hear the truth, is to hear lies and to be established and grounded therein through false miracles: and he that will not see, is worthy to be blind, and he that biddeth the spirit of God go from him, is worthy to be without him.

Paul, Peter, and all true Apostles preached Christ only. And the miracles did but confirm and establish their preaching and those everlasting promises and eternal testament that God had made between man and him in Christ's blood, and the miracles did testify also that they were true servants of Christ. Paul preached not himself: he taught not any man to trust in him or his holiness or in Peter or in any ceremony but in the promises which God hath sworn only, yea he mightily resisteth all such false doctrine both to the Corinthians, Galatians, Ephesians and everywhere. [a]If this be true (as it is true and nothing more truer) that if Paul had preached himself or taught any man to believe in his holiness or prayer or in anything, save in the promises that God hath made and sworn to give us for Christ's sake, he had been a false prophet: why am not I also a false prophet, if I teach thee to trust in Paul or in his holiness or prayer, or in anything save in God's word as Paul did?

[b]If Paul were here and loved me (as he loved them of his time to whom he was sent and to whom he was a servant to preach Christ), what good could he do for me or wish me, but preach Christ and pray to God for me, to open mine heart, to give me his Spirit and to bring me unto the full knowledge of Christ? Unto which port or haven, when I am once come, I am as safe as Paul, fellow with Paul, joint heir with Paul of all the promises of God, and God's truth heareth my prayer as well as Paul's.[392] I also now could not but love Paul and wish him good, and pray for him, that God would strength him in all his temptations and give him victory, as he would do for me. [c]Nevertheless there are

---

a. He that teacheth to trust in a saint is a false hypocrite.
b. What he should pray that prayeth for his neighbour.
c. The weak should be taught and not deceived.

many weak and young consciences all ways in the congregation which they that have the office to preach ought to teach and not to deceive them.

[a]What prayers pray our clergy for us which stop us and exclude us from Christ and seek all the means possible to keep us from knowledge of Christ? They compel us to hire friars, monks, nuns, canons, and priests, and to buy their abominable merits, and to hire the saints that are dead to pray for us, for the very saints have they made hirelings also: because that their offerings come to their profit. What pray all those? That we might come to the knowledge of Christ, as the Apostles did? Nay verily. For it is a plain case, that all they which enforce to keep us from Christ, pray not that we might come to the knowledge of Christ. And as for the saints (whose prayer was when they were alive that we might be grounded, established and strengthed in Christ only) if it were of God that we should this wise worship them contrary unto their own doctrine, I dare be bold to affirm that by the means of their prayers we should have been brought long ago unto the knowledge of God and Christ again, though that these beasts had done their worst to let it. Let us therefore set our hearts at rest in Christ and in God's promises, for so I think it best, and let us take the saints for an example only and let us do as they both taught and did. [b]Let us set God's promises before our eyes, and desire him for his mercy and for Christ's sake to fulfil them. And he is as true as ever he was, and will do it, as well as ever he did. For to us are the promises made as well as to them.

Moreover the end of God's miracles is good, the end of these miracles are evil. [c]For the offerings which are the cause of the miracles do but minister and maintain vice, sin and all abomination, and are given to them that have too much so that for very abundance, they foam out their own shame and corrupt the whole world with the stench of their filthiness.

Thereto whatsoever is not of faith is sin (Romans 14). Faith cometh by hearing God's word (Romans 10). When now thou fastest or doest

a. The spirituality pray not that we might
come to the knowledge of Christ.
b. The saints are but an example.
c. Offerings cause the miracles.

anything in the worship of any saint believing to come to the favour of God or to be saved thereby if thou have God's word, then is it true faith and shall save thee. If thou have not God's word, then is it a false faith, superstitiousness and idolatry and damnable sin.

Also in the collects of the saints with which we pray God to save us through the merits or deservings of the saints (which saints yet were not saved by their own deservings themselves) we say *per Christum dominum nostrum*, that is for Christ our Lord's sake. We say save us good Lord through the saints' merits for Christ's sake. How can he save us through the saints' merits for Christ's sake and for his deserving merits and love? Take an example. A gentleman saith unto me: I will do the utmost of my power for thee, for the love which I owe unto thy father. Though thou hast never done me pleasure, yet I love thy father well, thy father is my friend and hath deserved that I do all that I can for thee etc. Here is a testament and a promise made unto me in the love of my father only. If I come to the said gentleman in the name of one of his servants which I never saw never spake with neither have any acquaintance at all with and say: Sir I pray you be good master unto me in such a cause. I have not deserved that ye should so do. Nevertheless I pray you do it for such a servant's sake: yea I pray you for the love that you owe to my father do that for me for such a servant's sake. If I this wise made my petition, would not men think that I come late out of Saint Patrick's Purgatory,[393] and had left my wits behind me? This do we. For the testament and promises are all made unto us in Christ. And we desire God to fulfil his promises for the saints' sake yea that he will for Christ's sake do it for the saints' sake.

[a]They have also martyrs which never preached God's word neither died therefore: but for privileges and liberties which they falsely purchased contrary unto God's ordinances. Yea and such saints though they be dead, yet rob now as fast as ever they did neither are less covetous now than when they were alive. I doubt not but that they will make a saint of my lord cardinal[394] after the death of us that be alive and know his juggling and crafty conveyance and will shrine him gloriously, for his

---

a. All such martyrs are the Pope's martyrs and not God's. For martyr signifieth a witness bearer: now is he not God's witness that testifieth not his word.

might defending of the right of holy church, except we be diligent to leave a commemoration of that Nimrod[395] behind us.

[a]The reasons wherewith they prove their doctrine are but fleshly and as Paul calleth them,[396] enticing words of man's wisdom, that is to wit, sophistry and blawling arguments of men with corrupt minds and destitute of the truth, whose God is their belly,[397] unto which idol whosoever offereth not, the same is an heretic, and worthy to be burnt.

The saint was great with God when he was alive, as it appeareth by the miracles which God showed for him, he must therefore be great now say they. This reason appeareth wisdom, but is very foolishness with God. For the miracle was not showed that thou should put thy trust in the saint, but in the word which the saint preached, which word if thou believedest it, would save thee, as God hath promised and sworn, and would make thee also great with God, as it did the saint.

If a man have a matter with a great man or a king, he must go first unto one of his mean servants and then higher and higher till he come at the king. This enrising argument is but a blind reason of man's wit. It is not like[398] in the kingdom of the world and in the kingdom of God and Christ.

[b]With kings for the most part we have none acquaintance neither promise. They be also most commonly merciless. Moreover if they promise, they are yet men as unconstant as are other people and as untrue. But with God, if we have belief, we are acquainted and have an open way in unto him by the door of Christ which is never shut but through unbelief, neither is there any porter to keep man out. By him saith Paul (Ephesians 2) that is to say, by Christ, we have an open way in unto the father. So are ye now no more strangers and foreigners (saith he) but citizens with the saints and of the household of God. God hath also made us promises and hath sworn: yet hath made a testament or a covenant and hath bound himself and hath sealed[399] his obligation with Christ's blood and confirmed it with miracles. He is also merciful and kind, and complaineth that we will not come unto him. He is mighty and able to perform that he promiseth. He is true and cannot be but

---

a. The reasons which they make for the worshipping of saints are solved.

b. It is not like with kings and God.

true, as he cannot be but God. Therefore is it not like with the king and God.

We be sinners say they, God will not hear us. Behold how they flee from God as from a tyrant merciless. Whom a man counteth most merciful unto him he soonest fleeth. But these teachers dare not come at God. Why? For they are the children of Cain.[400] If the saints love whom God hateth, then God and his saints are divided. When thou prayest to the saints, how do they know, except that God, whom thou countest merciless, tell them? If God be so cruel and so hateth thee it is not likely that he will tell the saints that thou prayest unto them.

[a]When they say we be sinners: I answer, that Christ is no sinner, save a satisfaction, and an offering of sin. Take Christ from the saints and what are they? What is Paul without Christ? Is he anything save a blasphemer, a persecutor, a murderer, and a shedder of Christian blood?[401] But as soon as he came to Christ he was no more a sinner but a minister of righteousness. He went, not to Rome to take penance upon him, but went and preached unto his brethren[402] the same mercy which he had received free, without doing penance or hiring of saints or of monks or friars. Moreover if it be God's word that thou should put thy trust in the saints' merits or prayers, then be bold. For God commendeth by Moses (Deuteronomy 12) saying: what I command you that I observe and do, and put nothing to, nor take ought therefrom: yea and Moses warneth straightly in an hundred places that we do that only which God commandeth and which seemeth good and righteous in his sight and not in our own sight. For nothing bringeth the wrath of God so soon and so sore on a man, as the idolatry of his own imagination.

Last of all these arguments are contrary to the arguments of Christ and of his Apostles. Christ disputeth (Luke 11) saying: if the son ask the father bread, will he give him a stone? Or if he ask him fish, will he give him a serpent? And so forth. If ye then (saith he) which are evil can give good gifts to your children, how much rather shall your heavenly father give a good Spirit unto them that ask him? And a little before in the same chapter he saith: If a man came never so out of season to his neighbour to borrow bread: even when he is in his chamber and the door

a. Christ is no sinner.

shut, and all his servants with him. Nevertheless yet if he continue knocking and praying, he will rise and give him as much as he needeth, though not for love, yet to be rid of him that he may have rest: As who should say, what will God do if a man pray him, seeing that prayer overcometh an evil man? Ask therefore (saith he) and it shall be given you, seek and ye shall find, knock and it shall be opened unto you. And (Luke 18) he putteth forth the parable or similitude of the wicked judge which was overcome with the importune prayer of the widow. And concludeth saying: Hear what the wicked judge did. And shall not God avenge his elect which cry unto him night and day? Whether therefore we complain of the intolerable oppression and persecution that we suffer, or of the flesh that cumbreth and resisteth the spirit, God is merciful to hear us and to help us. Seest thou not also how Christ cureth many and casteth out devils out of many unspoken to,[403] how shall he not help if he be desired and spoken to?

When the old Pharisees, whose nature is to drive sinners from Christ, asked Christ why he did eat with publicans and sinners, Christ answered that the whole needed not the physician but the sick.[404] [a]That is, he came to have conversation with sinners to heal them. He was a gift given unto sinners, and a treasure to pay their debts. And Christ sent the complaining and disdaining Pharisees to the prophet [b]Hosea saying, go and learn what this meaneth, I desire or require mercy and not sacrifice.[405] As who should say, ye Pharisees love sacrifice and [c]offering for to feed that god your bellies withal, but God commandeth to be merciful. Sinners are ever captives and a prey unto the Pharisees and hypocrites, for to offer unto their bellies, and to buy merits, pardons and forgiveness of sins of them. And therefore fear they them away from Christ with arguments of their belly wisdom. For he that receiveth forgiveness free of Christ will buy no forgiveness of them. I came (saith Christ) to call, not the righteous, but the sinners unto repentance.[406] The Pharisees are righteous and therefore have no part with Christ, neither need they. For they are gods themselves and saviours. But sinners that repent pertain to Christ. If we repent, Christ hath made satisfaction for us all ready.

a. Christ is a gift to give to sinners.
b. God loveth mercy.
c. Hypocrites love offerings.

God so loved the world, that he gave his only son, that none that believe on him should perish, but should have everlasting life. For God sent not his son into the world, to condemn the world, but that the world through him might be saved. He that believeth on him shall not be damned, but he that believeth not he is damned already (John 3).

Paul (Romans 5) saith: Because we are justified through faith, we are at peace with God through our Lord Jesus Christ, that is, because that God, which cannot lie, hath promised and sworn to be merciful unto us and to forgive us for Christ's sake, we believe and are at peace in our consciences, we run not hither and thither for pardon, we trust not in this friar nor that monk neither in anything save in the word of God only. As a child when his father threateneth him for his fault, hath never rest, till he hear the word of mercy and forgiveness of his father's mouth again, but as soon as he heareth his father say, go thy ways, do me no more so, I forgive thee this fault, then is his heart at rest, then is he at peace, then runneth he to no man to make intercession for him. Neither though there come any false merchant saying, what wilt thou give me and I will obtain pardon of thy father for thee, will he suffer himself to be beguiled, no he will not buy of a wily fox that which his father hath given him freely.

It followeth, God setteth out his love that he hath to us, that is, he maketh it appear, that men may perceive love, if they be not more than stock blind.[407] Inasmuch saith Paul as while we were yet sinners, Christ died for us.[408] Much more now, saith he, saying we are justified by his blood shall we be preserved from wrath through him. For if when we were enemies we were reconciled to God by the death of his son: much more seeing we are reconciled, we shall be preserved by his life. As who should say, if God loved us when we knew him not, much more loveth he us now we know him. If he were merciful unto us while we hated his law, much more merciful will he be now, seeing we love it and desire strength to fulfil it. And in the eighth he argueth. If God spared not his own son but gave him for us all, how shall he not with him give us all things also?

Christ prayed (John 17) not for the Apostles only, but also for as many as should believe through their preaching, and was heard: whatsoever we ask in his name the father giveth us (John 16). Christ is also as merciful as the saints. [a]Why go we not straightway unto him? Verily because we feel not the mercy of God neither believe his truth. God will at the least way (say they) hear us the sooner for the saints' sake. Then loveth he the saint better than Christ and his own truth. Heareth he us for the saints' sake? So heareth he us not for his mercy. For merits and mercy cannot stand together.

Finally if thou put any trust in thine own deeds or in the deeds of any other man of any saint, then diminishest thou the truth, mercy and goodness of God. For if God look unto thy works or unto the works of any other man or goodness of the saint: Then doeth not he all things of pure mercy and of his goodness and for the truth's sake which he hath sworn in Christ. Now saith Paul in the last to Titus: Not of the righteous deeds which we did: but of his mercy saved he us.

Our blind disputers will say, if our good deeds justify us not, if God look not on our good deeds neither regard them nor love us the better for them what need we to do good deeds? [b]I answer God looketh on our good deeds and loveth them, yet loveth us not for their sakes. God loveth us first in Christ of his goodness and mercy, and poureth his spirit into us, and giveth us power to do good deeds. And because he loveth us, he loveth our good deeds: yea because he loveth us, he forgiveth us our evil deeds which we do of frailty and not of purpose or of the nonce. Our good deeds do but testify only that we are justified and beloved. For except we were beloved and had God's spirit we could neither do nor yet consent unto any good deed. [c]Antichrist turneth the roots of the tree upward. He maketh the goodness of God the branches and our goodness the roots. We must be first good after Antichrist's doctrine, and move God and compel him to be good again for our goodness' sake: so must God's goodness spring out of our goodness. Nay verily God's goodness is the root of all goodness and our goodness, if we have any, springeth out of his goodness.

a. Why we come not to Christ.
b. God looketh on our good deeds.
c. Antichrist turneth the roots of the tree upward.

Prayer.

Of prayer and good deeds and of the order of love or charity I have abundantly written in my book of the justifying of faith.[409] Neverthelater that thou mayest see what the prayers and good works of our monks and friars and of other ghostly people are worth, I will speak a word or two and make an end. Paul saith (Galatians 3), All ye are the sons of God through faith in Jesu Christ. For all ye that are baptized have put Christ on you (that is ye are become Christ himself). There is no Jew (saith he) neither Greek: neither bond nor free: neither man nor woman: but ye are all [a]one thing in Christ Jesu. In Christ there is neither French nor English: but the Frenchman is the Englishman's own self, and the English the Frenchman's own self. In Christ there is neither father, nor son: neither master nor servant: neither husband, nor wife: neither king, nor subject: but the father is the son's self and the son the father's own self, and the king is the subject's own self, and the subject is the king's own self, and so forth. I am thou thyself and thou art I myself and can be no nearer or kin. We are all the sons of God, all Christ's servants bought with his blood and every man to other Christ his own self. And (Colossians 3), Ye have put on the new man which is renewed in the knowledge of God after the image of him that made him (that is to say Christ) where is (saith he) neither Greek nor Jew, circumcision nor uncircumcision, barbarous or Scythian, bond or free: but [b]Christ is all in all things. I love thee not now, because thou art my father and hast done so much for me or my mother and hast borne me and given me suck of thy breasts (for so do Jews and Saracens) but because of the great love that Christ has showed me. I serve thee not because thou art my master or my king; for hope of reward or fear of pain, but for the love of Christ. [c]For the children of faith are under no law (as thou seest in the Epistles to the Romans, to the Galatians, in the first of Timothy) but are free. The spirit of Christ hath written the lively[410] law of love in

a. In Christ we are one as good as another equally beloved and indifferently heard.
b. Christ is all to a Christian man.
c. The children of faith work of love and need no law to compel them.

their hearts which driveth them to work of their own accord freely and willingly, for the great love's sake only which they see in Christ, and therefore need they no law to compel them.[411] Christ is all in all[412] things to them that believe, and the cause of all love. [a]Paul saith (Ephesians 6) servants obey unto your carnal or fleshly masters with fear and trembling as unto Christ. Not with eye service as menpleasers: but as the servants of Christ: doing the will of God from the heart: even as though ye served the Lord and not men. And remember that whatsoever good thing any man doeth, that shall he receive again of the Lord, whether he be bond or free. Christ thus is all in all things and cause of all to a Christian man. And (Matthew 25) saith Christ: inasmuch as ye have done it to any of the least of these my brethren, ye have done it to me. And inasmuch as ye have not done it unto one of the least of these, ye have not done it to me. Here seest thou that we are Christ's brethren and even Christ himself, and whatsoever we do one to another that do we to Christ.[413] If we be in Christ we work for no worldly purpose, but of love. As Paul saith (2 Corinthians 5), The love of Christ compelled us (as who should say we work not of a fleshly purpose). For (saith he) we know henceforth no man fleshly: no though we once knew Christ fleshly we do so now no more. We are otherwise minded, than when Peter drew his sword to fight for Christ. We are now ready to suffer with Christ and to lose life and all for our very enemies to bring them to Christ. If we be in Christ we are minded like unto Christ, [b]which knew nothing fleshly or after the will of the flesh, as thou seest (Matthew 12) when one said to him: Lo thy mother and thy brethren stand without desiring to speak with thee. He answered, who is my mother and who are my brethren? And stretched his hand over his disciples saying: see my mother and my brethren. For whosoever doeth the will of my father which is in heaven, the same is my brother my sister and my mother. He knew not his mother in that she bare him, but in that she did the will of his father in heaven. So now as God the father's will and commandment is all to Christ, even so Christ is all to a Christian man.

Christ is the cause why I love thee, why I am ready to do the uttermost

a. We are all Christ's servants and serve Christ.
b. Christ knoweth nothing worldly no not his very mother.

of my power for thee, and why I pray for thee. And as long as the cause abideth, so long lasteth the effect even as it is always day, so long as the sun shineth. Do therefore the worst thou canst unto me: take away my goods: take away my good name: yet as long as [a]Christ remaineth in mine heart, so long I love thee not a whit the less and so long art thou as dear unto me as mine own soul, and so long am I ready to do thee good for thine evil, and so long I pray for thee with all mine heart. For Christ desireth it of me and hath deserved it of me. Thine unkindness compared unto his kindness is nothing at all, yea it is swallowed up, as a little smoke of a mighty wind, and is no more seen or thought upon. Moreover that evil which thou doest to me, I receive not of thine hand, but of the hand of God, and as God's scourge to teach me patience and to nurture me. And therefore have no cause to be angry with thee more than the child hath to be angry with his father's rod or a sick man with a sore or bitter medicine that healeth him, or a prisoner with his fetters or he that is punished lawfully with the officer that punisheth him.

Thus is Christ all and the whole cause why I love thee, and to all can nought be added. [b]Therefore cannot a little money make me love thee better or more bound to pray for thee nor make God's commandment greater. Last of all, if I be in Christ then the love of Christ compelleth me. And therefore I am ready to give thee mine and not to take thine from thee: if I be able I will do the service freely: if not, then if thou minister to me again, that receive I of the hand of God which ministereth it to me by thee. [c]For God which careth for his and ministereth all things unto them and moveth Turks and Saracens and all manner infidels to do thee good, as thou seest in Abraham, Isaac and Jacob, and how God went with Joseph into Egypt and got him favour in the prison and in every place, which favour Joseph received of the hand of God and to God gave thee thanks. This is God and Christ all in all: good and bad receive I of God. Them that are good I love, because they are in Christ: and the evil, to bring them to Christ. When any man doeth well I rejoice, that God is honoured, and when any man doeth evil I sorrow because

a. As long as Christ abideth so long a Christian man loveth.
b. Money bindeth not Christian to pray.
c. God careth for his.

that God is dishonoured. Finally inasmuch as God hath created all and Christ bought all with his blood, therefore ought all to seek God and Christ in all and else nothing.

ᵃBut contrarywise unto monks, friars, and to the other of our holy spirituality the belly is all in all and cause of all love. Offer thereto, so art thou father, mother, sister, and brother unto them. Offerest thou not, so know they thee not, thou art neither father, mother, sister, brother nor any kin at all to them. She is a sister of ours, he is a brother of ours, say they: he is verily a good man, for he doeth much for our religion. She is a mother to our convent: we be greatly bound to pray for them. And as for such and such (say they) we know not whether they be good or bad or whether they be fish or flesh, for they do nought for us: we be more bound to pray for our benefactors (say they) and for them that give us, than for them that give us not. For them that give little are they little bound and them they love little and for them that give much are they much bound and them they love much. And for them that give nought are they nought bound and them they love not at all. And as they love thee when thou givest: so hate they thee when thou takest away from them, and run all under a stole⁴¹⁴ and curse thee as black as pitch. So is cloister love ᵇbelly love, cloister prayer belly prayer, and cloister brotherhood belly brotherhood. Moreover love that springeth of Christ seeketh not her own self (1 Corinthians 13) but ᶜforgetteth herself and bestoweth her upon her neighbour's profit as Christ sought our profit and not his own. He sought not the favour of God for himself, but for us: yea he took the wrath and vengeance of God from us unto himself and bare it on his own back to bring us unto favour. Likewise doth a Christian man give to his brethren and robbeth them not as friars and monks do: but as Paul commandeth (Ephesians 4)⁴¹⁵ laboureth with his hands some good work to have wherewith to help the needy. They give not but receive only. They labour not but live idly of the sweat of the poor. There is none so poor a widow, though she have not to find herself and her children nor any money to give: yet shall the friar snatch

a. The belly is a God and cause of all unto our spirituality.

b. All is of the belly and nothing of Christ.

c. Christ's love forgetteth herself: but monks' love thinketh on the belly.

a cheese or somewhat. They preach, sayest thou, and labour in the word. [a]First I say they are not called and therefore ought not: for it is the curate's office. The curate cannot, sayest thou. What doeth the thief there then? Secondarily a true preacher preacheth Christ's testament only and maketh Christ the cause and reward of all our deeds and teacheth every man to bear his cross willingly for Christ's sake. But these are enemies unto the cross of Christ and preach their belly which is their God (Ephesians 3) and they think that lucre is the serving of God (1 Timothy 6). That is, they think them Christian only which offer unto their bellies, which when thou has filled then spew they out prayers for thee, to be thy reward, and yet wot not what prayer meaneth. Prayer is the longing for God's promises, which promises as they preach them not, so long they not for them nor wish them unto any man. Their longing is to fill their paunch whom they serve and not Christ, and through sweet preaching and flattering words deceive the hearts of the simple and unlearned (Romans 16).

[b]Finally as Christ is the whole cause why we do all things for our neighbour, even so is he the cause why God doeth all things for us, why he receiveth us into his holy testament and maketh us heirs[416] of all his promises, and poureth his spirit into us, and maketh us his sons, and fashioneth us like unto Christ and maketh us such as he would have us to be. [c]The assurance that we are sons, beloved and heirs with Christ and have God's spirit in us, is the consent of our hearts unto the law of God. [d]Which law is all perfection and the mark where at all we ought to shoot. And he that hitteth that mark, so that he fulfilleth that law with all his heart, soul and might and with full love and lust without all let or resistance is pure gold and needeth not to be put any more in the fire:[417] he is straight and right and needeth to be no more shaven: he is full fashioned like Christ and can have no more added unto him. Nevertheless there is none so perfect in this life that findeth not let and resistance by the reason of original sin or birth poison that remaineth

a. Friars and monks ought not to preach.
b. Christ is the whole cause why God loveth us.
c. How to know that we are God's sons.
d. The law is the mark: yea and the touchstone from wherewith we ought to try ourselves and see how farforth we are purged.

in him, as thou mayest see in the lives of all the saints throughout all the scripture and in Paul (Romans 7). The will is present, saith he, but I find no means to perform that which is good: I do not that good thing which I would: but that evil do I which I would not. I find by the law that when I would do good, evil is present with me. I delight in the law, as concerning the inner man, but I find another law in my members rebelling against the law of my mind and subduing me unto the law of sin. ªWhich law of sin is nothing but a corrupt and a poisoned nature which breaketh into evil lusts and from evil lusts into wicked deeds and must be purged with the true Purgatory of ᵇthe cross of Christ: that is thou must hate it with all thine heart and desire God to take it from thee. And then whatsoever cross God putteth on thy back bear it patiently whether it be poverty, sickness or persecution or whatsoever it be, and take it for the right Purgatory and think that God hath nailed thee fast to it, to purge thee thereby. ᶜFor he that loveth not the law and hateth his sin and hath not professed in his heart to fight against it and mourneth not to God to take it away and to purge him of it, the same hath no part with Christ. ᵈIf thou love the law and findest that thou hast yet sin hanging on thee, when thou sorrowest to be delivered and purged as for an example, thou hast a covetous mind and mistrustest God and therefore art moved to beguile thy neighbour and art unto him merciless, not caring whether he sink or swim so thou mayest win by him or get from him that he hath: then get thee to the Observant[418] which is so purged from that sin that he will not once handle a penny and with that wile doth the subtle fox make the goose come flying into his hole ready prepared for his mouth without his labour or sweat and buy of his merits which he hath in store and give thy money not into his holy hands but to him that he hath hired, either with part of his prayers or part of his prey to take the sin upon him and to handle his money for him. In like manner if any person that is under obedience unto God's ordinance (whether it be son or daughter, servant, wife or subject), consent unto the ordinance and yet find contrary motions: let him go also to them

a. ☞
b. The right cross of Christ.
c. He that loveth not the law and hateth sin hath no part with Christ.
d. How to try the doctrine of our spirituality.

that have professed an obedience of their own making, and buy part of their merits. If thy wife give thee nine words for three, go to the Charterhouse[419] and buy of their silence and so. [a]If the abstaining of the Observant from handling money heal thine heart from desiring money, and the obedience of them that will obey nothing but their own ordinance heal thy disobedience to God's ordinance, and the silence of the Charterhouse monk tame thy wife's tongue: then believe that their prayers shall deliver thy soul from the pains of that terrible and fearful Purgatory which they have feigned to purge thy purse withal.

The spirituality increaseth daily. [b]More prelates, more priests, more monks, friars, canons, nuns and more heretics, I would say heremites[420] with like draff:[421] set before thee the increase of Saint Francis' disciples in so few years. Reckon how many thousand.[422] Yea, how many twenty thousands, not disciples only: but whole cloisters are sprung out of hell of them in so little space. Pattering of prayers increaseth daily. Their service as they call it, waxeth longer and longer and the labour of their lips greater, new saints, new service, new feasts and new holy days. What take all these away? Sin? Nay. For we see the contrary by experience and that sin groweth as they grow. [c]But they take away first God's word with faith, hope, peace, unity, love and concord then house and land, rent and fee, tower and town, goods and cattle, and the very meat out of men's mouths. All these live by Purgatory. [d]When others weep for their friends they sing merrily: when others lose their friends they get friends. The Pope with all his pardons is grounded on Purgatory. Priests, monks, canons, friars with all other swarms of hypocrites do but empty Purgatory and fill hell. Every mass, say they, delivereth one soul out of [e] Purgatory. If that were true, yet were the parish priests and curates of every parish sufficient to scour Purgatory. And the other costly workmen might well be spared.

a. If the prayers and merits of our religious purge our lusts then are they of value and else not.
b. ☞
c. What the spirituality taketh away with their prayers.
d. When others weep they sing and when others lose they win.
e. All is of Purgatory. These physicians give no other medicines save purgation only.

The four senses of the scripture.[423]

They divide the scripture into four senses, the literal, tropological, allegorical, anagogical. The literal sense is becoming nothing at all. For the Pope hath taken it clean away and hath made it his possession. He hath partly locked it up with the false and counterfeited keys of his traditions, ceremonies and feigned lies. And partly driveth men from it with violence of sword. For no man dare abide by the literal sense of the text, but under a protestation, if it shall please the Pope. The tropological sense pertaineth to good manners (say they) and teacheth what we ought to do. The allegory is appropriate to faith, and the anagogical to hope and things above. Tropological and anagogical are terms of their own feigning and altogether unnecessary. For they are but allegories[424] both two of them and this word allegory comprehendeth them both and is enough. For chopological[425] is but an allegory of manners and anagogical an allegory of hope. [a]And allegory is as much to say as strange speaking or borrowed speech. As when we say of a wanton child, this sheep hath maggots in his tail, he must be anointed with birchen salve[426] which speech I borrow of the shepherds.

Thou shalt understand therefore that the scripture hath but one sense which is the literal sense. [b]And that literal sense is the root and ground of all, and the anchor that never faileth whereunto if thou cleave thou canst never err or go out of the way. And if thou leave the literal sense thou canst not but go out of the way. Neverthelater the scripture useth proverbs, similitudes, riddles or allegories as all other speeches do, but that which the proverb, similitude, riddle or allegory signifieth is ever the literal sense which thou must seek out diligently. As in the English we borrow words and sentences of one thing and apply them unto another and give them new significations. We say let the sea swell and rise as high as he will yet hath God appointed how far he shall go: meaning that the tyrants shall not do what they would, but that only which God hath appointed them to do. Look ere thou leap, whose literal

---

a. Allegory and what it signifieth.
b. The scripture hath but one sense.

sense is, do nothing suddenly or without advisement. Cut not the bough that thou standest upon, whose literal sense is oppress not the commons and is borrowed of hewers. When a thing speedeth not well, we borrow speech and say, the bishop hath blessed it, because that nothing speedeth well that they meddle withal. If the porridge be burned too, or the meat over-roasted, we say, the bishop hath put his foot in the pot or the bishop hath played the cook, because the bishops burn whom they lust and whosoever displeaseth them. He is a pontifical fellow, that is, proud and stately. He is popish, that is, superstitious and faithless. It is a pastime for a prelate. It is a pleasure for a Pope. He would be free and yet will not have his head shaven. He would that no man should smite him and yet hath not the Pope's mark. And of him that is betrayed and wotteth not how, we say, he hath been at shrift. She is master parson's sister's daughter. He is the bishop's sister's son, he hath a cardinal to his uncle, she is a spiritual whore, it is the gentlewoman of the parsonage, he gave me a *Kyrie eleison*.[427] And of her that answereth her husband six words for one we say, she is a sister of the Charterhouse, as who should say, she thinketh that she is not bound to keep silence, their silence shall be a satisfaction to her. And of him that will not be saved by Christ's merits, but by the works of his own imagination we say it is a holyworkman. Thus borrow we and feign new speech in every tongue. All fables, prophecies and riddles are allegories and Aesop's fables and Merlin's[428] prophecies and the interpretation of them are the literal sense.

So in like manner the scripture borroweth words and sentences of all manner things and maketh proverbs and similitudes or allegories. As Christ saith (Luke 4), Physician heal thyself. Whose interpretation is do that at home which thou doest in strange places, and that is the literal sense. So when I say Christ is a lamb,[429] I mean not a lamb that beareth wool, but a meek and a patient lamb which is beaten for other men's faults. Christ is a vine,[430] not that beareth grapes: but out of whose root the branches that believe suck the spirit of life and mercy and grace and power to be the sons of God and to do his will. The similitudes of the gospel are allegories borrowed of worldly matter to express spiritual things. The Apocalypse or Revelations of John are allegories whose literal sense is hard to find in many places.[431]

^aBeyond all this, when we have found out the literal sense of the scripture by the process of the text or by a like text of another place, then go we, and as the scripture borroweth similitudes of worldly things even so we again borrow similitudes or allegories of the scriptures and apply them to our purposes, ^bwhich allegories are no sense of the scripture: but free things besides the scripture and altogether in the liberty of the Spirit. Which allegories I may not make at all the wild adventures:[432] but must keep me within the compass[433] of the faith and ever apply mine allegory to Christ and unto the faith. Take an example: thou hast the story of Peter how he smote off Malchus's ear[434] and how Christ healed it again. There hast thou in the plain text great learning, great fruit and great edifying which I pass over because of tediousness. Then come I, when I preach of the law and the gospel, and borrow this example to express the nature of the law and of the gospel and to paint it unto thee before thine eyes. And of Peter and his sword make I the law and of Christ the gospel saying, as Peter's sword cutteth off the ear so doth the law. The law damneth, the law killeth, and mangleth the conscience.

There is no ear so righteous that can abide the hearing of the law. There is no deed so good but that the law damneth it. But Christ, that is to say the gospel, the promises and testament that God hath made in Christ healeth the ear and conscience which the law hath hurt.[435] The gospel is life, mercy and forgiveness freely, and all together an healing plaster. And as Peter doth but hurt and make a wound where was none before: even so doth the law. For when we think that we are holy and righteous and full of good deeds if the law be preached aright, our righteousness and good deeds vanish away, as smoke in the wind, and we are left damnable sinners only. And as thou seest how that Christ healeth not till Peter had wounded, and as an healing plaster helpeth not till the corsie[436] hath troubled the wound, even so the gospel helpeth not, but when the law hath wounded the conscience and brought the sinner into the knowledge of his sin. ^cThis allegory proveth nothing neither can do. For it is not the scripture, but an example or a similitude

a. The right use of allegories.
b. Allegories are no sense of scripture.
c. Allegories prove nothing.

borrowed of the scripture to declare a text or a conclusion of the scripture more expressly, and to root it and grave it in the heart. For a similitude or an example doth print a thing much deeper in the wits of a man than doth a plain speaking, and leaveth behind him as it were a sting to prick him forward and to awake him with all. [a]Moreover if I could not prove with an open text that which the allegory doth express, then were the allegory a thing to be jested at and of no greater value than a tale of Robin Hood.[437] This allegory as touching his first part is proved by Paul in third chapter of his epistle to the Romans where he saith: The law causeth wrath. And in seventh chapter to the Romans: When the law or commandment came, sin revived, and I become dead. And in the second epistle to the Corinthians in third chapter, the law is called the minister of death and damnation etc. And as concerning the second part Paul saith to the Romans in the fifth chapter: In that we are justified by faith we are at peace with God. And in the second epistle to the Corinthians in the third chapter the gospel is called the ministration of justifying and of the spirit. And (Galatians 4), The spirit cometh by preaching of the faith etc. [b]Thus doth the literal sense prove the allegory and bear it, as the foundation beareth the house. And because that allegories prove nothing, therefore are they to be used soberly and seldom and only where the text offereth thee an allegory.

And of this manner (as I above have done) doth Paul borrow a similitude, a figure or an allegory of Genesis to express the nature of the law and of the gospel, and by Hagar and her son declareth the property of the law and of her bond children which will be justified by deeds, and by Sara[438] and her son declareth the property of the gospel and of her free children which are justified by faith, and how the children of the law which believe in their works persecute the children of the gospel which believe in the mercy and truth of God and in the testament of his son Jesus our Lord. And likewise do we borrow likenesses or allegories of the scripture, as of Pharaoh and Herod and of the scribes and Pharisees, to express our miserable captivity and persecution under Antichrist the Pope.

a. If thou cannot prove the allegory with
an open text then is it false doctrine.
b. The literal sense proveth the allegory.

[a]The greatest cause of which captivity and the decay of the faith and this blindness wherein we now are, sprang first of allegories. For Origen[439] and those of his time drew all the scripture unto allegories. Whose example they that came after followed so long, till at the last they forgot the order and process of the text, supposing that the scripture served but to feign allegories upon. Insomuch that twenty doctors expound one text twenty ways, as children make descant upon plain song. [b]Then came our sophisters with their anagogical and chopological sense and with an antetheme[440] of half an inch, out of which some of them draw a thread of nine days long. Yea thou shalt find enough that will preach Christ, and prove whatsoever point of the faith that thou wilt, as well out of a fable of Ovid [c]or any other poet, as out of Saint John's gospel or Paul's Epistles. Yea they are come unto such blindness that they not only say the literal sense profiteth not, but also that it is hurtful and noisome and killeth the soul. Which damnable doctrine they prove by a text of Paul (2 Corinthians 3) [d]where he saith the letter killeth but the spirit giveth life. Lo say they the literal sense killeth and the spiritual sense giveth life. We must therefore, say they, seek out some chopological sense.

Here learn what sophistry is and how blind they are, that thou mayest abhor them and spew them out of thy stomach forever. Paul by the letter meaneth Moses' law. Which the process of the text following declareth more bright than the sun. But it is not their guise to look on the order of any text but as they find it in their doctors so allege they it and so understand it. [e]Paul maketh a comparison between the law and the gospel and calleth the law the letter, because it was but letters graven in two tables of cold stone. For the law doth but kill and damn the consciences, as long as there is no lust in the heart to do that which the law commandeth. Contrarywise he calleth the gospel the administration of the spirit and of righteousness or justifying. For when Christ is preached and the promises which God hath made in Christ are believed,

a. The faith was lost through allegories.
b. Chopological sophisters.
c. Poetry is as good divinity as the scripture to our schoolmen.
d. The literal sense killeth say sophisters.
e. The letter killeth is expounded.

the spirit entereth the heart and looseth the heart and giveth lust to do the law and maketh the law a lively thing in the heart. [a]Now as soon as the heart lusteth to do the law, then are we righteous before God and our sins forgiven. Nevertheless the law of the letter graved in stone and not in the hearts was so glorious, that Moses' face shone so bright that the children of Israel could not behold his face for brightness. It was also given in thunder and lightning and terrible signs, so that they for fear came to Moses and desired him that he would speak to them and let God speak no more. Lest we die (said they), if we hear him anymore: as thou mayest see, Exodus twenty. Whereupon Paul maketh his comparison saying: if the ministration of death through the letters figured in stones was glorious, so that the children of Israel could not behold the face of Moses for the glory of his countenance: why shall not the administration of the Spirit be glorious? And again: if the administration of damnation be glorious: much more shall the administration of righteousness exceed in glory: That is, if the law that killeth sinners and helpeth them not be glorious: then the gospel which pardoneth sinners and giveth them power to be the sons of God and to overcome sin, is much more glorious. And the text that goeth before is as clear.

For the holy Apostle Paul saith, ye Corinthians are our epistle, which is understood and read of all men, in that ye are known how that ye are the epistle of Christ ministered by us and written: not with ink (as Moses' law) but with the Spirit of the living God: not in tables of stone (as the Ten Commandments) but in the fleshly tables of the heart, as who should say, we write not a dead law with ink and in parchment, nor grave that which damned you in tables of stone: but preach you that which bringeth the spirit of life unto your breasts, which spirit writeth and graveth the law of love in your hearts and giveth you lust to do the will of God. And furthermore, saith he, our ableness cometh of God which hath made us able to minister the New Testament, not of the letter (that is to say not of the law) but of the spirit. For the letter (that is to say the law) killeth: but the spirit giveth life (that is to say the spirit of God which entereth your hearts when ye believe the glad tidings that are preached you in Christ), quickeneth your hearts and giveth you life

a. To love the law is righteousness.

and lust and maketh you to do of love and of your own accord without compulsion, that which the law compelled you to do and damned you because ye could not do with love and lust and naturally. Thus seest thou that the letter signifieth not the literal sense and the spirit the spiritual sense. And (Romans 2) useth Paul this term *litera* for the law. And (Romans 7) where he setteth it so plain, that if the great wrath of God had not blinded them they could never have stumbled at it.

God is a spirit[441] and all his words are spiritual. His [a]literal sense is spiritual and all his words are spiritual. When thou readest (Matthew 1) she shall bear a son and thou shalt call his name Jesus: For he shall save his people from their sins. This literal sense is spiritual and everlasting life unto as many as believe it. And the literal sense of these words (Matthew 5) blessed are the merciful, for they shall have mercy, are spiritual and life. Whereby they that are merciful may of right by the truth and promise of God challenge mercy. And like it is of these words (Matthew 6), If you forgive other men their sins your heavenly father shall forgive you yours. And so is it of all the promises of God. Finally all God's words are spiritual, if thou have eyes of God to see the right meaning of the text and whereunto the scripture pertaineth and the final end and cause thereof.

[b]All the scripture is either the promises and testament of God in Christ and stories pertaining hereunto, to strengthen thy faith: either[442] the law and stories pertaining thereto to fear them from evil doing. There is no story nor gest,[443] seem it never so simple or so vile unto the world, but that thou shalt find therein spirit and life and edifying in the literal sense. For it is God's scripture written for thy learning and comfort. There is no cloth or rag there that hath not precious relics wrapped therein of faith, hope, patience and longsuffering and of the truth of God, and also of his righteousness. Set before thee the story of [c]Reuben which defiled his father's bed.[444] Mark what a cross God suffered to fall on the neck of his elect Jacob.[445] Consider first the shame among the heathen, when as yet there was no more of the whole world within the

---

a. The literal sense is spiritual.
b. What is to be sought in the scripture and in the literal sense.
c. The story of Reuben.

testament of God but he and his household. I report[446] me to our prelates which swore by their [a]honour whether it were a cross or no. Seest thou not how our wicked builders rage, because they see their buildings burn,[447] how they are tried by the fire of God's word, and how they stir up the whole world, to quench the word of God, for fear of losing their honour. Then what business[448] had he to pacify his children? Look what ado he had at the defiling of his daughter Dinah.[449] And be thou sure that the brethren there were no more furious for the defiling of their sister, than the sons here for the defiling of their mother. Mark what followed Reuben, to fear either that they shame not their fathers and mothers. He was cursed and lost the kingdom and also the priestdom, and his tribe or generation was ever few in number as it appeareth in the stories of the Bible.

[b]The adultery of David with Bathsheba[450] is an example, not to move us to evil: but if (while we follow the way of righteousness) any chance drive us aside, that we despair not. For if we saw not such infirmities in God's elect, we which are so weak and fall so often should utterly despair and think that God had clean forsaken us. It is therefore a sure and an undoubted conclusion, whether we be holy or unholy, we are all sinners. [c]But the difference is, that God's sinners consent not to their sin. They consent unto the law that it is both holy and righteous and mourn to have their sin taken away. But the devil's sinners consent unto their sin and would have the law and hell taken away and are enemies unto the righteousness of God.

Likewise in the homely gest[451] of [d]Noah, when he was drunk, and lay in his tent with his privy members open, hast thou great edifying in the literal sense. Thou seest what became of the cursed children of wicked Ham which saw his father's privy members and jested thereof to his brethren. Thou seest also what blessing fell on Shem and Japhet which went backward and covered their father's members and saw them not. And thirdly thou seest what infirmity accompanieth God's elect be they

a. Swore they by their honour. Then are they not ready
to suffer shame for Christ's sake.
b. The adultery of David.
c. The difference between God's sinners and the devil's.
d. Noah.

never so holy, which yet is not imputed unto them. For the faith and trust they have in God swalloweth up all their sins.

[a]Notwithstanding this text offereth us an apt and an handsome allegory or similitude to describe our wicked Ham, Antichrist the Pope, which many hundred years hath done all the shame that heart can think unto the privy member of God which is the word of promise or the word of faith as Paul calleth it (Romans 10) and the gospel and testament of Christ wherewith we are begotten, as thou seest (1 Peter 1 and James 1). And as the cursed children of Ham grew into giants so mighty and great that the children of Israel seemed but grasshoppers[452] in the respect of them: so the cursed sons of our Ham the Pope his cardinals, bishops, abbots, monks and friars are become mighty giants above all power and authority, so that the children of faith in respect of them, are much less than grasshoppers. [b]They heap mountain upon mountain, and will to heaven by their own strength and by a way of their own making and not by the way of Christ. Neverthelater those giants for the wickedness and abominations which they had wrought, did God utterly destroy, part of them by the children of Lot and part by the children of Esau,[453] and seven nations[454] of them by the children of Israel. So no doubt shall he destroy these for like abominations and that shortly. For their kingdom is but the kingdom of lies and falsehood which must needs perish at the coming of the truth of God's word, as the night vanisheth away at the presence of day. The children of Israel slew not those giants, but the power of God, God's truth and promises as thou mayest see in Deuteronomy. So it is not we that shall destroy those giants, as thou mayest see by Paul (2 Thessalonians 2) speaking of our Ham Antichrist. Whom the Lord shall destroy (saith he) with the spirit of his mouth (that is, by the words of truth) and by the brightness of his coming (that is, by the preaching of his gospel).

[c]And as I have said of allegories, even so it is of worldly similitudes which we make either when we preach either when we expound the scripture. The similitudes prove nothing, but are made to express more

a. The Pope is likened to Ham.
b. They will to heaven by a way of their own making.
c. The use of similitudes.

plainly that which is contained in the scripture and to lead thee in the spiritual understanding of the text. As the similitude of matrimony[455] is taken to express the marriage that is between Christ and our souls and what exceeding mercy we have there, whereof all the scriptures make mention. And the similitude of the members,[456] how every one of them careth for other is taken to make thee feel what it is to love thy neighbour as thyself. [a]That preacher therefore that bringeth a naked similitude to prove that which is contained in no text of scripture nor followeth of a text, count a deceiver, a leader out of the way and a false prophet, and beware of his philosophy and persuasions of man's wisdom as Paul everywhere warneth thee. [b]Paul (1 Corinthians 2) saith: my words and my preaching were not with enticing words and persuasions of man's wisdom but in showing of the spirit and power, that is, he preached not dreams confirming them with similitudes: but God's word confirming it with miracles and with working of the spirit the which made them feel everything in their hearts. That your faith, saith he, should not stand in the wisdom of man: but in the power of God. [c]For the reasons and similitudes of man's wisdom make no faith, but wavering and uncertainty opinions only: one draweth in this way with his argument another that, and of what principle thou provest black another proveth white, and so am I ever uncertain, as if thou tell me of a thing done in a far land and another tell me the contrary, I wot not what to believe. [d]But faith is wrought by the power of God, that is, when God's word is preached, the Spirit entereth thine heart and maketh thy soul feel it and maketh thee so sure of it, that neither adversity nor persecution, nor death, neither hell, nor the powers of hell, neither yet all the pains of hell could once prevail[457] against thee or move thee from the sure rock of God's word, that thou shouldest not believe that which God hath sworn.

And Peter (2 Peter 1) saith we followed not deceivable [e]fables, when we opened unto you the power and coming of our Lord Jesus Christ: but with our eyes we saw his majesty. And again, we have (saith he) a

a. A similitude without scripture is a sure token of a false prophet.
b. Paul preached not worldly wisdom.
c. Similitudes and reasons of man's wisdom make no faith but wavering opinion only.
d. God's word maketh sure faith for God cannot lie.
e. Peter preached not fables and false similitudes but the plain scripture.

more sure word of prophecy, whereunto if ye take heed, as unto a light shining in a dark place, ye do well. The word of prophecy was the Old Testament which beareth record unto Christ in every place, without which record the Apostles made neither similitudes nor arguments of worldly wit. Hereof seest thou, that all the allegories, similitudes, persuasions and arguments which they bring without scripture, to prove praying to saints, Purgatory, ear confession, and that God will hear thy prayer more in one place than in another, and that it is more meritorious to eat fish than flesh, and that to disguise thyself and put on this or that manner coat is more acceptable than to go as God hath made thee, and that widowhood is better than matrimony and virginity than widowhood, and to prove the assumption of Our Lady and that she was born without original sin, yea and with a kiss[458] say some, are but false doctrine.

[a]Take an example how they prove that widowhood and virginity exceed matrimony: they bring this worldly similitude. He that taketh most pain for a man deserveth most and to him a man is most bound, so likewise must it be with God and so forth: now the widow and virgin take more pain in resisting their lusts than the married wife, therefore is their state holier. [b]First I say, that in their own sophistry a similitude is the worst and feeblest argument that can be and proveth least, and soonest deceiveth. Though that one son do more service for his father than another, yet is the father free and may with right reward them all alike. For though I had a thousand brethren and did more than they all, yet do I not my duty. The fathers and mothers also care most for the least and weakest and them that can do least: yea for the worst care they most and would spend, not their goods only: but also their blood to bring them to the right way. And even so is it of the kingdom of Christ as thou mayest well see in the similitude of the riotous son (Luke 15). Moreover Paul saith (1 Corinthians 7), it is better to marry than to burn. For the person that burneth cannot quietly serve God inasmuch as his mind is drawn away and the thoughts of his heart occupied with wonderful and monstrous imaginations. He can neither see, nor hear, nor read but

a. School doctrine.
b. Similitudes are no good arguments
among the sophisters' own selves.

that his wits are rapt and he clean from himself. And again, saith he, circumcision is nothing, uncircumcision is nothing: but the keeping of the commandment is all together. Look wherein thou canst best keep the commandments, thither get thyself and therein abide, whether thou be widow, wife or maid, and then hast thou all with God. ᵃIf we have infirmities that draw us from the laws of God, let us cure them with the remedies that God hath made. If thou burn, marry. For God hath promised thee no chastity, as long as thou mayest use the remedy that he hath ordained: no more than he hath promised to slake thine hunger without meat.

Now to ask of God more than he hath promised cometh of a false faith and is plain idolatry:⁴⁵⁹ and to desire ᵇa miracle where there is natural remedy, is tempting of God. And of pain taking, this wise understand. He that taketh pain to keep the commandments of God is sure thereby that he loveth God and that he had God's Spirit in him. And the more pain a man taketh (I mean patiently and without grudging) the more he loveth God and the perfecter he is, and near unto that health which the souls of all Christian men long for, and the more purged from the infirmity and sin that remaineth in the flesh: but to look for any other reward or promotion in heaven or in the life to come than that which God hath promised for Christ's sake and which Christ hath deserved for us with his pain taking, is abominable in the sight of God.⁴⁶⁰ For Christ only hath purchased the reward, and our pain taking to keep the commandments doth but purge the sin that remaineth in the flesh, and certify us that we are chosen and sealed with God's Spirit unto the reward that Christ hath purchased for us.

I was once at the creating of doctors of divinity, where the opponent brought the same reason to prove that the widow had more merit than the virgin, because she had greater pains forasmuch as she had once proved the pleasures of matrimony. *Ego nego domine doctor*⁴⁶¹ said the respondent. For though the virgin have not proved, yet she imagineth that the pleasure is greater than it is indeed and therefore is more moved

a. We must cure our infirmities with the remedies
that God hath ordained and not tempt God.
b. What tempting of God is.

and hath greater temptation and greater pain. Are not these disputers they that Paul speaketh of in the sixth chapter of the first epistle to Timothy? That they are not content with the wholesome words of our Lord Jesus Christ, and doctrine of godliness? And therefore know nothing: but waste their brains about questions and strife of words, whereof spring envy, strife and railing of men with corrupt minds destitute of the truth.

As pertaining to Our Lady's body, where it is or where the body of Elias, of John the Evangelist and of many other be, pertaineth not to us to know. One thing are we sure of, that they are where God hath laid them. If they be in heaven, we have never the more in Christ: If they be not there, we have never the less. Our duty is to prepare ourselves unto the commandments and to be thankful for that which is opened unto us, and not to search the unsearchable secrets[462] of God. Of God's secrets can we know no more than he openeth unto us. If God shut, who shall open? How then can natural reason come by the knowledge of that which God hath hid unto himself?

Yet let us see one of their reasons wherewith they prove it. The chief reason is this, every man doth more for his mother, say they, than for other, in like manner must Christ do for his mother, therefore hath she this pre-eminence, that her body is in heaven.[463] And yet Christ in the twelfth chapter of Matthew knoweth her not for his mother: but as farforth as she kept his father's commandments. And Paul in the second epistle to the Corinthians in fifth chapter knoweth not Christ himself fleshly or after a worldly purpose. Last of all God is free and no further bound than he biddeth himself. If he have made her any promise he is bound, if not, then he is not. Finally if thou set this above-rehearsed chapter of Matthew before thee where Christ would not know his mother, and the second of John where he rebuked her, and the second of Luke where she lost him and how negligent she was to leave him behind her at Jerusalem unawares and to go a day's journey ere she sought for him thou mightest solve many of their reasons which they make of this matter, and that she was without original sin: read also Erasmus's annotations[464] in the said places. And as for me I commit all such matter unto those idle bellies which have nought else to do, than to move such questions and give them free liberty to hold what they list, as long as it hurteth not the faith, whether it be so or no: exhorting yet with Paul all that will please God and obtain that salvation that is in Christ, that they give no heed unto unnecessary and brawling disputations, and that they labour for the knowledge of those things without which they cannot be saved. And remember that the sun was given us to guide us in our way and works bodily. Now if thou leave the natural use of the sun and will look directly on him to see how bright he is and suchlike curiosity then will the sun blind thee. So was the scripture given us to guide us in our ways and works ghostly. The way is Christ and the promises in him are our salvation if we long for them and the law is our work. Now if we shall leave that right use and turn ourselves unto vain questions and to search the unsearchable secrets of God: then no doubt shall the scripture blind us as it hath done our schoolmen and our subtle disputers.

And as they are false prophets which prove with allegories, similitudes and worldly reasons that which is nowhere made mention of in the scripture. Even so count them for false prophets which expound the scriptures drawing them unto a worldly purpose clean contrary unto the [a]example, living, and practising of Christ and of his Apostles and of all the holy prophets. For saith Peter (2 Peter 1) no prophecy in the scripture hath any private interpretation. For the scripture came not by the will of man:[465] but the holy men of God spake, as they were moved by the Holy Ghost. No place of the scripture may have a private exposition, that is it may not be expounded after the will of man or after the will of the flesh or drawn unto a worldly purpose contrary unto the open texts and the general articles of the faith and the whole course of the scripture, and contrary to the living and practising of Christ and the Apostles and holy prophets. For as they came not by the will of man, so may they not be drawn or expound after the will of man: but as they came by the Holy Ghost, so must they be expounded and understood by the Holy Ghost.

The scripture is that wherewith God draweth us unto him and not wherewith we should be led from him. The scriptures spring out of God and flow unto Christ, and were given to lead [b]us to Christ. Thou must

a. In expounding of the scripture we must have a respect unto the living and practising of Christ and of his Apostles and prophets.
b. The scripture was given to lead us unto Christ.

therefore go along by the scripture as by a line, until thou come at Christ, which is the way's end and resting place. If any man therefore use the scripture to draw thee from Christ and to nosel[466] thee in anything save in Christ, the same is a false prophet. And that thou mayest perceive what Peter meaneth, it followeth in the text. There were false prophets among the people (whose prophecies were belly wisdom) as there shall be false teachers among you: which shall privily bring in damnable ^asects (as thou seest how we are divided into monstrous sects or orders of religion) even denying the Lord that hath brought them. (For every one of them taketh on him to sell thee for money that which God in Christ promiseth freely) and many shall follow their damnable ways, by whom the way of truth shall be evil spoken of (as thou seest how the way of truth is become heresy, seditious or cause of insurrection and breaking of the King's peace and treason unto His Highness). And through covetousness with feigned words shall they make merchandise of you. Covetousness ^bis the conclusion: for covetousness and ambition that is to say, lucre and desire of honour is the final end of all false prophets and of all false teachers. Look upon the Pope's false doctrine, what is the end thereof and what seek they thereby? Wherefore serveth ^cPurgatory but to purge thy purse and to poll thee and rob both thee and thy heirs of house and lands and of all thou hast, that they may be in honour. Serveth not ^dpardons for the same purpose? Whereto pertaineth ^epraying to saints but to offer unto their bellies? Wherefore serveth ^fconfession, but to sit in thy conscience and to make thee fear and tremble at whatsoever they dream and that thou worship them as Gods: and so forth in all their traditions, ceremonies, and conjurations they serve not the Lord: but their bellies. And of their false expounding the scripture and drawing it contrary unto the example of Christ and the Apostles and holy Prophets unto their damnable covetousness and filthy ambition take an example.

a. Sects or orders.
b. Covetousness and desire of honour is the end of all
false doctrine and that which false prophets seek.
c. Purgatory.
d. Pardons.
e. Praying to saints.
f. Confession.

^a(Matthew 16) When Peter saith to Christ thou art the son of the living God, and Christ answered, thou art Peter and upon this rock I will build my congregation: By the rock interpret they Peter. And then cometh the Pope and will be Peter's successor, whether Peter will or will not, yea whether God will or will not and though all the scripture say nay to any such succession, and saith, lo I am the rock, the foundation and head of Christ's church. ^bNow saith all the scripture that the rock is Christ, the faith and God's word. As Christ saith (Matthew 7) he that heareth my words and doeth thereafter is like a man that buildeth on a rock. For the house that is built on God's words will stand, though heaven should fall. And (John 15) Christ is the vine and we the branches: so is Christ the rock, the stock and foundation whereon we be built. And Paul (1 Corinthians 3) calleth Christ our foundation and all other, whether it be Peter or Paul, he calleth our servants to preach Christ and to build us on high. ^cIf therefore the Pope be Peter's successor, his duty is to preach Christ only and other authority hath he none.[467] And Paul (1 Corinthians 2) marrieth us unto Christ and driveth us from all trust and confidence in man. And (Ephesians 2) saith Paul: Ye are built on the foundation of the Apostles and prophets, that is on the word which they preached, Christ being, saith he, the head cornerstone, in whom every building coupled together groweth up into an holy temple in the Lord, in whom also ye are built together and made an habitation for God in the Spirit. And Peter in the second of his first epistle buildeth us on Christ, contrary unto the Pope which buildeth us on himself. Hell gates shall not prevail against it, that is to say, against the congregation that is built upon Christ's faith and upon God's word. Now were the Pope the rock, hell gates could not prevail against him. For the house could not stand if the rock and the foundation whereon it is built did perish: but the contrary see we in our Popes. For hell gates have prevailed against them many hundred years, and have swallowed them up: if God's word be true and the stories that are written of them: yea or if it be true that we see with our eyes. I will give thee the keys of heaven, saith Christ,

a. An example of false expounding the scriptures.
b. Christ the faith and God's word is the rock and not the Pope.
c. The authority of Peter's successor is but to preach.

and not I give. And (John 20) after the resurrection paid it and gave the keys to them all indifferently. Whatsoever thou bindest on earth, it shall be bound in heaven, and whatsoever thou loosest on earth it shall be loosed in heaven. Of this text maketh the Pope what he will, and expoundeth it contrary to all the scripture, contrary to Christ's practising, and the Apostles, and all the prophets. Now the scripture giveth record to himself and ever expoundeth itself by another open text. ᵃIf the Pope then cannot bring for his exposition the practising of Christ or of the Apostles and prophets or an open text, then is his exposition false doctrine. Christ expoundeth himself (Matthew 18) saying: If thy brother sin against thee, rebuke him betwixt him and thee alone. If he hear thee thou hast won thy brother: but if he hear thee not then take with thee one or two and so forth as it standeth in the text. He concludeth saying to them all whatsoever ye bind in earth it shall be bound in heaven and whatsoever ye loose on earth it shall be loosed in heaven. Where binding is but to rebuke them that sin and loosing to forgive them that repent. And (John 20), Whose sins ye forgive they are forgiven and whose sins ye hold they are holden. And Paul (1 Corinthians 5) bindeth, and (2 Corinthians 2) looseth after the same manner.

ᵇAlso this binding and loosing is one power, and as he bindeth so looseth he: yea and bindeth first ere he can loose. For who can loose that is not bound? Now whatsoever Peter bindeth or his successor (as he will be called and is not, but indeed the very successor of Satan) is not so to be understood, that Peter or the Pope hath power to command a man to be in deadly sin or to be damned or to go into hell saying: be thou in deadly sin, be thou damned, go thou to hell, go thou to Purgatory. For that exposition is contrary to the everlasting testament that God hath made unto us in Christ. He sent his son Christ to loose us from sin and damnation and hell, and that to testify unto the world sent he his disciples (Acts 1). Paul also hath no power to destroy, but to edify (2 Corinthians 10 and 13). How can Christ give his disciples power against himself and against his everlasting testament? Can he send them

a. That exposition is false which is against the open scripture or against the practising of Christ and of his Apostles.
b. Binding and loosing is one power.

to preach salvation and give them power to damn whom they lust? What mercy and profit have we in Christ's death and in his gospel, if the Pope which passeth all men in wickedness hath power to send whom he will to hell, and to damn whom he lusteth? We had then no cause, to call him [a]Jesus, that is to say saviour: but might of right call him destroyer. Wherefore then this binding is to be understood as Christ interpreteth it in the places above rehearsed and as the Apostles practised it [b]and is nothing but to rebuke men of their sins by preaching the law. A man must first sin against God's law ere the Pope can bind him: yea and a man must first sin against God's law ere he need to fear the Pope's curse. [c]For cursing and binding are both one and nothing save to rebuke a man of his sins by God's law. [d]It followeth also that the loosing is of like manner, and is nothing but forgiving of sin to them that repent through preaching of the promises which God hath made in Christ in whom only we have all forgiveness of sins, as Christ interpreteth it and as the Apostles and prophets practised it. So is it a false power that the Pope taketh on him to loose God's laws, as to give a man licence to put away his wife to whom God hath bound him, and to bind them to chastity which God commandeth to marry, that is to wit them that burn and cannot live chaste. It is also a false power to bind that which God's word maketh free, making sin in the creatures which God hath made for man's use.

[e]The Pope which so fast looses and purgeth in Purgatory, cannot with all the low signs and purgations that he hath either loose or purge our appetites and lust and rebellion that is in us against the law of God. And yet the purging of them is the right Purgatory. If he cannot purge them that are alive, wherewith purgeth he them, that are dead? The Apostles knew no other ways to purge, but through preaching God's word which word only is that that purgeth the heart, as thou mayest see (John 15). Ye are pure, saith Christ, through the word. Now the Pope preacheth not to them whom they feign to lie in Purgatory, no more than he doth to

a. What Jesus signifieth.
b. What binding meaneth.
c. What cursing meaneth.
d. What loosing meaneth.
e. ☞

us that are alive. How then purgeth he them? [a]The Pope is kin to Robin Goodfellow[468] which sweepeth the house, washeth the dishes and purgeth all by night. But when day cometh there is nothing found clean.

Some man will say the Pope hindereth them not, they bind themselves. I answer he that bindeth himself to the Pope and have lever have his life and soul ruled by the Pope's will than by the will of God and by the Pope's word than by the word of God, is a fool. And he that had lever be bond than free is not wise. And he that will not abide in the freedom wherein Christ hath set us, is also mad. And he that maketh deadly sin where none is and seeketh causes of hatred between him and God is not in his right wits. Furthermore no man can bind himself further than he hath power over himself. He that is under the power of another man cannot bind himself without licence, as son, daughter, wife, servant and subject. Neither canst thou give God that which is not in thy power. Chastity canst thou not give God further than God lendeth it thee: if thou cannot live chaste thou art bound to marry or to be damned. Last of all for what purpose thou bindest thyself must be seen. If thou do it to obtain thereby that which Christ hath purchased for thee freely, so art thou an infidel[469] and hast no part with Christ and so forth. If thou wilt see more of this matter look in Deuteronomy and there shalt thou find it more largely entreated.

[b]Take another example of their false expounding the scripture. Christ saith (Matthew 23), The scribes and the Pharisees sit on Moses' seat, whatsoever they bid you observe, that observe and do: but after their works do not. Lo say our sophisters or hypocrites, live we never so abominably, yet is our authority never the less. Do as we teach therefore (say they) and not as we do. And yet Christ saith they sit on Moses' seat, that is, as long as they teach Moses, do as they teach. For the law of Moses is the law of God. But for their own traditions and false doctrine Christ rebuked them and disobeyed them and taught other to beware of their leaven. So if our Pharisees sit on Christ's seat and preach him, we ought to hear them: but when they sit on their own seat, then ought we to beware as well of their pestilent doctrine as of their abominable living.

a. The Pope is Robin Goodfellow.
b. Another example.

Likewise where they find mention made of a sword, they turn it unto the Pope's power. The disciples said unto Christ (Luke 22), Lo here be two swords. And Christ answered two is enough. Lo, say they, the Pope hath two swords, the spiritual sword and the temporal sword. And therefore is it lawful for him to fight and make war.

Christ, a little before he went to his passion,[470] asked his disciples saying: when I sent you out without all provision lacked ye anything? And they said nay. And he answered, but now let him that hath a wallet take it with him and he that hath a scrip likewise, and let him that hath never a sword sell his coat and buy one: As who should say, it shall go otherwise now than then. Then ye went forth in faith of my word and my Father's promises and it fed you and made provision for you and was your sword and shield and defender: but now it shall go as thou readest (Zechariah 13), I will smite the shepherd and the sheep of the flock shall be scattered. Now shall my father leave me in the hands of the wicked and ye also shall be forsaken and destitute of faith, and shall trust in yourselves and in your own provision and in your own defence. Christ gave no commandment, but prophesied what should happen. And they because they understood him not, answered here are two swords. And Christ to make an end of such babbling answered two is enough. For if he had commanded every man to buy a sword, how had two been enough? Also if two were enough, and pertained to the Pope only, why are they all commanded to buy every man a sword? By the sword they should be last unto their own defence. And two swords were enough: yea never a one had been enough. For if every one of them had had ten swords they would have fled ere midnight.

In the same chapter of Luke not twelve lines from the foresaid text, the disciples even at the last supper asked who should be the greatest. And Christ rebuked them and said it was an heathenish thing and there should be no such thing among them, but that the greatest should be as the smallest, and that to be great was to do service as Christ did. But this text because it is brighter than the sun, that they can make no sophistry out of it, therefore will they not bear it nor let other know it.

Forasmuch now as thou partly seest the falsehood of our prelates, how all their study is to deceive us and to keep us in darkness, to sit as gods in our consciences and handle us at their pleasure and to lead us whither they lust: therefore, I rede thee, get thee to God's word and thereby try all doctrine and against that receive nothing. Neither any exposition contrary unto the open texts, neither contrary to the general articles of the faith, neither contrary to the living and practising of Christ and of his Apostles. [a]And when they cry fathers fathers,[471] remember that it were the fathers that both blinded and robbed the whole world and brought us into this captivity wherein these enforce to keep us still. Furthermore as they of the old time are fathers to us, so shall these foul monsters be fathers to them that come after us, and the hypocrites that follow us will cry of these and of their doings fathers, fathers, as these cry fathers, fathers of them that are past. And as we feel our fathers, so did they that are past feel their fathers: neither were there in the world any other fathers than such as we both see and feel this many hundred years, as their decrees bear record and the stories and chronicles well testify. If God's word appeared anywhere they agreed all against it. When they had brought that asleep, then strove they one with another about their own traditions and one Pope condemned another's decrees[472] and were sometime two, yea three Popes at once.[473] And one bishop went to law with another and one cursed another for their own fantasies and such things as they had falsely gotten. And the greatest saints are they that most defended the liberties of the church (as they call it) which they falsely got with blinding kings, neither had the world any rest of this many hundred years for reforming of friars and monks and ceasing of schisms that were among our clergy. And as for the holy doctors as Augustine, Jerome, Cyprian, Chrisostom and Bede,[474] will they not hear. If they wrote anything negligently (as they were men) that draw they clean contrary to their meaning and thereof triumph they. Those doctors knew of none authority that one bishop should have above another, neither thought or once dreamed that ever any such should be, or of any such whispering or of pardons, or scouring of Purgatory, as they have feigned.

[b]And when they cry miracles miracles,[475] remember that God hath made an everlasting testament with us in Christ's blood, against which

a. Fathers fathers.
b. Miracles miracles.

we may receive no miracles, no neither the preaching of Paul himself if he came again, by his own teaching to the Galatians,[476] neither yet the preaching of the angels of heaven. [a]Wherefore either they are no miracles but they have feigned them (as in the miracle that Saint Peter hallowed Westminster)[477] or else, if there be miracles that confirm doctrine contrary to God's word, then are they done of the devil (as the maid of Ipswich[478] and of Kent[479]) to prove us whether we will cleave fast to God's word and to deceive them that have no love to the truth of God's word nor lust to walk in his laws.

[b]And forasmuch as they to deceive withal arm themselves against thee with arguments and persuasions of fleshly wisdom, with worldly similitudes, with shadows, with false allegories, with false expositions of the scripture contrary unto the living and practising of Christ and the Apostles, with lies and false miracles, with false names, dumb ceremonies, with disguising of hypocrisy, with the authorities of the fathers and last of all with the violence of the temporal sword: [c]therefore do thou contrarywise arm thyself, to defend thee withal, as Paul teacheth in the last chapter to the Ephesians. Gird on the sword of the spirit which is God's word and take to thee the shield of faith, which is not to believe a tale of Robin Hood or *Gestus Romanorum*[480] or of the chronicles, but to believe God's word that lasteth ever.

And when the Pope with his falsehood challengeth temporal authority above king and emperor: set before thee the five and twentieth chapter of Saint Matthew. Where Christ commandeth Peter to put up his sword. And set before thee Paul (2 Corinthians 10) where he saith the weapons of our war are not carnal things but mighty in God to bring all understanding in captivity under the obedience of Christ, that is, the weapons are God's word and doctrine and not sword of iron and steel, and set before thee the doctrine of Christ and of his Apostles and their practice.

And when the Pope challengeth authority over his fellow bishops and over all the congregation of Christ by succession of Peter, set before thee the first of the Acts where Peter for all his authority put no man

a. The woman of Leinster was a solemn miracle.
b. The armour of the spirituality.
c. The armour of a Christian man is God's word and faith.

in the room of Judas, but all the Apostles chose two indifferently and cast lots desiring God to temper[481] them that the lot might fall on the most ablest. And (Acts 8) that Apostles sent Peter, and in the eleventh call him to reckoning and to give up accompts of that he hath done.

[a]And when the Pope's law commandeth saying: though that the Pope live never so wickedly and draw with him through his evil example innumerable thousands unto hell, yet see that no man presume to rebuke him, for he is head over all and no man over him: set before thee (Galatians 2) where Paul rebuketh Peter openly. And see how both to the Corinthians and also to the Galatians he will have no superior but God's word and he that could teach better by God's word. And because when he rehearsed his preaching and his doings unto the high Apostles, they could improve[482] nothing, therefore will he be equal with the best.

[b]And when the friars say, they do more than their duty when they preach and more than they are [c]bound to: to say our service are we bound (say they) and that is our duty and to preach is more than we are bound to. Set thou before thee how that Christ's blood-shedding hath bound us to love one another with all our might and to do the utmost of our power one to another. And Paul saith (1 Corinthians 9), Woe be unto me if I preach not: yea woe is unto him that hath wherewith to help his neighbour and to make him better and do it not. If they think it more than their duty to preach Christ unto you then they think it more than their duty to pray that ye should come to the knowledge of Christ. And therefore it is no marvel though they take so great labour: yea and so great wages also to keep you still in darkness.

And when they cry furiously hold the heretics unto the wall[483] and if they will not revoke burn them without any more ado, reason not with them, it is an article condemned by the fathers. Set thou before thee the saying of Peter (1 Peter 3), To all that ask you be ready to give an answer of the hope that is in you and that with meekness. The fathers of the Jews and the bishops, which had as great authority over them as ours have over us, condemned Christ and his doctors. If it be enough to say

a. ☞
b. ☞
c. Friars be not bound to preach.

the fathers have condemned it, then are the Jews to be hold excused: yea they are yet in the right way and we in the false. But and if the Jews be bound to look in the scripture and to see whether their fathers have done right or wrong, then are we likewise bound to look in the scripture whether our fathers have done right or wrong, and ought to believe nothing without a reason of the scripture and authority of God's word.

And of this manner defend thyself against all manner wickedness of our spirits,[484] armed always with God's word and with a strong and a steadfast faith thereunto. Without God's word do nothing. And to his word add nothing, neither pull anything therefrom, as Moses everywhere teacheth thee. ᵃServe God in the spirit, and thy neighbour with all outward service. ᵇServe God as he hath appointed thee and not with thy good intent and good zeal. Remember Saul[485] was cast away of God forever for his good intent. God requireth obedience unto his word and abhorreth all good intents and good zeals which are without God's word. For they are nothing else than plain idolatry and worshipping of false gods.[486]

ᶜAnd remember that Christ is the end of all thing. He only is our resting place and he is our peace (Ephesians second chapter). For as there is no salvation in any other name, so is there no peace in any other name. Thou shalt never have rest in thy soul neither shall the worm of conscience ever cease to gnaw thine heart till thou come at Christ: till thou hear the glad tidings, how that God for his sake hath forgiven thee all freely. If thou trust in thy words there is no rest. Thou shalt think, I have not done enough. Have I done it with so great love as I should do? Was I so glad in doing as I would be to receive help at my need, I have left this or that undone and such like. If thou trust in confession, then shalt thou think. Have I told all? Have I told all the circumstances? Did I repent enough? Had I as great sorrow in my repentance for my sins as I had pleasure in doing them? Likewise in our holy pardons and pilgrimage, gets thou no rest. For thou seest that the very gods themselves which sell their pardon so good cheap, or some whiles give them freely

a. How God ought to be served.

b. ☞

c. In Christ is rest of conscience only.

for glory sake, trust not therein themselves. They build colleges and make perpetuities to be prayed for forever and lade the lips of their beadsmen[487] or chaplains with so many masses and diriges[488] and so long service, that I have known of some that have bid the devil take their founders' souls for very impatience and weariness of so painful labour.

^aAs pertaining to good deeds therefore, do the best thou canst and desire God to give strength to do better daily, but in Christ put thy trust and in the pardon and promises that God hath made thee for his sake, and on that rock build thine house[489] and there dwell. For there only shalt thou be sure from all storms and tempests and from all wily assaults of our wicked spirits which study with all falsehood to undermine us. And the God of all mercy give thee grace so to do, unto whom be glory forever. Amen.

A compendious rehearsal of that which goeth before.

I have described unto you the obedience of children, servants, wives and subjects. These four orders are of God's making and the rules thereof are God's word. He that keepeth them shall be blessed: yea is blessed all ready and he that breaketh them shall be cursed. If any person of impatiency or of a stubborn and rebellious mind withdraw himself from any of these, and get him to any other order: let him not think thereby to avoid the vengeance of God in obeying rules and traditions of man's imagination. If thou pollest thine head in the worship of thy father and breakest his commandments, shouldest thou so escape? Or if thou paintest thy master's image on a wall and stakest up a candle before it, shouldest thou therewith make satisfaction, for the breaking of his commandments? Or if thou wearest a blue coat[490] in the worship[491] of the king and breakest his laws, shouldest thou so go quiet? Let a man's wife make herself a sister of the Charterhouse and answer her husband when he biddeth her hold her peace, my brethren keep silence for me, and see whether she shall so escape. And be thou sure God is

a. Do good deeds and trust in Christ.

more jealous over his commandments than man is over his or than any man is over his wife.

Because we be blind, God hath appointed in the scripture how we should serve him and please him. As pertaining unto his own person he is abundantly pleased when we believe his promises and holy testament which he hath made unto us in Christ, and for the mercy which he there showed us, love his commandments. All bodily service must be done to man in God's stead. We must give obedience, honour, gold, tribute, custom, and rent unto whom they belong. Then if thou have ought more to bestow, give unto the poor which are left here in Christ's stead that we show mercy on them. If we keep the commandments of love then are we sure that we fulfil the law in the sight of God and that our blessing shall be everlasting life. Now when we obey patiently and without grudging evil princes that oppress us and persecute us and be kind and merciful to them that are merciless to us and do the worst they can to us and so take all fortune patiently and kiss whatsoever cross God layeth on our backs: then are we sure that we keep the commandment of love.

I declared that God hath taken all vengeance into his own hands, and will avenge all unright himself: either by the powers or officers which are appointed thereto or else, if they be negligent, he will send his curses upon the transgressors and destroy them with his secret judgment. I showed also that whosoever avengeth himself is damned in the deed-doing and falleth into the hands of the temporal sword, because he taketh the office of God upon him and robbeth God of his most high honour in that he will not patiently abide his judgment. I showed you of the authority of princes, how they are in God's stead and how they may not be resisted do they never so evil, they must be reserved unto the wrath of God. Neverthelater if they command to do evil we must then disobey and say we are otherwise commanded of God: but not to rise against them. They will kill us then, sayest thou. Therefore I say is a Christian called, to suffer even the bitter death for his hope's sake and because he will do no evil. I showed also that the kings and rulers be they never so evil are yet a great gift of the goodness of God, and defend us from a thousand things that we see not.

I proved also that all men without exception are under the temporal sword,[492] whatsoever names they give themselves. Because the priest is chosen out of the lay men, to teach this obedience, is that a lawful cause for him to disobey? Because he preacheth that the lay man should not steal, is it therefore lawful for him to steal unpunished? Because thou teachest me that I may not kill, or if I do the king must kill me again, is it therefore lawful for thee to kill and go free? Or whether is it rather meet that thou which art my guide to teach me the right way shouldest walk therein before me? The priests of the old law with their high bishop Aaron and all his successors, though they were anointed by God's commandment and appointed to serve God in his temple and exempt from all offices and ministering of worldly matters, were yet nevertheless under the temporal sword, if they break the laws. Christ saith to Peter, all that take the sword, shall perish by the sword.[493] Here is none exception. Paul saith all souls must obey.[494] Here is none exception. Paul himself is here not except. God saith (Genesis 9), Whosoever sheddeth man's blood, by man shall his blood be shed again. Here is none exception.

Moreover Christ became poor to make other men rich, and bond to make other free. He left also with his disciples the law of love. [a]Now love seeketh not her own profit: but her neighbour's: love seeketh not her own freedom, but becometh surety and bond to make her neighbour free. Damned therefore are the spirituality by all the laws of God, which through falsehood and disguised hypocrisy have sought so great profit, so great riches, so great authority and so great liberties, and have so beggared the lay and so brought them in subjection and bondage and so despise them, that they have set up franchises in all towns and villages for whosoever robbeth, murdereth or slayeth them, and even for traitors unto the king's person also.

I proved also that no king hath power to grant them such liberty: but are as well damned for their giving, as they for their false purchasing. For as God giveth the father power of his children: even so giveth he him a commandment to execute it, and not to suffer them to do wickedly unpunished but unto damnation, as thou mayest see by Eli the high priest[495] etc. And as the master hath authority over his servants: even so hath he a commandment to govern them. And as the husband is

a. The Pope hath a law that none of his spirits may be surety.

head over his wife: even so hath he commandment to rule her appetites and is damned if he suffer her to be an whore and a misliver, or submit himself to her and make her his head. And even in like manner as God maketh the king head over his realm even so giveth he him commandment to execute the laws upon all men indifferently. For the law is God's and not the king's. The king is but a servant to execute the law of God and not to rule after his own imagination.

I showed also that the law and the king are to be feared, as things that were given in fire and in thunder and lightning and terrible signs, I showed the cause why rulers are evil and by what means we might obtain better. I showed also how wholesome those bitter medicines, evil princes, are to Christian men.

I declared how they which God hath made governors in the world ought to rule if they be Christian. They ought to remember that they are heads and arms, to defend the body to minister peace health and wealth and even to save the body, and that they have received their offices of God to minister and to do service unto their brethren. King, subject, master, servant, are names in the world: but not in Christ. In Christ we are all one[496] and even brethren. No man is his own but we are all Christ's servants bought[497] with Christ's blood. Therefore ought no man to seek himself or his own profit: but Christ and his will. In Christ no man ruleth as a king his subjects, or a master his servants: but serveth as one hand doth to another and as the hands do unto the feet and the feet to the hands, as thou seest (1 Corinthians 13). We also serve not as servants unto masters: but as they which are bought with Christ's blood serve Christ himself. We be here all servants unto Christ. For whatsoever we do unto another in Christ's name that do we unto Christ, and the reward of that shall we receive of Christ.[498] The king counteth his commons of Christ himself and therefore doth them service willingly seeking no more of them than is sufficient to maintain peace and unity and to defend the realm. And they obey again willingly and lovingly as unto Christ. And of Christ every man seeketh his reward.

I warned the judges that they take not an example how to minister their offices, of our spirituality, which are bought and sold to do the will of Satan: but of the scripture whence they have their authority. Let that which is secret abide secret till God open it, which is the judge of secrets.

For it is more than a cruel thing to break up into a man's heart and to compel him to put either soul or body in jeopardy or to shame himself. If Peter, that great pillar, for fear of death forsook his master,[499] ought we not to spare weak consciences?

I declared how the King ought to rid his realm from the wily tyranny of the hypocrites and to bring the hypocrites under his laws: yea and how he ought to be learned and to hear and to look upon the causes himself which he will punish and not to believe the hypocrites and to give them his sword to kill whom they will.

The King ought to count what he hath spent in the Pope's quarrel[500] since he was King. The first voyage cost upon fourteen hundred thousand pounds. Reckon since what hath been spent by sea and land between us and French men and Scots[501] and then in triumphs and in embassies and what hath been sent out of the realm secretly and all to maintain our holy father, and I doubt not but that will surmount the sum of forty or fifty hundred thousand pounds. For we had no cause to spend one penny but for our holy father. The King therefore ought to make them pay this money every farthing, and fetch it out of their mitres, crosses, shrines and all manner treasure of the church, and pay it to his commons again: not that only which the Cardinal and his bishops compelled the commons to lend, and made them swear with such an example of tyranny as was never before thought on: but also all that he hath gathered of them. Or else by the consent of the commons to keep it in store for the defence of the realm. Yea the King ought to look in the chronicles what the popes have done to kings in time past and make them restore it also, and ought to take away from them their lands which they have gotten with their false prayers and restore it unto the right heirs again or with consent and advisement turn them unto the maintaining of the poor and bringing up of youth virtuously and to maintain necessary officers and ministers for to defend the common with.

If he will not do it: then ought the commons to take patience and to take it for God's scourge and to think that God hath blinded the king for their sins' sake and commit their cause to God: And then shall God make a scourge for them and drive them out of his temple after his wonderful judgment.

On the other side I have also uttered the wickedness of the spirituality, the falsehood of the bishops and the juggling of the Pope, and how they have disguised themselves, borrowing some of their pomp of the Jews and some the gentiles, and have with subtle wiles turned the obedience that should be given to God's ordinance unto themselves. And how they have put out God's testament and God's truth and set up their own traditions and lies, in which they have taught the people to believe and thereby sit in their consciences as God, and have by that means robbed the world of lands and goods, of peace and unity, and of all temporal authority, and have brought the people into the ignorance of God and have heaped the wrath of God upon all realms and namely upon the kings. Whom they have robbed (I speak not of worldly things only) but even of their very natural wits. They make them believe that they are most Christian, when they live most abominably and will suffer no man in their realms that believeth on Christ, and that they are defenders of the faith, when they burn the gospel and promises of God, out of which all faith springeth.

I showed how they have ministered Christ, king and emperor out of their rooms, and how they have made them a several kingdom which they got at the first in deceiving of princes, and now pervert the whole scripture to prove that they have such authority of God. And lest the lay men should see how falsely they allege the places of the scripture, is the greatest cause of this persecution.

ᵃThey have feigned confession for the same purpose to establish their kingdom with all. All secrets know they thereby. The bishop knoweth the confession of whom he lusteth⁵⁰² throughout all his diocese. Yea and his chancellor commandeth the ghostly father to deliver it written. The Pope, his cardinals and bishops know the confession of the Emperor, kings and of all lords. And by confession they know all their captives. If any believe in Christ, by confession they know him. Shrive thyself where thou wilt, whether at Sion,⁵⁰³ Charterhouse, or at the Observants, thy confession is known well enough. And thou, if thou believe in Christ, art waited upon. Wonderful are the things that thereby are wrought. The wife is feared and compelled to utter not her own only but also the secrets of her husband and the servant the secrets of his master. Besides that through confession they quench the faith of all the promises of

a. Confession.

God and take away the effect and virtue of all the sacraments of Christ.

They have also corrupted the saints' lives with lies and feigned miracles and have put many things out of the sentence or great curse, as raising of rent and fines and hiring men out of their houses, and whatsoever wickedness they themselves do and have put a great part of the stories and chronicles out of the way lest their falsehood should be seen. For there is no mischief or disorder, whether it be in the temporal regiment or else in the spiritual whereof they are not the chief causes and even the very fountain and springs and as we say, the well head, so that it is impossible to preach against any mischief except thou begin at them or to set any reformation in the world except thou reform them first. Now are they indurate[504] and tough as Pharaoh[505] and will not bow unto any right way or order. And therefore persecute they God's word and the preachers thereof, and on the other side lie await unto all princes and stir up all mischief in the world and send them to war and occupy their minds therewith or with other voluptuousness, lest they should have leisure to hear the word of God and to set an order in their realms.

By them is all things ministered and by them are all kings ruled: yea in every king's conscience sit they ere he be king, and persuade every king what they lust, and make them both to believe what they will and to do what they will. Neither can any king or any realm have rest for the business. Behold King Henry the Fifth[506] whom they sent out for such a purpose as they sent out our King that now is.[507] See how the realm is inhabited. Ask where the goodly towns and their walls and the people that was wont to be in them are become, and where the blood royal of the realm is become also. Turn thine eyes whither thou wilt and thou shalt see nothing prosperous but their subtle polling. With that it is flowing water: yea and I trust[508] it will be shortly a full sea.

In all their doings though they pretend outwardly the honour of God or a commonwealth, their intent and secret counsel is only to bring all under their power and to take out of the way whosoever letteth[509] them or is too mighty for them. As when they send the princes to Jerusalem to conquer the holy land and to fight against the Turks.[510] Whatsoever they pretend outwardly their secret intent is, while the princes there conquer them more bishoprics, to conquer their lands in the mean season with their false hypocrisy and to bring all under them, which thou mayest easily perceive by that they will not let us know the faith of Christ. And when they are once on high, then are they tyrants above all tyrants, whether they be Turks or Saracens. How minister they proving of testaments? How causes of wedlock? Or if any man die intestate? If a poor man die and leave his wife and half a dozen young children and but one cow to find them, that will they have for a mortuary merciless: let come of wife and children what will. Yea let anything be done against their pleasure and they will interdict the whole realm, sparing no person.

Read the chronicles of England (out of which yet they have put a great part of their wickedness) and thou shalt find them always both rebellious and disobedient to the kings and also churlish and unthankful, so that, when all the realm gave the king somewhat to maintain him in his right, they would not give a mite. Consider the story of King John, where I doubt not but they have put the best and fairest for themselves and the worst of King John, for I suppose they make the chronicles themselves. Compare the doings there of holy church (as they ever call it) unto the learning of Christ and of his Apostles. Did not the legate of Rome[511] assoil[512] all the lords of the realm of their due obedience which they ought to the king by the ordinance of God? Would he not have cursed the king with his solemn pomp, because he would have done that office which God commandeth every king to do and wherefore God hath put the sword in every king's hand? That is to wit, because King John would have punished a wicked clerk[513] that had coined false money.[514] The lay men that had not done half so great faults must die, but the clerk must go scapefree.[515] Sent not the Pope also unto the King of France remission of his sins to go and conquer King John's realm?[516] So now remission of sins cometh not by faith in the testament that God hath made in Christ's blood: but by fighting and murdering for the Pope's pleasure. Last of all was not King John fain to deliver his crown unto the legate and to yield up his realm unto the Pope, wherefore we pay Peterpence?[517] They might be called the polling pence of false prophets well enough. They care not by what mischief they come by their purpose. War and conquering of lands is their harvest. The wickeder the people are the more they have the hypocrites in reverence, the more they fear them and the more they believe in them. And they that conquer other men's lands, when they die, make them their heirs, to be prayed for forever. Let there come one conquest more in the realm, and thou shalt see them get yet as much more as they have (if they can keep down God's word that their juggling come not to light) yea thou shalt see them take the realm whole into their hands and crown one of themselves king thereof. And verily I see no other likelihood, but that the land shall be shortly conquered. The stars of the scripture[518] promise us none other fortune, inasmuch as we deny Christ with the wicked Jews[519] and will not have him reign over us: but will be still children of darkness under Antichrist and Antichrist's possession, burning the gospel of Christ[520] and defending a faith that may not stand with his holy testament.

If any man shed blood in the church, it shall be interdicted,[521] till he have paid for the hallowing. If he be not able the parish must pay or else shall it stand always interdicted. They will be avenged on them[522] that never offended. Full well prophesied of them Paul in the second epistle to Timothy 3. Some man will say, wouldest thou that men should fight in the church unpunished? Nay but let the king ordain a punishment for them, as he doth for them that fight in his palace, and let not all the parish be troubled for one's fault. And as for their hallowing is the juggling[523] of Antichrist. A Christian man is the temple of God and of the Holy Ghost, and hallowed in Christ's blood. A Christian man is holy in himself by reason of the Spirit that dwelleth in him and the place wherein he is, is holy by reason of him, whether he be in the field or town. A Christian husband sanctifieth an unchristian wife and a Christian wife an unchristian husband (as concerning the use of matrimony) saith Paul to the Corinthians.[524] If now while we seek to be hallowed in Christ, we are found unholy and must be hallowed by the ground or place or walls, then died Christ in vain. Howbeit Antichrist must have wherewith to sit in men's consciences and to make them fear where is no fear and to rob them of their faith and to make them trust in that cannot help them, and to seek holiness of that which is not holy in itself.

After that the old King of France was brought down out of Italy, mark what pageants have been played and what are yet aplaying to separate us from the Emperor (lest by the help or aid of us he should be able to recover his right of the Pope) and to couple us to the Frenchmen whose might the Pope ever abuseth to keep the Emperor from Italy.[525] What prevaileth it for any king to marry his daughter or his son, or to make any peace or good ordinance for the wealth of his realm? For it shall no longer last than it is profitable to them. Their treason is so secret that the world cannot perceive it. They dissimule[526] those things which they are only cause of and simule[527] discord among themselves when they are most agreed. One shall hold this and another shall dispute the contrary: But the conclusion shall be that most maintaineth their falsehood, though God's word be never so contrary. What have they wrought in our days, yea and what work they yet, to the perpetual dishonour of the king and rebuke of the realm and shame of all the nation in whatsoever realms they go?

I uttered unto you partly the malicious blindness of the Bishop of Rochester, his juggling, his conveying,[528] his foxy wiliness, his Bo Peep,[529] his wresting, renting[530] and shameful abusing of the scripture, his oratory and alleging of heretics and how he would make the Apostles authors of blind ceremonies without signification contrary to their own doctrine, and have set him for an example to judge all other by. Whatsoever thou art that readest this, I exhort thee in Christ, to compare his sermon and that which I have written and the scripture together and judge. There shalt thou find of our holy father's authority, and what it is to be great and how to know the greatest.

Then followeth the cause why laymen cannot rule temporal offices which is the falsehood of the bishops. There shalt thou find of miracles and ceremonies without signification, of false anointing and lying signs and false names and how the spirituality are disguised in falsehood, and how they roll the people in darkness and do all things in the Latin tongue, and of their petty pillage. Their polling is like a soking[531] consumption[532] wherein a man complaineth of feebleness and of faintness and wotteth not whence his disease cometh: it is like a pock that fretteth inward[533] and consumeth the very marrow of the bones.

There seest thou the cause why it is impossible for kings to come to the knowledge of the truth. For the spirits[534] lay await for them and serve their appetites at all points and through confession buy and sell and betray both them, and all their true friends, and lay baits for them and never leave them till they have blinded them with their sophistry and have brought them into their nets. And then when the king is captive they compel all the rest with violence of his sword. For if any man will not obey them, be it right or wrong, they cite him, suspend him and curse or excommunicate him. If he then obey not they deliver him to Pilate, that is to say, unto the temporal officers to destroy him. Last of all there findest thou the very cause of all persecution, which is the preaching against hypocrisy.

Then come we to the sacraments, where thou seest that the work of the sacrament saveth not, but the faith in the promise which the sacrament signifieth justifieth us only. There hast thou that a priest is but a servant to teach only and whatsoever he taketh upon him more than to preach and to minister the sacraments of Christ (which is also preaching) is falsehood.

Then cometh how they juggle through dumb ceremonies and how they make merchandise with feigned words, penance, *a pena et a culpa*,[535] satisfaction, attrition, character, Purgatory pickpurse and how through confession they make the sacraments and all the promise of none effect or value. There seest thou that absolving is but preaching the promises and cursing or excommunicating preaching the law, and of their power, and of their keys, of false miracles and of praying to saints. There seest thou that ceremonies did not the miracles but faith: even as it was not Moses' rod[536] that did the miracles but Moses' faith in the promise of God. Thou seest also that to have a faith where God hath not a promise is idolatry. And there also seest thou how the Pope exalteth himself above God and commandeth him to obey his tyranny. Last of all thou hast there that no man ought to preach but he that is called.

Then followeth the belly brotherhood of monks and friars. For Christ hath deserved nought with them. For his sake gettest thou no favour. Thou must offer unto their bellies and then they pray bitterly for thee. There seest thou that Christ is the only cause: yea and all the cause why God doeth ought for us and heareth our complaint. And there hast thou doctrine how to know and to be sure that thou art elect and hast God's spirit in thee. And hast there learning to try the doctrine of our spirits.

Then follow the four senses of the scripture of which three are no sense and the fourth that is to wit the literal sense which is the very sense hath the Pope taken to himself. It may have no other meaning than as it pleaseth his fatherhood. We must abide his interpretation. And as his bells tink,[537] so must we think, though it be impossible to gather any such meaning of the scripture. Then hast thou the very use of allegories and how they are nothing but examples borrowed of the scripture to express a text or an open conclusion of the scripture and as it were to paint it before thine eyes, that thou mayest feel the meaning and the power of the scripture in thine heart. Then cometh the use of worldly similitudes, and how they are false prophets which bring a worldly similitude for any other purpose, save to express more plainly that which is contained in an open text. And so are they also which draw the scripture contrary to the open places and contrary to the example living and practising of Christ, the Apostles and of the holy Prophets. And then finally hast thou of our holy father's power and of his keys and of his binding and excommunicating and of his cursing and blessing with examples of everything.

The table of the book.

At Marlborow in the land of Hesse The second day of October.
Anno. M. CCCCC. xxviij, by me Hans Luft.

NOTES

Quotations from the New Testament are from the most accessible version of Tyndale, the modern-spelling edition of his revised New Testament of 1534 (*Tyndale's New Testament*, Yale University Press, 1989). By the time that revision was made, six years after the *Obedience* was written, Tyndale had learned Hebrew, and this had led to his greater understanding of the influence of the Old Testament on the Greek of the New. It is indicated below where a reading in his first, 1526, New Testament (which he seems often to quote here from memory) differs significantly from his revision. Quotations from the Old Testament as far as the end of 2 Chronicles are from the modern-spelling edition (*Tyndale's Old Testament*, Yale University Press, 1992). Tyndale gives chapter references. Verses are numbered as they were for the first time in English Bibles in the Geneva Bible of 1560, and in all thereafter. The source of references to the second half of the Old Testament is shown as they occur.

W.T. unto the reader

1. New Testament authority for the word is given, for example, in 2 Corinthians 2:9, Ephesians 6:5–7, Titus 2:9, Philemon 21, Hebrews 13:17, 1 Peter 1:2 and 14, and 1 Peter 2:13.
2. i.e. cunning contrivances of all deceivers.
3. A branch of the Gloucestershire Tyndales took the name Hutchins as well: see *WTB*, pp. 9 and 392. The author of the *Obedience* is not hiding.
4. This opening blessing is paralleled at an early point in almost every one of the New Testament epistles. 2 Peter 1:2 has 'Grace with you, and peace be multiplied in the knowledge of God and of Jesus our Lord' ('. . . of the saviour Jesus Christ', 1526). Tyndale used similar words to begin *Mammon* and *Answer*.
5. Colossians 1:10.
6. Romans 10:13 and *passim*.
7. 1 Timothy 1:5.

8. The two 'Lollard' manuscript translations from the Latin Bible into English made in the 1580s under the inspiration of John Wyclif resulted in the ban proclaimed by Archbishop Arundel in the 'Constitutions of Oxford', 1408. By it, translating, owning, or reading a Bible in English was forbidden, and severely punishable – including by being burned alive, under a statute, *De Hæretico Comburendo*, of Henry IV, 1401 (*A&M*, III, 239–40). John Bale as a boy of eleven watched the burning of a young man in Norwich for possessing the Lord's Prayer in English (*A treatise made by Johan Lambert*, 1548, 3ᵛ). Foxe records, among much else that is relevant, seven Lollards burned at Coventry in 1519 for teaching their children the Lord's Prayer in English: *A&M*, IV, 557. (Tyndale, in the Prologue to Jonah, declares that the rejection of Wyclif had dire political effects; *TOT*, 634–5). His abandoned 1525 and completed 1526 New Testaments have to be put into this context.

9. 1 Thessalonians 2:2. That passage continues 'to speak unto you the gospel of God'. As here, boldness and the word of God are linked.

10. The comforting (i.e. refreshing) of hearts is found in Genesis 18:5, Judges 19:5 and 8; but more significantly from the Greek παρακαλεω (*parakaleo*), to call alongside, help, at Ephesians 6:22, Colossians 4:8, and 2 Thessalonians 2:17, each in a context of praying for strength for the communal readers of an epistle, as Tyndale does here.

11. A Tyndale word in translating both the Old and New Testaments: e.g. Genesis 41:29, Luke 1:1 and *passim*. Tyndale uses it to refer forwards grammatically, rather than, more familiarly, backwards.

12. Philippians 1:28 – the King James Version adds 'evident' to Tyndale's 'token'; the double phrase was already known (*OED*, evident, A.1.b).

13. For the life in Christ leading to persecution, see 2 Timothy 3:12.

14. *word of God*: frequent in the New Testament, e.g. Acts 4:31.

15. Echoing and richly developing John 1:10, 'the world knew him not'.

16. A rhetorical flourish. But see the murder of Abel at Genesis 4:5–8; the death of Christ himself at Matthew 26:59–60, 27:23; and the death of Stephen at Acts 7:54.

17. The start of this long sentence may echo Luke 8:14, Jesus's amplification of the defeat of 'the word' in the Parable of the Sower.

18. Another word Tyndale likes: he had used 'wiles' at Ephesians 6:11, and will use 'wilily' at Joshua 9:4.

19. Words and phrases together in this paragraph are strongly biblical: 'authority', Matthew 21:23 and *passim*; 'bear a rule', 1 Kings 9:23; 'persecuteth', Acts 22:4 and *passim*; 'curseth', Romans 12:14 and *passim*; 'belief . . . damned . . .', Romans 13:2; 'doctrine', Romans 16:17 and *passim*; 'deceive', Matthew 24:4, 5, and *passim*; 'blind powers', see Matthew 15:14; 23:16, 24; 23:26; there are others. These rise to break the surface, as it were, in the quotation from John 15:19. This not only clinches Tyndale's point about the hostility of 'the world', but sets it in the context of John's chapter, which is about union in the love of Christ, of the Father, and of each other. Tyndale omits a short phrase from the passage.

20. i.e. strength alongside. John 14:16 (see n. 10 above).

21. Luke 9:43.

22. Titus 2:10.

23. Tyndale is quoting the refrain in Psalm 107, verses 8, 15, 21 and 31. See n. 91 below.

24. As Mark 6:2, 'virtues that are wrought'.

25. Hebrews 8:3.

26. John 9:32, where the phrase is used of the power of God doing a wonderful deed beyond reason, even on the Sabbath.

27. Again, the run of scripture words climaxes in a direct quotation which focuses the thought: the words in parenthesis are Tyndale's.

28. Matthew 22:18.

29. Genesis 4.

30. A commonplace, usual in the New Testament as 'the last days', e.g. Acts 2:17.

31. *elders . . . Jews*: Tyndale first (1525, 1526) translated the Greek πρεσβυτερος (*presbuteros*), at Matthew 15:2 and thereafter, as 'seniors': he soon, as here, changed to 'elders'. The Vulgate has 'seniorum', and Wyclif 'eldere men'. πρεσβυτερος is the comparative of πρεσβυς (*presbus*), an old man, to make the sense of 'an elder'.

32. John 19:12.

33. Luke 23:12.

34. 1 Corinthians 1:20. The name of Mr Worldly Wiseman, like other names in Bunyan's *Pilgrim's Progress* (1678), is taken directly from the New Testament.

35. To make afraid.

36. John 9:22.

37. As recorded in John 2, Jesus drove out the merchants and money-men who were polluting the holy place. Tyndale's point is that the worldly powers ('hypocrites', as they are supposed to be of God's church) reverse the significance, excommunicating the true believers in the Word.

38. John 19:12.

39. Matthew 26:55.

40. Acts 3:14.

41. Tyndale's coinage (not recorded in *OED*).

42. 2 John 9.

43. Two kinds of battle-axe.

44. Helped.

45. Genesis 22:16, and Hebrews 6:13–18; . . . *to David*, 2 Samuel 7, and see Isaiah 9:7; for these two figures as central to biblical argument, see Romans 4:3–7; *prophets*, see Amos 9:11–15.

46. Romans 15:4.

47. Exodus 5.

48. Numbers 13:31–33.

49. Romans 8:31.

50. Exodus 1, 2.

51. See n. 8 above.

52. Exodus 14:19–22.

53. 1 Samuel 17:51.

54. Hebrews 11:29.

55. *Remember . . . nought*: the passage is a free rendering of Deuteronomy 7:17–24.

56. Deuteronomy 29:12–13.

57. Hebrews 11, *passim*. 'Promises' is a key word in Tyndale's theology.

58. *If we ask . . . knock . . . find*: Tyndale's slightly free rendering of Matthew 7:7.

59. John 7:37–38; 'lust' does not have its modern sexual sense. Like the German *Lust*, it means 'wanting', in any direction.

60. *Christ . . . end*: Matthew 28:20.

61. Luke 12:32. The phrase *little flock*, used a dozen times by Tyndale, was common among the reformers for the congregations of believers, often persecuted. A lyrical passage in *Answer* beginning 'But little flock . . .' (108–9) makes 'little flock' the true believing man or woman, living in Christ.

62. Romans 8:31.

63. *Mark . . . neighbour*. The paragraph has obvious reference to the book of Jonah. That minor prophet especially interested the reformers, as demonstrating their vocation. Luther had translated it separately in 1526. Probably in 1531, Tyndale printed his translation of this prophecy, with a preface longer than the book itself. It is striking that he expects his readers to follow the reference. See *TOT*, 628–43.

64. Hebrews 12:6. The following sentences are not scriptural, except as they are a free elaboration of God's dealing with Christ: so *exalteth*, Acts 5:31; *damneth . . . hell* has reference to Ephesians 4:9–10, and the tradition of Christ's Harrowing of Hell, as in the Creed, 'he descended into Hell'.

65. Ephesians 5:9.

66. Luke 20:13–15.

67. Genesis 37:9, and chapters 39–41.

68. Exodus 3:8 and in the Pentateuch *passim*.

69. A free rendering of Deuteronomy 8:2–3; *latter end*, Ruth 3:10 and 2 Samuel 2:26.

70. 1 Samuel 16:1, 11–13; chapters 18–23.

71. 2 Peter 1:10.

72. 1 John 1:8.

73. *die with Christ . . . live with him . . . suffer . . . reign*: a slightly free rendering of 2 Timothy 2:11–12.

74. Deuteronomy 1:30.

75. John 10:11.

76. These sayings of Christ are selected from Matthew 10:16–25.

77. Luke 14:33.

78. Acts 14:22, Romans 8:35.

79. Sense (surviving in 'have the wit to . . .').

80. Matthew 5:10.

81. i.e. giving strength.

82. Matthew 20:25.

83. James 3:10.

84. Matthew 55:48.

85. Colossians 1:12.

86. 2 Corinthians 9:15.

87. 2 Corinthians 1:22.

88. John 18:37.

89. i.e. pledge.

90. Hebrews 12:7–8.

91. Misprint for Psalm 50 (v. 15). Tyndale was martyred before he reached the Psalms in his translation of the Old Testament. He is probably translating from the Greek of the Septuagint. The following quotation from 'Psalm 46' is from Psalm 33:18–19; 'Psalm 47' is Psalm 34:8–10, and, at the end of the paragraph, 'Psalm 71' is Psalm 55:22. Why the numbering is wrong at this point is not known.

92. 1 Peter 5:7.

93. 1 Corinthians 13:52.

94. 1 Thessalonians 5:2.

95. Surround.

96. 1 Thessalonians 5:3.

97. Hebrews 3:8, 15 and in the Old Testament *passim*.

98. Five broad-brush references. *Noah*: Genesis 5:29 and chapters 6–9; *Lot*: Genesis 19; *Moses . . . Egyptians*: Exodus 7; *images . . . prophets*: 1 Kings 18; *his own Son*, Luke 20:9–15.

99. A monk who, about AD 550, recorded 'simplistically and with very dubious factual accuracy' what happened in the power vacuum after the Romans had left and the Anglo-Saxons 'turned on the native population and devastated the towns and countryside' (both quotations from Christopher Daniell, *A Traveller's History of England* (1991), 22). Gildas's book *De excidio et conquestu Britonum* is the only surviving account of Britain in the fourth century. This 'Destruction and conquest of the British' is a warning of what apocalyptic divine retribution might again happen if the rulers and churchmen did not mend their ways. Tyndale could have known the book as it was incorporated into Bede's *Ecclesiastical History*, written in 731.

100. Adulterous.

101. Acts 9 and 22; 26:4–5; Philippians 3:5–6. His thirteen epistles in the New Testament.

102. Matthew 26:69–75; Mark 14:66–72; Luke 22:54–62.

103. *Delivered* to, or *secretly* from, the church authorities.

104. The spiritual, that is, all clergy.

105. John 1:17, referring to Exodus 20 and in the Pentateuch *passim*.

106. Romans 5:14.

107. The word occurs four times in the New Testament, in 1 John 2:18 and 22, and 4:3; and in 2 John 7. For parallel New Testament teaching about the antagonist to the gospel, see Matthew 24:24, Mark 13, 2 Thessalonians 2, 2 Timothy 3, 2 Peter 2:1–3, and Revelation 13. Expectation of the Antichrist was powerful in the Middle Ages. Luther first identified the Pope with Antichrist, followed in English by both John Frith and Tyndale in various works. *Mammon* virtually opens with an exposition of Antichrist (41–4).

108. Before Christ.

109. Tyndale will vividly translate the Hebrew word at Deuteronomy 6:7 in his Pentateuch of 1530, though the older versions, including the Latin Vulgate and the Greek Septuagint, had had 'tell'. The King James Version gave 'teach', with 'whet or sharpen' in the margin. Luther had *schaerfen*, 'sharpen'. Tyndale's word implies vigour.

110. 1 Peter 3:15.

111. Know.

112. Perhaps.

113. Magpie and parrot, both famous for chatter.

114. Confirmed by the contemporary Archbishop of Canterbury, William Warham, as quoted in J. F. Mozley, *William Tyndale* (1937), 33.

115. John 5:39.

116. Matthew 7:22–23.

117. 1 John 2:28.

118. Matthew 7:16, where Tyndale in 1526, and all following versions to the King James Version (1611), have 'fruits'.

119. Separate.

120. The tenth part of stock or produce given to the church.

121. Particular kind.

122. Taxes.

123. Offering of money made at mass.

124. Payment for a set of thirty masses.

125. Dirge money, paid for singing the dirge, the Office of the Dead.

126. List of persons to be specially prayed for.

127. Acts 1:15–17, 2:14–36, 3:12–26, and *passim*.

128. Jerome unified the Latin versions of the Bible from 382 with his own translation, which became the Vulgate.

129. Undeveloped.

130. Because it is not so syntactically tight as Latin – in not placing the verb at the end, for example.

131. Hebrew word-order matches English.

132. Go round.

133. Not identified. Athelstan (reigned AD 925–39) followed the example of his grandfather Alfred (reigned AD 871–99) in his enthusiasm for learning and the education of the nation. William of Malmesbury's account in his *Gesta regum anglorum* (*c.* 1120) of Athelstan, who had been a benefactor of Malmesbury Abbey, might support Tyndale. William was librarian of that Abbey, a dozen miles from Tyndale's birthplace.

134. Duns Scotus, the Scottish Franciscan philosopher who taught at Oxford at the beginning of the fourteenth century. Tyndale's implied point is the multiplicity of his followers' arguments as opposed to the simplicity of God (see *Mammon*, 108 and *Answer*, 48). His followers were opposed to Aquinas.

135. Thomas Aquinas (1225–74), the Dominican whose *Summa Theologica* became the basis of church doctrine but was scorned by Tyndale because it used Aristotle to expound the gospel. (See *Mammon*, 46, 108.)

136. Franciscan 'seraphic doctor', contemporary with, and less Aristotelian than, Aquinas.

137. Thirteenth-century Franciscan 'irrefragible doctor' whose lectures on theology were not on the Bible but on Peter Lombard's *Sentences* (1215), the standard textbook of Catholic theology.

138. Spanish Dominican, whose *Summa de casibus poenitentia* (*c.* 1225) was much consulted in the development of the penitential system.

139. Nicolas de Lyra (*c.* 1270–1349), a rabbi who converted to Christianity and became a Franciscan. His 'postils', written between 1293 and 1330, were the first biblical commentaries to be printed and were influential in late medieval scholarship.

140. Probably Brigitta, the fourteenth-century Swedish author of eight popular books of revelations; see Duffy, plates 61–2.

141. Nicholas de Orbellis, a fifteenth-century Franciscan theologian and follower of Duns Scotus.

142. Robert Holcot, Oxford Dominican, wrote on Lombard's *Sentences*, 1497.

143. Nicholas Gorranus, commentator on Gospels and Epistles, 1473.

144. Fifteenth-century Franciscan follower of Duns Scotus.

145. Prolific twelfth-century abbot.

146. Fifteenth-century mathematician.

147. Learned physician, astrologer and alchemist, early sixteenth century.

148. Thirteenth-century Oxford Franciscan, accused of heresy in Paris. Tyndale's point in this list is that few of these fashionable figures used the scriptures.

149. Echoing 1 Corinthians 12:4.

150. Measuring-rod.

151. Origen (*c.* 185–254) was the most prolific, significant and controversial of the early theologians and biblical critics. Most of his work is either lost or known only in translation. Augustine: see prologue n. 5, below.

152. *philautia*: probably Tyndale's borrowing from Erasmus's *Praise of Folly* (1509), where it also mocks scholastic vocabulary, coined from the Greek adjective φιλαυτος (*philautos*), loving oneself, to stand in the place of φιλοσοφια (*philosophia*), the love of wisdom.

153. Aristotle, *De coelo*, 283b6.

154. *first . . . be*: Aristotle, *De generatione et corruptione*, 317b3 *et sqq.*

155. A general summary of Aristotle's teaching.

156. Genesis 1:1, 2.

157. Romans 8:28–30.

158. 1 Corinthians 1:51–7.

159. Romans 14:12.

160. *Nichomachean Ethics*, ed. Bekker, II.1.4 (1103b1).

161. Romans 3:20–24; 7:7–8.

162. As n. 155, above.

163. *Nichomachean Ethics*, ed. Bekker, I.4.2–3 (1095a20) and I.13.1 (1102a4).

164. 1 Corinthians 1:30.

165. Galatians 5:22.

166. Romans 5:3–6.

167. John 7:37.

168. Echoing Matthew 7:7.

169. Apparently Tyndale's coinage for original sin, though possibly a translation of Luther.

170. The sentence is a compression of the theology of Paul. Here and elsewhere, Tyndale's emphasis on a feeling response to the work of God in salvation is striking.

171. Parables.

172. Train, nurture, bring up; the word is related to 'nuzzle', associated with 'nurse' (*vb.*).

173. A sure foundation.

174. Tyndale was not alone in scorning the metaphysical disputes of his time which were splitting European universities. Erasmus, in chapter 53 of *The Praise of Folly* (1509), had also mocked the Scholastic theologians: but that was in Latin. Tyndale was the first in English. He is more hard-hitting, and his point is always their barrenness and the foolish passions roused contrasted with the life-giving scripture. See *WTB*, 30.

175. The realist *via antiqua* belonged to Duns Scotus; the nominalist *via moderna* came from Ockham. Both had been Oxford philosophers.

176. Things predicated; Aristotle's 'categories'.

177. Predicated to form a class. Disputes over the term split medieval philosophers into Realists, Nominalists or Conceptualists, with the most profound disagreements.

178. In logic, implying precise intention.

179. Barbarous terms of the schoolmen for *quidditas*, the 'what-ness' of a thing, its real nature or essence, and *haecceitas*, 'just-this-ness', individuality, of which its *quidditas* consists.

180. Predicated of two or more.

181. A farrago of some of the barbarous terms used by the quibbling schoolmen. The barely discernible sense seems to be, roughly, whether something imaginary can be said to not-exist, and whether being is ambiguous and not-created, and generates itself. Tyndale intends the reader to give up.

182. A region supposed to be on the fringe of hell where the just who died before Christ (*patrum*, of the fathers, patriarchs) await his coming.

183. Dominican and Franciscan. Tyndale throughout his books mocks monks and friars for their corruption and false theology of works before faith, and their failure to teach and preach. In *Answer* (107–8), in a scornful passage about fashions in clothing, he refers to friars 'white, black, grey and pied' supposedly serving God by their external appearance. Milton echoes Tyndale's tone in *Paradise Lost*, III, 474–5: '... Friars/White, Black and Grey, with all their trumpery'.

184. Echoing Galatians 3:21–22.

185. Psalm 119:2. Tyndale is now numbering according to the Vulgate, which he translates here.

186. Stories of this legendary hero were probably common before the first written reference to him, in *Piers Plowman* in the late 1370s; the many ballads about him probably date from the fifteenth century. See Stephen Knight, *Robin Hood: A Complete Study of the English Outlaw* (Oxford, 1994), chapter 3.

187. A longwinded but colourful verse romance written about 1300, with many fabulous events and passions.

188. Roman legendary hero of great strength. One of the Nine Worthies of ancient and medieval lore.

189. Trojan hero, leader of the forces besieging Troy, a central figure in Homer's *Iliad*. His legendary fame as another Worthy did not depend on a knowledge of Homer.

190. A prince of Troy, of minor significance in Homer. Chaucer's *Troilus and Criseyde* (*c.* 1385) elaborates the later legends about their tragic love affair.

191. The preface to Erasmus's 1516 edition of the New Testament in Greek and Latin, the *Novum instrumentum*, and his later, widely circulated, gospel annotations.

The prologue unto the book

1. Spiritual friars or monks.

2. Understanding scripture as it was first written.

3. Jeremiah 44:18, 20–28, paraphrased.

4. For example, Acts 17:7.

5. *Cyprian*, Bishop of Carthage and a widely admired theologian, martyred in 258; *Augustine*, Bishop of Hippo from 396, the most influential of the Western Fathers. See below, notes 126 and 127 to *Obedience*.

6. To lay the fault or blame upon (*OED*, wite, *v.*¹.3, citing this passage).

7. Welfare.

8. Plunder and tax excessively.

9. Matthew 22:21; Mark 12:17; Luke 20:25.

10. Matthew 5:25; 26:52.

11. Matthew 5:44.

12. Romans 12:19.

13. Matthew 6:15.

14. As Tyndale was writing these words, Turks were threatening Christian Europe; conquering Hungary and about to besiege Vienna.

15. As one of the only contemporary English Hebrew scholars, Tyndale returns to the issue of the Jews in most of his writing, especially in *Answer*. Primarily he rejects their doctrine of works, shared with Turks and Catholics. Even so, he deplores any policy of killing religious opponents.

16. Infectious disease in cattle.

The obedience of all degrees

1. Relative positions; ranks.

2. In these paragraphs, Tyndale's point, strange to us, is that the church's practice of the parties marrying partners of choice goes against the needful obedience to parents: *saute*, leap.

3. Legal quibbles to defraud.

4. Matthew 22:39.

5. The buying or selling of a benefice.

6. Genesis 12:10–20.

7. Ephesians 5:23. Tyndale, here and in his New Testaments, correctly translates the Greek word ἐκκλεσια (*ekklesia*) as *congregation* and not as 'church', angering his enemies.

8. Grumble, complain.

9. Philemon 13.

10. In the 1546 list of 'Heresies and Errors, collected by the bishops out of Tyndale's book named "The Obedience of a Christian Man"', this sentence, abridged to 'He saith that vows are against the ordinance of God', was denounced as Article III. Foxe prints the twenty-five articles, with his own brief trenchant retorts, in *A&M*, V, 577–82.

11. Tyndale gives these first ten verses of Romans 13 exactly as they appear in his 1526 Worms New Testament. The sixteen pages following the quotation are all commentary on this passage.

12. Adultery.

13. Neutral.

14. So in Exodus 22 (and John 10:34–35, quoting Psalm 82:6) as in Tyndale's Pentateuch (1530), the King James Version (1611) and elsewhere. The Geneva Bible (1560) gave the alternative 'judges', and some later versions followed that. The Hebrew word is one of the names of God.

15. The two books of Samuel and of Kings were originally one book in the Hebrew. They were then divided into two, and then into four in the Septuagint, known there as the 1st, 2nd, 3rd and 4th Books of the King(dom)s, so retained in the Vulgate, which nomenclature Tyndale follows. Hence this reference is to 1 Samuel 24:1–15. Tyndale will not prepare his translation of the historical books

for some years, and here translates freely, perhaps already from the Hebrew, though the Septuagint, the Vulgate and Luther's translation were available.

16. Tyndale seems to show knowledge of the Hebrew.

17. 1 Samuel 22:18.

18. 2 Samuel 1 and 4.

19. Article IV of the bishops' list (see n. 10 above) abridges this sentence to 'He saith, that a Christian man may not resist a prince, being an infidel and an ethnic. This taketh away freewill.' Foxe's reply contrasts St Peter (1 Peter 2:13–15), and St Paul not resisting Nero (as Romans 13:1–3), with the Pope resisting even Christian princes (*A&M*, V, 578).

20. Romans 13:1.

21. In ninth- and thirteenth-century canon law.

22. Romans 13:4: *wealth*, welfare.

23. These lines easily apply to Richard II in the chronicles. The word 'shadow' is used by Shakespeare at a climactic moment in his *Richard II*, IV.i.292–5.

24. Romans 13:4.

25. Place of refuge.

26. By reading the beginning of the fifty-first psalm in Latin, *Miserere mei, Deus . . .*, a criminal could assert that he was about to take holy orders, thus claiming 'benefit of clergy', exemption from trial before a secular judge.

27. Exodus 32.

28. Exodus 34:29–35.

29. Romans 7:14–21.

30. Differently.

31. At nightfall.

32. For Tyndale, the work of God is shown also in feelings.

33. Article V of the bishops' list (see n. 10 above) declares that this sentence is 'against moral virtues'. Foxe, appealing to Aristotle's *Ethics*, finds no heresy.

34. In Roman legend, Lucrece gloried in her chastity. Having suffered rape by Tarquin, she took her own life. Her story had been told by Chaucer in his *Legend of Good Women* (1387–92) and by Gower in his *Confessio Amantis* (1386–93). Shakespeare, some sixty-five years after Tyndale, made Lucrece the subject of his second long poem (1594).

35. Rather.

36. Article VI of the bishops' list (see n. 10 above) declares that: 'He reproveth men that make holy saints their advocates to God; and there he saith, that saints were not rewarded in heaven for their holy works.' Foxe replies simply with two sentences from this paragraph, including the last (*A&M*, V, 578).

37. Deuteronomy 13:9–16.

38. Germany.

39. Tyndale sketches Italian history from the accession of Pope Julius II in 1503 up to the time of writing.

40. Probably Switzers; Tyndale puns on succour.

41. Henry VIII had received a golden rose, such as was blessed annually by the Pope on the first Sunday in Lent, from Julius II in 1510, to induce him to attack France.

42. Symbol of high rank.

43. In 1511 Julius II had offered to give this title, already given to the kings of France in 1469, to Henry VIII.

44. Title conferred on Henry VIII by Pope Leo X in 1521 for his personal attack on Luther. English monarchs have held the title ever since, and 'F.D.' still appears on all British coins.

45. Title given to the kings of France because Clovis, the third Merovingian king, had embraced the Catholic church in a battlefield conversion, probably in 496.

46. Proclaims, spreads abroad.

47. Bologna.

48. Muslims.

49. Four years before Tyndale wrote the *Obedience* Cardinal Wolsey had undertaken to induce the House of Commons to raise £800,000 if Henry VIII would claim his right to be king of France. The Commons refused. Wolsey settled for less than a quarter of that sum; Thomas More was Speaker of the House and was given £100 by Wolsey for his efforts. Wolsey used his authority as papal legate to make the clergy give a quarter of their goods. Swearing to the value caused them extreme difficulty, both of not being forsworn and of credence of the value. Tyndale attacks Wolsey frequently, in *Practice* calling him 'Wolfsee': pp. 307, 310, 311, 313.

50. Knows.

51. Revelation 17:1–5. Babylon was also a symbolic name for Rome (Revelation 17–18, and see 1 Peter 5:13). The reformers used the phrase for the pope and the Roman church.

52. The evil craft of attempting to reveal the future by calling up and questioning the spirits of the dead. 1 Samuel 28 tells how Saul, before the battle of Gilboa, visited the Witch of Endor to have raised for him the spirit of the dead Samuel: he then heard, correctly, of imminent defeat and his own death.

53. Mark 12:42.

54. John Fisher, Bishop of Rochester from 1504, preached a celebrated and much printed sermon against Luther on the occasion of the public burning of Luther's books at St Paul's Cross on 12 May 1521. Later in the *Obedience* Tyndale will go on to attack Fisher at length on the point of the precedence of Peter,

and thus the supremacy of the pope (pp. 69–81). Fisher, with More, was made a saint in 1935.

55. Matthew 18:1–4. Tyndale expects his readers to observe that in the gospel this passage immediately follows the verses by which Fisher aims to exalt Peter.

56. Romans 13:5. Tyndale is steadily working through the passage he quoted at the start of the section.

57. Riches.

58. Separate, different.

59. For the betraying of confession, see below, pp. 94, 117–19, and *Practice*, 305, where Tyndale reports the passing of political information learned in confession through Cardinal Morton and Bishop Fox to Henry VII. Half a dozen passages in *Answer* attack confession as not scriptural.

60. Continuing Romans 13, from verse 6. This and the next paragraph conclude the comment up to verse 10.

61. Specious and deliberately fallacious reasoners.

62. Aiming at or pretending to holiness on the ground of works.

63. Acquitters.

64. Echoing 2 Corinthians 3:3.

65. Romans 13:9–10.

66. A frequent New Testament word (see, for example, Romans 15:8) central to Tyndale's thought.

67. Echoing Romans 5:3–5 and 1 Timothy 6:11.

68. 1 Samuel 12.

69. 1 Peter 2:14.

70. Psalm 107:33–34.

71. Psalm 105:25.

72. Article VII (see n. 10 above) reads: 'God moved the hearts of the Egyptians to hate the people; likewise he moved kings, etc.' Foxe in retort quotes Tyndale's words and Bible references (*A&M*, V, 578–9).

73. 2 Samuel 24.

74. Probes.

75. Cauterizes, burns.

76. Corrosives.

77. Pustules, pimples containing pus.

78. Matthew 16:24.

79. This sentence is printed in diminishing lines to mark a conclusion, as it is the end of the discussion of the obedience of 'them that are under power and rule'. The new section, on those who rule, begins with an illuminated letter.

80. Reprove angrily.

81. Article II of the bishops' list (see n. 10 above) declares: 'He saith that children

ought not to marry without the consent of their parents.' Foxe quotes these dozen lines in ample retort (*A&M*, V, 577–8).

82. Hindered.

83. Echoing Ephesians 1:14.

84. Deuteronomy 16:19.

85. Unique.

86. Deuteronomy 17:17–20.

87. Bailiff-errants, appointed by the sheriff to travel the county to execute writs and summon the courts.

88. Popery and puppetry combined; possibly popery and poetry (i.e. falsehood).

89. Destroy; Matthew 5:17.

90. Tyndale's word here, in his 1526 New Testament, had been the first instance of the correct translation into English of the Greek at Acts 2:38, μετανοησατε (*metanoesate*). The Vulgate, followed by the Wyclif versions, had had *poenitentiam agite*, 'do penance'.

91. Matthew 16:6.

92. Territory held by the pope in Italy.

93. Not traced; probably from an anonymous English jurist.

94. John Fisher, Bishop of Rochester from 1504, and a Cambridge scholar instrumental in getting Erasmus there to teach Greek. As confessor to Queen Catherine, he vigorously opposed Henry VIII's divorce and was imprisoned in the Tower. He was made a cardinal by the pope in 1535, and was soon after beheaded by Henry's order. With More, he was canonized in 1935.

95. The title is in various forms in different editions. The fullest is: *A sermon had at Paul's by the commandment of the most reverend father in god my lord legate* [i.e. Wolsey] *and said by John the bishop of Rochester upon quinquagesima Sunday* [12 May 1521] *concerning certain heretics which then were abjured for holding the heresies of Martin Luther that famous heretic and for the keeping and retaining of his books against the ordinance of the bull of Pope Leo the tenth.* See *The English Works of John Fisher*, ed. John E. B. Mayor, Part 1 (EETS, Oxford University Press, 1876/1935), 308.

96. Type, allegory.

97. Fisher, *English Works*, 315–16.

98. Hebrews 7:24–28; chapter 9.

99. John 3:14; Genesis 3.

100. Revelation 5:5; 1 Peter 5:8.

101. Matthew 13:33; 16:6.

102. Hebrews 3:1–6.

103. Hebrews 9:19–28.

104. Exodus 32.

105. Fisher, *English Works*, 317–18.

106. 1 Corinthians 3:22 and *passim*.

107. Matthew 20:27.

108. Article VIII of the bishops' list (see n. 10 above) charges Tyndale with saying: 'Paul was of higher authority than Peter.' As a reply Foxe quotes Tyndale's previous dozen lines (*A&M*, V, 579).

109. Or.

110. Echoing Romans 5:14–17.

111. Adapting Ephesians 4:4–6. Fisher had argued that the church 'is one, having one head, the pope'. *English Works*, 314.

112. Acts 8:14; 13:1–3; Acts 15:22.

113. Friars licensed to beg within certain limits, and sell partnerships in the convent. Tyndale refers at the end of the *Obedience* to 'the belly-brotherhood of monks and friars': such fraternity is carnal.

114. Priests and monks, with tonsures.

115. Clergyman.

116. 'You are sent'; the last words of the mass.

117. Fisher, *English Works*, 314.

118. Several.

119. Galatians 1:12.

120. Corinthians 15:8.

121. Acts 15:1–12.

122. Citing this passage as the first recorded, *OED* has: 'A nursery play with a young child, who is kept in excitement by the nurse or playmate alternately concealing herself (or her face), and peeping out for a moment at an unexpected place, to withdraw again with equal suddenness.'

123. Hebrews 10. Fisher, *English Works*, 315.

124. Fisher, *English Works*, 337.

125. ibid., 338.

126. Bishop of Carthage, d. 258. His writings were significant for later disputes about papal claims.

127. 354–430. Bishop of Hippo and the most influential theologian of the church Fathers. The point of Tyndale's references to these is that they do not support the pope's authority, in spite of what Fisher said; *English Works*, 327, 334, 341, 344.

128. *c.* 339–97. Bishop of Milan, and, with Jerome, Augustine and Gregory, one of the four first 'Doctors of the Church'. Ambrose was a fine preacher and orthodox theologian. Fisher, *English Works*, 335.

129. *c.* 342–420. Bible scholar who standardized Old Latin versions to produce the 'common version', the Vulgate, still extant. Tyndale understands correctly that Jerome was not the author of the Vulgate: 'the translation that we take for saint Jerome's' (*TNT*, 9). Fisher, *English Works*, 341.

130. See *W.T. unto the reader*, n. 151. Fisher, *English Works*, 320, 333–4.

131. *c.* 549–604. Pope from 590 with far-reaching effects, including the conversion of England. Fisher, *English Works*, 319–20.

132. Cicero.

133. *c.* 673–*c.* 735. Biblical scholar and historian at the monastery of Jarrow. A main authority for early English history. His commentaries on Genesis (he had some Hebrew) and on Mark, Luke and Acts (using Greek for the latter) were very influential.

134. Feed, from John 21:15–17. Fisher, *English Works*, 316.

135. Cut.

136. Make them owners of, surrender them to.

137. Fisher, *English Works*, 332.

138. Ephesians 5:22–24.

139. 1 Corinthians 11:6.

140. 1 Timothy 2:11.

141. 1 Timothy 2:9.

142. 1 Timothy 3:4; Ephesians 6:1.

143. Ephesians 6:5; Colossians 3:22.

144. Ephesians 6:1.

145. 2 Thessalonians 3:10.

146. Acts 13:2–3.

147. Colossians 4:2.

148. Because of.

149. Perhaps from Luke 12:35–40 and 1 Thessalonians 5:6.

150. 1 Corinthians 16:20.

151. 1 Corinthians 14:27.

152. Ephesians 4:14.

153. Colossians 4:3.

154. Ephesians 4:11–12.

155. Fisher, *English Works*, 309.

156. Probably referring to the notorious case of Richard Hunne; see W. R. Cooper, 'Richard Hunne', *Reformation* 1 (1996), 221–51.

157. Decrees, especially of the pope. On 10 December 1520, in front of the Elster Gate in Wittenberg, Luther burned the bull excommunicating him, *Exsurge Domine* ('Rise, O Lord'), and, more significantly and decisively, the decretals, the canon law.

158. Fisher, *English Works*, 345.

159. More properly.

160. Copies of Tyndale's first English New Testament were burned at St Paul's in October 1526.

161. Stunned, stupefied.

162. Fisher's sermon includes four 'instructions': Tyndale mocks.

163. Fisher, *English Works*, 331.

164. In Latin grammar, deponent verbs are passive in form but active in meaning. Tyndale quotes Erasmus's version of Galatians 5:6, with *operans* as present participle. The Greek at that point gives 'faith which by love is mighty in operation': that is, it is faith which works (ενεργουμενε, *energoumene*), through love. Lewis and Short, *A Latin Dictionary* (1955), note *operor* as possibly active in ecclesiastical Latin, quoting the Vulgate.

165. Galatians 5:6.

166. *The Parable of the Wicked Mammon.*

167. Fisher, *English Works*, 328.

168. *salt . . . bells . . . wax . . . boughs . . . candles . . . ashes*: see Duffy, 279–83, also *Answer*, 70, 109, 176 and elsewhere.

169. Chrisom cloth, a white cloth put on the child at baptism. If the child died within a month, it became a shroud: if it lived, the mother gave the cloth, or money, to the priest.

170. Neckerchief or jacket: Acts 19:12.

171. Signs, especially of something about to happen.

172. Reckoning and grimacing.

173. Monkey.

174. Dumb show.

175. Wearing wool next to the skin as a penance.

176. Stricter Franciscan (Grey) friars. They were to beg for necessities, not money.

177. Bereft of hair, tonsured.

178. This sentence echoes the prayer of consecration and other phrases of the communion service.

179. Article I of the bishops' list (see n. 10 above) charges Tyndale with saying: 'We are bound to make satisfaction to our neighbour, but not to God', apparently referring to this passage, against the sense (*A&M*, V, 577).

180. Tyndale was abused by Thomas More for translating the Greek with these English words. Tyndale explained that he used 'elder' for the Greek πρεσβυτερος (*presbuteros*, presbyter), and reserved 'priest' for the Greek ιερος (*hieros*, Latin *sacerdos*). So Tyndale had translated 1 Timothy 3:2 in 1526.

181. *OED* first records the word in this 1528 passage. It is not recorded after 1632. It was possibly Gloucestershire dialect.

182. Greek διαβολος (*diabolos*). A New Testament word for the opponent of God, that is, the Devil. In common use it is an adversary or accuser in a court of law.

183. Breviaries, the daily service books of the Roman Catholic church.

184. Find the place.

185. Article IX of the bishops' list (see n. 10 above) charges Tyndale with saying: 'A priest ought to have a wife for two causes.' Foxe in retort simply prints this paragraph (*A&M*, V, 579). Tyndale returns angrily a number of times to the compulsory celibacy of bishops and all clergy, quoting 1 Timothy 3:2 again (p. 88 below), and dealing with the subject at length in *Answer*, 151–67.

186. Position, rank.

187. 1 Timothy 3.

188. 'O Almighty God, who didst give the blessed Laurence victory over the fires of his torments, grant to us, we beseech thee, that we may extinguish the flames of our vices.' Laurence (d. 258) was said to have been roasted to death on a gridiron.

189. 'Grant us, O Lord, we beseech thee, that we may imitate what we reverence, and may learn to love even our enemies; since we are celebrating the birth of him, who learnt to implore mercy for his prosecutors from our Lord Jesus Christ . . .' For Stephen, see Acts 7:60.

190. In the breviary, those collects were for the two 'St Mary days'.

191. Foxe, *A&M*, I, 206–7.

192. See *W.T. unto the reader*, n. 107 above. Here in *Obedience* Tyndale is particularly concerned with the present operative effects of Antichrist at work as popes and prelates secretly usurp monarchs, falsely interpret scripture and teach the primacy of works.

193. Clips the hair or beard (as in 'shorn').

194. 1 Timothy 3:2.

195. 1 Corinthians 7:9.

196. An Oxford tradition still in force in 1659, explained then as making them shod with the preparation of the gospel: see Walter, PS, n. 232, and Ephesians 6:15.

197. Disgrade, or possibly disgrace.

198. Remove from rank or degree.

199. See for example *A&M*, IV, 363–5: 'the bishop scraped the nails of both his [the martyr's] hands with a piece of glass' to symbolize the taking away of the power 'to sacrifice, to consecrate and to bless'. Tyndale was himself degraded just before his martyrdom.

200. The text, as spoken in English to the people, is given by Strype, *Ecclesiastical Memorials* (1821), 22, and Appendix xlvi.

201. Particularly, especially.

202. Terrified continually.

203. Rogation week. It comes before Ascension Day, which is ten days before

Whitsunday, which is the seventh Sunday after Easter. See Duffy, 279–80, who quotes a parallel passage in *Answer*.

204. The word is stronger than it is today, containing the sense of 'innate character'.

205. Know.

206. Back to 1 Timothy 3 and the office of bishop, here verse 3. The King James Version has 'no striker'.

207. Vestments; and see n. 169 above.

208. The custom whereby on a death the priest could claim from the household the most valuable item as fee, a source of great contention. See below, p. 93. The practice was famously challenged by Richard Hunne in 1511. See W. R. Cooper, 'Richard Hunne', *Reformation* 1 (1996), 221–51.

209. The Court of Arches, the ecclesiastical court of appeal for the province of Canterbury, formerly held at St Mary-le-Bow, and named from the arches that supported its steeple.

210. To cause contention; from the strife which a bone causes between dogs.

211. One of the four judges of the Court of Appeal.

212. Wolsey, at this time: succeeded by Sir Thomas More.

213. *They*: as subject throughout this section, those sent by Antichrist, particularly the bishops.

214. Living.

215. Jacques le Goff, in *The Birth of Purgatory*, trans. Goldhammer (Chicago University Press, 1981), traced the few notions of purgatory before its codification at councils at Lyons (1274), Florence (1438), and, after Tyndale, at Trent (1545–63). Tyndale attacks the concept in other works: in *The exposition of Matthew V, VI, VII* he says it is no more real than Utopia (*Expositions . . . Tyndale . . .*, Parker Society, Cambridge University Press, 1849, p. 84). His friend John Frith in 1531 published *A Disputation of Purgatory*, arguing clearly against the current arguments of, among others, More and Fisher. For that heresy he was burned alive; see *WTB*, 217–19.

216. Holding two or more benefices at once.

217. Joining two or more benefices into one.

218. Literally, as many as there may be: dispensation to hold as many benefices as the holder pleases; unlimited pluralism.

219. Revelation 16:2; the beast (Revelation 11:7) is the anti-Christian power of Rome.

220. Greed extending from a tenth to a third.

221. Unit of assessment of land, the amount that can be tilled by one team of eight oxen in a year.

222. A military-religious order owning large tracts of English land. Dissolved in

England at the Reformation, the order survived for centuries on Malta, and still exists as a Catholic order.

223. Chapels not subject to jurisdiction by a bishop, having been founded by the king.

224. Wills, bequests.

225. Quarter days, traditionally for paying rents.

226. Private.

227. 'Cuthbert at Durham [like Edmund at Bury], the foundations on which were reared mighty ecclesiastical corporations, whose continuing power and wealth depended on continuing loyalty to the patron'; Duffy, 196.

228. St Alban was the first English Christian martyr (either *c.* 209 or *c.* 305); his shrine in Hertfordshire was greatly venerated.

229. Linking the shrine of St Edmund at Bury with Cuthbert; Duffy, as n. 227 above.

230. The papal states in Italy. Tyndale's point is that the four estates he lists are extremely wealthy.

231. Likewise, also.

232. See *W.T. unto the reader*, n. 126.

233. A white cloth put on a child at baptism; see n. 169 above.

234. Partnerships.

235. Persons licensed to sell papal pardons or indulgences. Chaucer's portrait of such a man, 'that streit was comen from the court of Rome', in the Prologue and the Pardoner's Tale in his *Canterbury Tales*, does much to show his corruption. See *The Poetical Works of Chaucer*, ed. F. N. Robinson (Oxford, n.d., pp. 26–7, 178–87). The European Reformation was sparked by Luther's theses against indulgences in 1518.

236. Masses for the soul of a dead person.

237. See *W.T. unto the reader*, n. 125.

238. Commemoration of a deceased person on a day one month, or one year, after death.

239. See *W.T. unto the reader*, n. 124.

240. *Hallowing* is consecrating to God; by contrast, *conjuring* is putting on a magic spell.

241. Incense boat.

242. *sheareth . . . polleth . . . pareth*: clips, cuts, trims.

243. Officers representing a bishop.

244. Officers who summon persons to appear in court. Like the pardoners, they were feared and hated: Chaucer's Summoner is, if that be possible, even more revolting than his Pardoner (Chaucer, op. cit., pp. 20, 112–20).

245. Officers in attendance at a court, to execute orders.

246. Procuring for sex.

247. Episcopal edicts, which cost a lot of money, presumably to their advantage.

248. Canker worms; larvae which eat crops.

249. Matthew 7:15.

250. Probably observe closely for a while (*OED*, wait, *v*[1].1.3).

251. Spiritual.

252. Either.

253. 1 Corinthians 6:15.

254. Matthew 12:50.

255. John 6:55−56.

256. Romans 8:17.

257. 2 Corinthians 1:22.

258. Immediately.

259. At the first stroke, immediately.

260. Above all (*OED*, namely, 1).

261. John 4:1.

262. John 18:30.

263. Matthew 27:25.

264. Violently (*OED*, hardly, 1).

265. John 19:7.

266. Psalm 2:10−12. This sentence will chime again at the end of some paragraphs below.

267. Echoing Isaiah 59:4.

268. Romans 4:16.

269. As an example close to home, the Bishop of London burned as many of Tyndale's 1526 New Testaments as he could find for the 'heresy' in them: see Introduction, p. xviii.

270. Matthew 5:26; legal tender until January 1961, a farthing was a quarter of a penny.

271. See n. 26 above. An exempted criminal would have his thumb branded with 'M' for murder or 'T' for theft: Tyndale puns on the mark of the beast.

272. Recite rapidly (*OED*, roll, *v*[2].1.4.a).

273. In a few words, a summary of the New Testament.

274. Make afraid.

275. The pope.

276. *Scala celi*: an indulgence attached to St Botolph's church at Boston in Lincolnshire which allowed those members of the Guild of Our Lady, who went every Friday to the attached chapel of Our Lady (or to any other chapel), to say a Paternoster, Ave Maria and Creed, to have as full remission of sins as if he or she went to the chapel of Our Lady called Scala Celi (that is, 'ladder to heaven') in Rome: see *A&M*, V, 364−5.

277. John 10:7–9.

278. 1 Samuel.

279. Acts 20:35.

280. Hinder.

281. For example, by papal law, marriage between even the children of godparents to the same child was forbidden, as being of spiritual family.

282. Confess.

283. Article X of the bishops' list (see n. 10 above) says of this paragraph, 'He condemneth auricular confession' (*A&M*, V, 579).

284. As the pope.

285. Proverbial; to do something openly and think no one can see. The first recorded use. Also in *Answer*, 247.

286. Thus breaking the communicant's fast which was, until relatively recently, compulsory for twelve hours before communion in the Roman Catholic, and similar, churches.

287. The wafer was placed on the stretched-out tongue, avoiding contact with the teeth, which would cause bleeding in the body of Christ. It was not uncommon for the wafer, while being placed, to touch the nose.

288. Most probably the priest, in the spirit of numerous continental woodcuts showing the ignorant priest as an ass, or a bishop with long furry ears sticking out from his mitre, performing ceremonies. The ass here just might be from the Nativity scenes, always important to the Catholic church; with the ox, the ass was customarily understood to keep the Christ child warm by breathing on him (see next note). In the context, however, that is more obscure. Tyndale attacks such superstitious anxieties elsewhere, for example in *Answer*, 8.

289. Gilbert Burnet, in his *History of the Reformation of the Church of England*, Part II (1681), Book 1, in 'Collection of Records', no. 33, p. 165, 'Articles to be followed and observed, according to the King's Majesty's [Edward VI] Injunctions and Proceedings', prints a list of a dozen things not to be done by the minister to 'counterfeit the Popish Mass': the items include 'breathing upon the bread or chalice'.

290. For the reading of the gospel during the mass, the book is brought specially forward to the lectern, with one, or two, acolytes standing alongside with a candle.

291. Chapels endowed for the chanting of masses.

292. See notes 234 and 239, above.

293. Endow.

294. In 1208, in retaliation for King John asserting his royal power, Pope Innocent III forbade the sacraments in England except for persons in danger of death. No church services, marriages or funerals took place in England for five years.

For his struggle against Rome, John was later used as a symbol in the play by John Bale (1537–40) and also by Shakespeare (*c.* 1594).

295. Starve as a punishment.

296. The four verbs are prescient of Tyndale's own end; a probable sequence that can have rarely been far from his mind.

297. Matthew 23:14.

298. Romans 2:25–29; 4:9–12.

299. Romans 10:6.

300. Pretence of piety; sanctimoniousness.

301. At the side (of the pope); that is, virtually the pope himself.

302. Crozier, pastoral staff or hook.

303. Linen vestment like a surplice worn by bishops and abbots.

304. Matthew 7:15–16.

305. Genesis 9:12–17.

306. A bunch of ivy as a vintner's sign, or the signboard of a tavern generally. Its use here antedates *OED*.

307. Parrot.

308. *credo ... volo ... baptismum*: the responses that the godparents are to make; 'I believe', 'I will' and 'baptism', with a play on mumming.

309. 1 John 1:7.

310. Romans 5:14; 6:6.

311. Allegorically, by the Song of Songs, and in Revelation 19:7–9.

312. *mustard seed, leaven, a net, keys, bread, water*: Christ's words at Matthew 13:31, 33, 47; 16:19; John 6:48; 4:14. In view of the obliqueness of the marriage references (see the note above), Tyndale's point, quoting Christ himself, is a fair one. Thomas More ridiculed the sentence (*Confutation* on Tyndale's Preface), and suggested adding to the list 'a sack': one wonders whether he had recognized, or did not expect his readers to recognize, the source of the words.

313. Rather.

314. Article XII of the bishops' list (see n. 10 above) is: 'He destroyeth the sacraments of matrimony and orders', related to this section (*A&M*, V, 579). Tyndale argues that orders, from subdeacon to pope, cannot be sacraments because Christ's promise of salvation is not coupled with them. Tyndale maintains that the 'priesthood of all believers', as the reformers understood the New Testament, is clear as relating to the spiritual needs of others, and can include women (*Answer*, 29–30, 98).

315. As Aaron.

316. Hebrews 5:6.

317. 1 Peter 2:5–9. Article XI of the bishops' list (see n. 10 above) abridges Tyndale's sentence to: 'Every man is a priest, and we need no other priest to be

a mean for us unto God.' Foxe prints Tyndale's paragraph as far as 'unto God' (*A&M*, V, 579).

318. Hebrews 6:19.

319. As 'mercy seat' in Exodus 25 and *passim*; Hebrews 9:5. The word is Tyndale's coinage, first in print at this place in the *Obedience* and following Luther's *Gnadenstuhl*, itself following the Hebrew rather than the Latin *propriatorium*.

320. See *W.T. unto the reader*, nn. 31 and 180 above.

321. In his *Confutation* (8/1.192–3) Thomas More wrote that Tyndale 'mocketh and scoffeth out the words of St Paul, written unto Timothy, in which the sacrament of orders is so plainly proved that all the world cannot deny it . . .'. In those letters Paul writes of the practicalities of appointing bishops, deacons and elders. More traditionally takes 1 Timothy 4:14 and 2 Timothy 1:6, which mention in passing 'the laying on of hands', as clearly proving 'the holy order of priesthood a sacrament'. For Luther, as other reformers, orders were not sacraments. See also *Answer*, 16–20.

322. Impartially.

323. Luke 6:12–13.

324. Matthew 28:19–20; Mark 16:14–18; Luke 24:27, 45, 47.

325. Matthew 16:19.

326. 1 Corinthians 11:24.

327. Understood.

328. An Old English reflexive verb that goes back at least to 1300, meaning to change the direction of one's thoughts, to experience a change of mind or purpose, to repent: it is accurate for the Greek μετανοεω (*metanoeō*).

329. Tyndale could mean Caxton's *Chronicles of England*, the *Polychronicon* of Ralph Higden, Roger of Wendover's *Flores historiarum*, or Fabian, or Grafton.

330. Various.

331. Romans 10.

332. Acknowledge.

333. Tyndale's emphasis on feeling is, as always, striking.

334. See *W.T. unto the reader*, n. 128.

335. A late fourth-century scandal that seems to have been well enough known in 1528 for Tyndale to make only this intriguing reference. The two historical accounts are printed as an Appendix to this edition, pp. 234–6 below.

336. As (to take early examples) at Acts 3:8; 5:1–11.

337. The openings of most of Paul's epistles after 2 Corinthians support this.

338. *Venerabilis Bedae, Patrilogiae Latinae*, ed. J.-P. Migne, Tomus 92, 301–632.

339. Nor.

340. From the Latin for 'wearing down by rubbing', theologically an imperfect sorrow for sin out of fear of punishment, a sense invented by scholastic theologians in the twelfth century.

341. The Latin Vulgate rendering of the Hebrew *kapporeth*, translated by Tyndale in Exodus 25 and thereafter as 'mercy seat'. See *TOT*, xxii, 122 and n. 319 above.

342. John 10:11: *lopen*, leaped.

343. Luke 15:10.

344. Grumble, complain.

345. Ordinary people, not ordained.

346. Matthew 11:15.

347. Article XIII of the bishops' list (see n. 10 above) says: 'He saith that purgatory is the pope's invention, and therefore, he may do there whatsoever he will.' Foxe notes the absence of Purgatory in the scriptures, and the lack of belief in it in the fathers (*A&M*, V, 579).

348. Migne, *Patrilogia Latina*, vol. 26, col. 118B. Tyndale accurately paraphrases, but extends 'bishops' to the bishop of Rome.

349. Echoing 1 John 1:9.

350. Matthew 28:18.

351. (Absolution) 'from punishment and from guilt'; coined by Peter Lombard and taken over in Aquinas's *Summa*.

352. In 1350 a bull made by Clement VI, incorporated into papal law, gave power to the church 'to grant pardons or indulgences, out of a supposed treasure of merits at its disposal' (Walter, PS, 74n.).

353. Those who avowed their faith in the face of persecution, without suffering martyrdom.

354. Article XIII of the bishops' list (see n. 10 above) quotes this sentence as heresy or error (*A&M*, V, 579).

355. See n. 200 above.

356. James 3:10, as translated by Tyndale in 1526, 'Out of the mouth proceedeth blessing and cursing. My brethren these things ought not so to be.'

357. Across the river Severn from the place, in western Gloucestershire, where Tyndale was born and grew up; *marches* = borders.

358. To act in dumb-show (*OED*, mum, *v*.4). The bishops, failing to preach the gospel, were thus in disguise, and silent.

359. Assistant bishops, with no jurisdiction.

360. *privy seal*: used by the sovereign in subordinate matters, those not passed to the *great seal*, used for documents of the highest importance issued in the name of the sovereign.

361. See the section in *Answer*, 68–75.

362. James 5:14.

363. As at Acts 26:1.

364. Anointing with oil, particularly at the moment of death.

365. I wish it.

366. A common appellation for any priest.

367. See Introduction, p. xvii.

368. Echoing Romans 8:31.

369. The doctrine of transubstantiation was defined as an article of faith in 1215, and classically elaborated by Aquinas.

370. Supposed relics of Christ and others were everywhere.

371. Those who exalt works above faith.

372. 1 Kings 18.

373. Carthusians, an order founded in 1086, noted for strictness and silence.

374. Partner. The heats of thwarted passions contrast with insipid 'cold phlegm'.

375. A carved tablet to be kissed by the priest at mass, in those days also to be kissed by the people; see Duffy, 125.

376. Monastery.

377. Trader.

378. Article XV of the bishops' list (see n. 10 above) has: 'He saith, "No man may be hired to pray."' Foxe in retort quotes the whole sentence (A&M, V, 580).

379. A common phrase of Luther's, in discussing the New Testament teaching of the fulfilling of the law, *Herz von Grund*.

380. The shrine of 'Sant Iago' at Compostela in Spain was a fashionable place of pilgrimage.

381. Enjoin.

382. Matthew 21:23–24.

383. Revelation 17:2.

384. John 8:44; Revelation 12:9.

385. Tyndale, like Wyclif before him and all the reformers, maintained the New Testament doctrine that baptism and eucharist were the only sacraments, both instituted by Christ in the gospels, and developed by Paul in Romans 6:3–4 and 1 Corinthians 11:26.

386. Probably a scornful misspelling: 'bisshapes' occurs seven lines below.

387. 1 John 2:1.

388. Walter omits these words, noting: 'A coarse expression, originating with the once popularly credited story of pope Joan, is here omitted' (PS, 285). It was believed that incumbent popes, after that, were so tested for maleness.

389. 1 John 1:7–8.

390. The peculiarity of the marginal note probably alludes to More's *Dialogue*, in imitation of the myriad 'quoth he's' in that book. The end 'while they' suggests words fallen out in printing. *OED*, however, records a transitive verb, 'while',

meaning 'to pass the time tediously', which perhaps might fit: it is not recorded before 1890, but being from Thomas Hardy it could have been West Country dialect and known to Tyndale nearly four hundred years before.

391. See also *Answer*, 115–16.

392. Article XVI of the bishops' list (see n. 10 above) says: 'He saith, "Why should I trust in Paul's prayer or holiness?" If St Paul were alive, he would compare himself to St Paul, and be as good as he.' Foxe, commenting that 'The words of Tyndale import no such meaning as in the article', quotes this passage from 'why am not I . . .' to '. . . Paul's' (*A&M*, V, 580).

393. A cavern on an island in Lough Derg, Donegal. There, Irish legend had it, Christ appeared to St Patrick. He showed him a deep pit, saying that whoever spent a day and a night in it would see the torments of hell and the joys of heaven. It was said that those who had tried it emerged insane.

394. Wolsey.

395. 'The mighty hunter', Genesis 10:9. Tyndale refers to Wolsey's persecution of 'Lutherans' in England. The phrase from 'except . . .' means that Wolsey will be gloriously shrined as a saint unless the reformers record the truth of his ruthless pursuits. See *Answer*, 81–2, for worship of Wolsey's supposed relics.

396. 1 Corinthians 2:4.

397. Philippians 3:19.

398. The same.

399. 2 Corinthians 1:21–22.

400. Cain was the first fratricide and murderer: Genesis 4.

401. Acts 9 and 26:9–12.

402. Acts 28:30; 2 Timothy 4:17.

403. Mark 6:7–13.

404. Luke 5:30–31.

405. Matthew 9:13, quoting Hosea 6:6.

406. Luke 5:32.

407. Blind as a block of wood (*OED*, stock, sb^1.1.b).

408. Romans 5:8.

409. *Mammon*; see Introduction, pp. viii–ix, xi.

410. Living.

411. Article XVIII of the bishops' list (see n. 10 above) says: 'He saith, that the children of faith be under no law.' Foxe, commenting, 'The article is true, being truly taken', quotes Tyndale's two sentences ending here (*A&M*, V, 580).

412. Colossians 3:11.

413. Article XVII of the bishops' list (see n. 10 above) says: 'He saith, that all that be baptized, become Christ himself.' Foxe refers to Tyndale's words here from 'Matthew 25' to 'in Christ'.

414. Hide in a robe; Walter mistakenly prints 'stool' (PS, 299).

415. Tyndale means Philippians: perhaps a small clue about how much he works from memory.

416. Galatians 3:29; Hebrews 6:17.

417. For trying gold by fire, see 1 Corinthians 3:13; 1 Peter 1:7; Revelation 3:18.
418. See n. 176 above.

419. The English name for the Carthusian order, in which the monks were vowed to silence: n. 373 above.

420. Hermits: Tyndale makes play with *heretics*.

421. Dregs.

422. Tyndale does not exaggerate. Christopher Haigh has estimated that in the early 1530s there were 100,000 in orders in England, out of a population of 2.5 million. Of these, 10,000 were monks and friars (Christopher Haigh, *English Reformations* (1993), 5–6).

423. All the reformers, even from within the church, attacked these methods of interpreting scripture, universal in the church of the time, dating at least from Origen.

424. For Tyndale's dislike of allegorizing, see his Prologue to the Pentateuch (*TOT*, 4, 8).

425. Tyndale's invention, playing on 'chop logic', contentious argument.

426. Beaten with birch rods.

427. 'Lord have mercy', that is, he gave me nothing but words, as James 2:16.

428. Legendary soothsayer of the time of King Arthur; his name was used as the title of almanacks.

429. John 1:29, 36.

430. John 15:1.

431. Revelation (with Acts) is a book for which Tyndale wrote no introduction in his 1534 New Testament. Like the church of the time, the earliest reformers did not know what to do with it. The largely Hussite interpretation of it as referring to world history did not arrive in England until John Bale's *The image of both churches* in about 1545.

432. Chances.

433. Bounds, limits.

434. John 18:10.

435. Article XIX of the bishops' list (see n. 10 above) has Tyndale say: 'There is no deed so good, but that the law condemneth it.' Foxe, asking 'What heresy is this?', prints these sentences (*A&M*, V, 580).

436. Corrosive.

437. See *W.T. unto the reader*, n. 186 above.

438. Galatians 4:22–31; referring to Genesis 16 and 21.

439. See *W.T. unto the reader*, n. 151.

440. The text prefixed to a sermon. Walter prints 'antitheme'.

441. John 4:24.

442. Or.

443. Romance, tale of adventure.

444. Genesis 35:22.

445. Genesis 29:15, 30; 42:36.

446. Refer (*OED*, report, V.1.111.6.c).

447. An allegory about churchmen, 'now tried in the fire of God's word'.

448. Trouble.

449. Genesis 34.

450. 2 Samuel 11.

451. Domestic deed; see Genesis 9:21–27.

452. Numbers 13:33.

453. Deuteronomy 2.

454. Deuteronomy 7:1.

455. Matthew 22:1–15; Ephesians 5:22–33; Revelation 19:1–9, 21:1–4.

456. 1 Corinthians 12.

457. Echoing Matthew 16:18.

458. As in the widely-known anonymous Middle English poem in rhyming couplets, *Cursor Mundi* (1340).

459. Article XX of the bishops' list (see n. 10 above) quotes the previous sentences. Foxe asks, 'What heresy is this?' (*A&M*, V, 581).

460. Article XXI of the bishops' list abridges, and distorts, this sentence. See *A&M*, V, 581, where Foxe comments, 'Consider the place.'

461. The addition of the pronoun, in classical Latin unnecessary, is from the rough Latin of the schools: 'I deny it, master doctor.'

462. Echoing Ephesians 3:8.

463. Belief in the assumption of Mary dates from the sixth century. It is not in the New Testament. It became official doctrine of the Roman Catholic church in 1950.

464. Erasmus's often long notes on the text (in Latin) were expanded in successive editions of his *Novum Testamentum*. Tyndale refers to the third edition of 1522.

465. Echoing John 1:13.

466. Nurse.

467. Article XXII of the bishops' list (see n. 10 above) says: 'The pope hath no authority but to preach only.' Foxe replies forcefully from scripture (*A&M*, V, 581).

468. A capricious goblin, 'Hobgoblin', believed in the sixteenth and seventeenth centuries to haunt the English countryside. He was also called Puck, and a good account of him is in Shakespeare, *A Midsummer Night's Dream*, II.i.33ff.

469. Article XXIII of the bishops' list (see n. 10 above) abridges and distorts this sentence. Foxe replies by quoting Tyndale in full (*A&M*, V, 581).

470. Luke 22:35.

471. The church Fathers, presumed older authorities. *Rede*, advise.

472. Honorius I, Pope 625–38, condemned by his successors.

473. For example, in 897, and 1378–1429. Walter's notes 2 and 3, PS, 324–5, clarify.

474. See notes 127, 129 and 133 above. Chrysostom ('the golden-mouthed'), *c.* 347–407, Bishop of Constantinople and preacher, opposed allegorical exegesis of scripture.

475. Article XXIV of the bishops' list (see n. 10 above) says: 'He denieth, rebuketh and damneth miracles': in retort, Foxe simply prints Tyndale's sentences (*A&M*, V, 581–2). See *Answer*, 83–4.

476. Galatians 3:5.

477. For St Peter's spectacular visit to London, 'with a great multitude of angels by night . . . more than five hundred years ago', see Thomas More's unfinished *History of King Richard the Third*, ed. Richard S. Sylvester (1976), 28.

478. Anne Wentworth, one of a number of 'holy maids' mentioned by More in his *Dialogue Concerning Heresies* (*Complete Works*, III.1, 87–94). Not all of them 'prophesied', but this Ipswich adolescent seemed to be 'psychic' in her unexpected insights and utterances about distant events, perhaps associated with epilepsy.

479. Elizabeth Barton, a Benedictine nun from the convent of St Sepulchre's in Canterbury, connected with Bishop John Fisher: also discussed by More (see *Answer*, 90–92), and Burnet (III.ii, 100). Probably also epileptic, her later 'prophesyings' were found to be treason. She was hanged, with her confessor and associates, at Tyburn on 20 April 1534. For both, see Diane Watt, *Secretaries of God* (1997), 51–74.

480. *Gestus Romanorum*: properly *Gesta Romanorum*, a popular medieval collection of tales, loosely attached to Roman times and intended to point a moral. There were vernacular translations, the first printed version in English being from Wynkyn de Worde in 1510.

481. Present, show; Acts 1:24.

482. Censure (*OED*, improve, *v.*2).

483. To the last extremity.

484. The spirituality, churchmen.

485. Acts 9; 13:9.

486. Article XXV of the bishops' list (see n. 10 above) charges Tyndale, 'He saith, that no man should serve God with good intent or zeal; for it is plain idolatry.' Foxe simply prints Tyndale's two sentences (*A&M*, V, 582).

487. Someone paid to pray for others.

488. See *W.T. unto the reader*, n. 125.

489. Matthew 7:24.

490. As soldier or sailor (*OED*, blue coat, 2).

491. Honour.

492. Matthew 26:52.

493. Above, p. 49.

494. Romans 13:1.

495. Through his sons; 1 Samuel 2:12 to 4:11.

496. Romans 12:5.

497. 1 Corinthians 6:20.

498. Matthew 25:40, 45; Mark 9:37.

499. Matthew 26:56.

500. In 1511, Pope Julius II initiated the Holy League against France, which Henry VIII joined two years after he came to the throne.

501. Henry's fleet inflicted damage on the French and conveyed his army, which later mutinied, home. He defeated the Scots at Flodden on 12 September 1513.

502. The confession of whatever person he wants to know of.

503. Brigittine monastery.

504. Hardened.

505. Exodus 3–11.

506. He defeated the French at Harfleur and Agincourt in 1522.

507. See n. 500 above.

508. Believe.

509. Hinders.

510. For three hundred years from 1095, when Pope Urban II initiated the first, there had been a score of Crusades.

511. Stephen Langton.

512. Absolve, acquit. *Ought*, owed.

513. Cleric, priest or religious.

514. *King John . . . money*: see *A&M*, II, 329.

515. Escape freely.

516. In April 1213.

517. An annual tax or tribute, probably dating from the ninth century, levied from every householder with land above a certain value, paid to the papal see at Rome. It was discontinued from 1534.

518. Matthew 24:29; Revelation 6:13–17.

519. As Matthew 27:22–25.

520. As Tyndale's New Testaments had been burned by the Bishop of London; see Introduction, p. xix.

521. Its use prohibited.

522. The parishioners.

523. Trickery, deception.

524. 1 Corinthians 7:13–14.

525. The French king Louis XII died in 1514; his successor, Francis I, invaded Italy. Cardinal Wolsey, at great expense, supported him and opposed the Emperor Maximilian, who then agreed with France and Spain on a partition of Italy in 1517. In 1520 Wolsey staged the magnificent Field of the Cloth of Gold for Francis I and Henry VIII, and the new emperor, Charles V, visited England. In June 1527 Charles V occupied, and sacked, Rome.

526. Conceal, disguise (*OED*, dissimule, 1).

527. Simulate or feign (*OED*, simule).

528. See *W.T. unto the reader*, n. 2.

529. See n. 122 above.

530. Tearing.

531. Soaking, sucking; draining or exhausting (*OED*, soak, *v*.111.8.c).

532. Wasting disease.

533. Compare *Hamlet*, IV.iv.27–8, 'th' impostume [abscess] ... that inward breaks, and shows no cause without/Why the man dies.'

534. See n. 484 above.

535. See n. 351 above.

536. Exodus 4–17.

537. *tink*: emit a sound as from a cracked bell (*OED*, tink, *v*¹1; Walter gives 'bellies think' (PS, 343).

APPENDIX

Confession in Constantinople

With reference to note 335 (page 225), here follow the texts of both Socrates (c. 380–450) and Sozomenus (early fifth century) as they give the story about the woman of Constantinople. It is possible to date the event at about AD 391/2. Sozomenus drew on Socrates' account.

How Tyndale knew the story is not recorded. Greek or Latin editions of both writers would have been available to him. According to comment by Valesius on the passage in Socrates, the abolition of confession was the most discussed topic in all early church history: if that is correct, then Tyndale could have known it from a late secondary source. Sozomenus's account might have appealed to him for its description of such operatic rites of confession in the Roman church.

I am especially grateful to Robert Ireland for help with these passages, and for the translations which follow.

D.D.

a. Socrates, *Historia ecclesiastica*, Book V, chapter 19
(*Patrilogia Graeca* 67, cols. 613–19)

At about that time it was decided to abolish the church priests who were in charge of confession, for the following reason. After the Novatians had separated themselves from the church, because they were unwilling to partake with those who had lapsed during the persecution under Decius, the bishops added a confessor [literally, 'a priest of confession'] to the list of ecclesiastical officials, so that those who had gone astray after baptism could confess their sins to a priest appointed for that purpose. This rule persists even now amongst other sects. Only those of the Homoousian persuasion, and the Novatians who share their opinion in matters of faith, refused to accept a confessor. The Novatians rejected the idea from the first: those who now rule the church [i.e. the Homoousians] retained the custom for a long time, but finally gave it up in the time of bishop Nectarius [of Constantinople, 381–98] because of an event which shook the church. A certain noblewoman went to the confessor, and confessed, one by one, the sins which she had committed since her baptism. The priest ordered the woman to fast and pray constantly, so that, in addition to her confession, she might show some physical sign of repentance. Eventually the woman confessed to another lapse: she said that she had slept with [exactly the Greek verb] a deacon of the church. This confession brought about the removal of the deacon from the church, and the laity were extremely concerned. They were angry not only at the crime, but also because of the disrepute and damage which had been inflicted on the church. Representations were made to saintly men in the matter, and Eudaemon, a priest of the church, a native of Alexandria, delivered it as his opinion to Nectarius that the [office of] confessor should be abolished, and that he [Nectarius] should permit individuals to take communion according to their own will and conscience: only in this way could the church escape infamy. I myself heard this from Eudaemon, and have had no hesitation in admitting it into this History.

b. Sozomenus, *Historia ecclesiastica*, Book VII, chapter 16 (*Patrilogia Graeca* 67, cols. 1457 *et sqq.*)

At that time Nectarius, bishop of the church of Constantinople, was the first to abolish the confessor [literally, 'the priest appointed for those who repent']. Almost all bishops subsequently followed his example. What this institution is, where it came from, and why it was discontinued, are differently stated by different authors: I will give my own version. It requires divine, rather than human, nature never to commit a fault, and yet God has commanded that the repentant shall be forgiven, even though they have erred many times; and since, when asking pardon, it is necessary for the fault to be confessed, priests considered it, from the first, improper that guilt should be proclaimed openly, as if in a theatre, with the whole congregation standing round. Consequently, they appointed for this purpose a priest conspicuous for the purity of his life, his wisdom, and his ability to preserve a confidence, to whom those who had done wrong might confess the sins of their past life. He would prescribe what each must do or give by way of amends for their sins, and would absolve them, leaving them to punish themselves for their wrongdoing. The Novatians required nothing of this kind, since they have no concept of repentance; but the custom persists among other sects. In Western congregations it is carefully observed, especially in the Roman church. There, the place for penitents is in public view: they stand there, sorrowful and (as it were) in mourning. When the ceremony of the Mass is finished, those who are excluded from the communion which is administered to the faithful throw themselves flat on the ground with groans and wailing. Then the bishop, in tears, comes towards them and falls to the ground himself; and the whole church cries out together, bursting into tears. Then the bishop rises first and lifts up the prostrate bodies; and having offered up an appropriate prayer for the repentant sinners, he dismisses them. Each of them voluntarily undergoes some personal privation – fasting, abstinence from washing, going without meals, or whatever is required of him – for as long as the bishop appoints; and when the stated day comes round, he is released from the penalty for his fault, as though he had paid his debt in full, and rejoins the rest of the congregation. Bishops of Rome have observed this custom from remotest antiquity to our own time: but in the church of Constantinople a particular priest was deputed to take charge of penitents – that is, until a certain noble lady was commanded by this priest to fast and pray humbly to God on account of the sins which she had committed; and when she was in the church for this purpose, she revealed that she had committed fornication with one of the deacons. When this was known, the people became bitterly angry, because an insult had been offered to the church, and clerks in holy orders had been exposed to grave reproach. After long and careful consideration of what should be done in the matter, Nectarius stripped the offending deacon of his office; and, since a number of people had advised him to allow everyone unrestricted access to the sacred rites, in accordance with their self-knowledge and confidence, he abolished the office of confessor. This custom has remained in force ever since.